Bravo for the Marshallese

Regaining Control in a Post-Nuclear, Post-Colonial World

Holly M. Barker

Embassy of the Republic of the Marshall Islands

Case Studies on Contemporary Social Issues: John A. Young, Series Editor

THOMSON

™

WADSWORTH

Australia • Canada • Mexico • Singapore • Spain
United Kingdom • United States

THOMSON

WADSWORTH

Acquisitions Editor: *Lin Marshall*
Editorial Assistant: *Kelly McMahon*
Technology Project Manager: *Dee Dee Zobian*
Marketing Manager: *Diane Wenckebach*
Marketing Assistant: *Michael Silverstein*
Advertising Project Manager: *Linda Yip*
Project Manager, Editorial Production:
   Catherine Morris
Print/Media Buyer: *Rebecca Cross*

Permissions Editor: *Joohee Lee*
Production Service: *Buuji, Inc.*
Photo Researcher: *Pat Quest*
Copy Editor: *Cheryl Hauser*
Illustrator: *Eunah Chang, Buuji, Inc.*
Cover Designer: *Rob Hugel*
Cover Image: *Holly Barker*
Compositor: *Buuji, Inc.*
Text and Cover Printer: *Webcom*

The logo for the Contemporary Social Issues series is
based on the image of a social group interacting around
a central axis, referring both back to a tribal circle and
forward to a technological society's network.

For more information about our products,
contact us at:
Thomson Learning Academic Resource Center
1-800-423-0563

For permission to use material from this text,
contact us by:
Phone: 1-800-730-2214 **Fax:** 1-800-730-2215
Web: http://www.thomsonrights.com

Library of Congress Control Number: 2003109617

ISBN 0-534-61326-8

Wadsworth/Thomson Learning
10 Davis Drive
Belmont, CA 94002-3098
USA

Asia
Thomson Learning
5 Shenton Way #01-01
UIC Building
Singapore 068808

Australia/New Zealand
Thomson Learning
102 Dodds Street
Southbank, Victoria 3006
Australia

Canada
Nelson
1120 Birchmount Road
Toronto, Ontario M1K 5G4
Canada

Europe/Middle East/Africa
Thomson Learning
High Holborn House
50/51 Bedford Row
London WC1R 4LR
United Kingdom

Latin America
Thomson Learning
Seneca, 53
Colonia Polanco
11560 Mexico D.F.
Mexico

Spain/Portugal
Paraninfo
Calle/Magallanes, 25
28015 Madrid, Spain

*This book is dedicated to
the students of the Nuclear Institute at the College
of the Marshall Islands and to
the people of the Marshall Islands
who live each day with a firsthand understanding
of the effects of nuclear weapons testing.*

*In loving memory of
Walter Lawton Barker*

Contents

Foreword

ABOUT THE SERIES

This series explores the practical applications of anthropology in understanding and addressing problems faced by human societies around the world. Each case study examines an issue of socially recognized importance in the historical, geographical, and cultural context of a particular region of the world, while adding comparative analysis to highlight not only the local effects of globalization, but also the global dimensions of the issue. The authors write with a readable narrative style and include references to their own participation, roles, and responsibilities in the communities they study. Their engagement with people goes beyond being merely observers and researchers, as they explain and sometimes illustrate from personal experience how their work has implications for advocacy, community action, and policy formation. They demonstrate how anthropological investigations can build our knowledge of human societies and at the same time provide the basis for fostering community empowerment, resolving conflicts, and pursuing social justice.

ABOUT THE AUTHOR

Holly M. Barker began her work with the Marshallese when she served as a Peace Corps volunteer from 1988 to 1990 on Mili Atoll in the Republic of the Marshall Islands (RMI). After a brief stint with the Senate Foreign Relations Committee on Capitol Hill, Holly joined the RMI's embassy in Washington, DC, where she is employed today. Holly lived and worked in Washington, DC, for the first 10 years of her work with the embassy, and currently resides with her family in Seattle, Washington, where she telecommutes. While working full-time at the embassy in Washington, DC, Holly earned an M.A. in Education and a Ph.D. in Anthropology from American University. Holly has represented the RMI at community, national, bilateral, and international forums, including conferences at the United Nations such as the extension of the Nuclear Non-Proliferation Treaty.

ABOUT THIS CASE STUDY

In this book, you will find an absorbing story of how the people of the Marshall Islands have struggled to understand the effects of radiation contamination from nuclear weapons testing and to mobilize themselves against efforts by the U.S. government to limit U.S. responsibilities for the damages and injuries caused by the testing program. Author and applied anthropologist, Holly Barker, presents the accounts she collected from Marshallese families to reveal the enduring impacts of radiation on a fragile ecosystem, including intergenerational consequences for human health and the breakdown of social and cultural life. She explains how she worked with the people she studied, using her research to help document the human costs of radiation exposure and to support their legal claims for just compensation from the United States government. In a global context she examines the consequences and questions raised when powerful nations compromise basic principles of human rights in the name of pursuing strategic military interests.

John A. Young
Series Editor
Department of Anthropology
Oregon State University
jyoung@oregonstate.edu

Preface

I chose the title of this book for two reasons. First, I want to document how the Bravo test, an atmospheric thermonuclear test the equivalent of 1,000 Hiroshima bombs, and the U.S. nuclear weapons testing program fundamentally altered the health, environment, language, economy, politics, and social organization of the Marshall Islands. Second, I want readers to know the Marshallese not as helpless victims rendered powerless by the events that took place in their land, but as the fighters and advocates for their communities they are. The Marshallese people deserve praise (bravo!) for the ways they resist U.S. government efforts to minimize or keep secret the true extent of damages and injuries from the testing program and for their efforts to tell the world about their plight, to seek medical care and environmental restoration, and to return to their home islands.

The story of the Marshallese people's collisions with U.S. strategic and Cold War interests is a powerful and complex one, a story that cannot be told in a single book. This book provides an overview of the problems created by the U.S. nuclear weapons testing program conducted in the Marshall Islands from 1946–1958 from the perspective of the Marshallese people. Through the words and voices of the Marshallese, I hope readers will gain an appreciation for the firsthand knowledge that the Marshallese have about the effects and consequences of radiation exposure and nuclear weapons testing.

The United States achieved global superpower status as a result of its weapons testing in the Marshall Islands. The tests demonstrated the capabilities of the U.S. nuclear arsenal—capabilities that Marshallese will know for generations to come, such as the Marshallese and their offspring whose health is affected by radiation exposure; the communities whose homelands are too contaminated to inhabit; the resettled portion of Enewetak's community living adjacent to an unmonitored nuclear storage facility; and the Marshallese subjects who unknowingly participated in secret U.S. government experiments to understand the effects of radiation on human beings. Superpower status for the United States came at the cost of the health of the Marshallese people and their environment.

The costs to the Marshallese, and the Marshallese responses to the problems thrust upon them by the nuclear weapons testing program, are the primary focus of this book. Readers will see that the story of the Marshall Islands illustrates many of the most fundamental concepts of environmental justice. The U.S. government chose the Marshall Islands as a testing group for sixty-seven atmospheric atomic and thermonuclear tests because the Marshall Islands is far from the United States and American citizens who could have been harmed by radioactive fallout, to allay growing concerns about the use of Nevada as a proving ground, and to conduct secret experiments in a remote location. From the perspective of the U.S. government, the Marshallese people and their environment were expendable. The U.S. government deemed the health and well-being of the Marshallese people and the vitality of their land as less important than the strategic interests of the United States at the time. In Chapter 5, readers will learn what the loss of land, access to resources, and exile mean to one community, the people of Rongelap.

Instead of acknowledging the full extent of damages and injuries caused by the testing program, the U.S. government continues to withhold information, and to downplay the effects of radiation exposure on the people and their land. Instead of accepting U.S. government efforts to control the scope of radiological problems, the Marshallese actively challenge U.S. government assertions. This is particularly evident in the unique radiation language created by the Marshallese—a language that demonstrates the breadth of radiological problems experienced by the people, and that enables the Marshallese people to claim events as their own. Readers will note in Chapters 6 and 7 that the Marshallese have created language to convey their experiences with radiation—experiences they did not need language to convey to one another prior to the arrival of the United States and nuclear weapons. The Marshallese have developed language to describe their illnesses and the changes to their environment, and to express their frustrations and the blame they place on the United States for their predicaments. This language is particularly well developed by the Marshallese women, who have created words to discuss the gross reproductive abnormalities they began to experience after the weapons testing program.

Whether readers are interested in environmental justice, anthropology, Cold War history, Pacific Islands, oral history, or public policy, the nuclear legacy in the Marshall Islands is a story people should know. As an American citizen, it is a history and a story I cannot walk away from. Marshallese people continue to die from illnesses linked to the testing program without access to health care, and without full or partial compensation for their sufferings. Marshallese people continue to live in exile from their home islands more than fifty years after the testing program began. In the last generation, however, the Marshallese have begun to assert their right and ability to take control of their own destiny. They are restoring contaminated lands and making plans to reinhabit their islands. They are building their capacity to self-govern the nation after hundreds of years of foreign occupation by establishing institutions that guarantee democracy and that will guide them into the future. The testing program and its consequences are only part of the story; what the Marshallese do in response to the challenges created by the testing program is the remainder of the tale. This story is not over.

ACKNOWLEDGMENTS

Without the support and input of many people, this book would not exist. I want to express my deepest appreciation to Jeilar and Mejjan Kabinmeto, my Marshallese family on Mili Atoll, for showing me the beauty of the Marshallese people, culture, and environment. I am also grateful to my siblings and my mom for their lifelong support and love. In addition, I wish to thank Banny deBrum and Wilfred Kendall, the best bosses anyone could hope to work for; Tony deBrum, for mentoring and encouragement; Newton Lajuan, Abacca Anjain-Maddison, and Tina Stege, for their friendship and interest in these ideas; and Bill Leap, Brett Williams, Peter Kuznik, Barbara Rose Johnston, Bill Graham, John Young, Julie Walsh, Alfred Capelle,

Joanne Everett, and Christopher Barker, for their professional encouragement. Finally, I want to express my deep appreciation to Bill Sherman, for the love, editing, and tireless support.

Please share any comments or thoughts about this book with the author at hbarker@rmiembassyus.org.

INTRODUCTION

I've told this story many times before, but there is no other way to begin to explain my work and 15-year relationship with the people of the Marshall Islands.

In 1987, I graduated from college with a B.A. in English. I had absolutely no idea what to do with an English major, but I was anxious to get out into the world and see what I could find. By some stroke of luck—at least I perceived it as such—an English major is a prerequisite for teaching English in the Peace Corps. Throughout high school I watched the television advertisements for the Peace Corps. The combination of travel, living overseas, and the opportunity to get to know a completely different way of life always appealed to me. So, I filled out my application and waited.

After several months and many interviews, I received a package in the mail from the Peace Corps. They sent me a letter of invitation, and a glossy booklet about being a Peace Corps volunteer in the Republic of the Marshall Islands. The cover picture of the kids playing on a long coconut tree arching over a beautiful beach and lagoon was all I needed to see. I was ecstatic!

The next day I went to the airport to pick up my mother, who was returning from a trip. I couldn't wait to tell her about my assignment; I told her in the parking lot before we even got to the car. When I told my mother I was accepted by the Peace Corps, she was thrilled! I then told her I was going to the Marshall Islands. What I did not expect, and what I will never forget, is her response: "Oh, honey, you can't go to the Marshall Islands!" My mother proceeded to tell me that the Marshall Islands was the location where the United States tested its atomic and thermonuclear weapons during the Cold War. I had absolutely no idea. I managed to get through high school and college without learning this. That information was not contained in the glossy brochure and I certainly could not see any signs of radiological contamination in the photographs.

My parents and I decided that I should get more information from the U.S. government about lingering radiation in the Marshall Islands and the possible effects on human life. I called the Peace Corps and I called the U.S. State Department. Both offices told me that I would be in no danger if I lived and ate local foods in the Marshall Islands because radiation levels were too low to be of concern. I was not completely confident in the answers I received, but I assumed that my government would have my best interest in mind if it was going to send me to the Marshall Islands. Besides, I really wanted to live on the tropical islands that I envisioned. So, I decided to go.

I asked the same questions about residual radiation levels during the summer-long training for my group of new recruits and received the same answers. When it came time for the Peace Corps director in the Marshall Islands to give us our assignments at the end of our training, I asked to be placed as far away from the testing sites as possible. The testing sites were located in the northwest of the country, and I was placed on an island that was in the southeast, literally the furthest distance possible from the testing sites.

After splitting off from my Peace Corps friends (we were all assigned to separate islands), I concentrated all of my energies on trying to assimilate into my life as a volunteer on the island of Nallu, Mili, and didn't think too much about the radiological issues. I was too busy struggling to learn a language, teach eight grades of students, and adjust to being the only outsider on a mile-long, half-mile-wide village. Nallu, Mili consists of one church, one school, and 15 houses. There are no stores, no electricity, and no one who admits to speaking English. Of the 150 or so residents of the island, approximately 100 of them were children. The kids were always happy to swim with me in the lagoon, play games, and teach me the language.

After I adjusted to my life as a Peace Corps volunteer, I remember sitting in the cooking house of the family compound where I lived one day. I was reading the weekly edition of the country's only newspaper, *The Marshall Islands Journal.* There was an article about foreign ships that were believed to be dumping radioactive materials into the Pacific Ocean in areas not too far from the Marshall Islands. At this point in my Peace Corps experience, I talked about everything with my Marshallese host-Papa. There was no television or other distractions in the evenings, so my Papa and I would talk from dinnertime until midnight almost every evening. He would share local myths and legends, and stories about the Marshallese people with me, and I would tell him about current events in the United States ranging from the U.S. defense program, Star Wars, located on another atoll in the RMI, to nuclear deterrence, or whatever news items that appeared in the outdated copies of *Newsweek* magazine that the Peace Corps could get to me on Nallu. I had no way of knowing at the time that these would become the subjects of many years of research, including this book.

On this particular day that I read the newspaper article about ocean dumping of radioactive materials, I wanted to share the news with my Papa. I looked through the paper for the translation of the article in Marshallese since the newspaper normally prints major stories in both English and Marshallese. There was no translation of the story, and I was upset because I thought the Marshallese people, and not the English speakers in the nation, had a right to know if their environment was being compromised by the dumping of radioactive materials. With encouragement from my Marshallese Papa, I wrote a letter to the newspaper telling them so.

The following week I went to use the only two-way radio on the island of Nallu to participate in a Peace Corps radio hour reserved for volunteers throughout the nation to check in with the country director based in the capitol, Majuro. The director told me that my letter to the editor appeared in that week's newspaper (which I would not receive for a few more weeks when my mail could be flown, boated, and walked to my island). I was pleased to hear this and asked the director to send me a few extra copies of my letter. The country director agreed and also told me he would write me a letter about the subject.

When my mail package did arrive, I hurried to open the letter from the director. I guess I thought he would be pleased that I was advocating for the interests of the people we had come to serve. Instead, I received a letter saying that as a representative of the U.S. government I was forbidden to talk about any issues related to the U.S. nuclear weapons testing program, and that if I continued to discuss these matters the Peace Corps would terminate me.

The reaction of the director made it obvious that there was a reason why the U.S. government did not want me to talk about the testing program. It was then that I began to question the official responses to my earlier queries about radiological safety. I continued to talk about nuclear issues with my Marshallese Papa and friends, but I stopped writing to the newspaper because I loved the Peace Corps and certainly did not want the director to terminate me. By the same token, I felt my Papa and all Marshallese had a right to know about and question any information about the consequences of the radiation exposure. Little did I know that this would become my full-time job when I returned to the United States.

When my two years of Peace Corps service came to an end, I was devastated because I did not want my relationship with the Marshallese people to end, but I knew I could not spend the rest of my life teaching English on a remote island. I literally curled up on the floor of the airport in Majuro and cried because I could not imagine that I was leaving the people that I had become so close to.

A few months later I went to Washington, DC, with my Peace Corps friends to see what jobs we could find in the international arena. I worked briefly on Capitol Hill, but the culture shock of returning home at the same time Congress was feverishly engaged in the U.S. war agenda in Iraq was too much for me. In the midst of the chaos on Capitol Hill, I called the Marshall Islands' embassy in Washington, DC. I spoke in Marshallese to the Deputy Chief of Mission and told him that I worked on the Hill and would love to be able to help the Marshall Islands but my role as a glorified receptionist didn't put me in a position where I could effect change. The Deputy Chief of Mission asked me to come to the embassy that day during my lunch break. I did. Two weeks later I was working at the embassy. The Deputy Chief of Mission, Banny deBrum, is now the ambassador and he is my boss today, 13 years later.

I never thought I would grow up and work on nuclear issues at an embassy, but here I am. I had to go back to school to get a degree that would enable me to conduct research and influence public policy. As an applied anthropologist working for the embassy, I conduct research with populations affected by the nuclear weapons testing in the Marshall Islands, and I help these populations seek the remedies for their problems they deem most appropriate. My time with the Marshallese has been tremendously rewarding and I feel fortunate and honored to have the chance to work with them. There are many people in the Marshall Islands who know much more about this subject than I ever will; this book is my effort to explain just a piece of the story.

1/Setting the Stage
Geography, Social/Political Organization, and the Language of the Marshall Islands

From 1946 to 1958, the U.S. government tested 67 atomic and thermonuclear weapons in the Marshall Islands. All of the tests were atmospheric and spread radiation throughout the nation. The nuclear weapons testing program caused extensive damage and injury to the people and the environment in the Marshall Islands.

Before discussing the impact of the U.S. nuclear weapons testing program on the Marshallese people, it is important to examine the history and geography, which were factors contributing to the U.S. government's decision to test its nuclear weapons in the Marshall Islands. It is also important to understand the Marshallese relationship to their land and environment, as well as their language to see how the testing program changed the lived experiences of the Marshallese.

LOCATION AND ECOLOGY

What is it about the geography of the Marshall Islands that made the U.S. government interested in the tiny atoll nation as a testing site for its nuclear weapons? The following discussion shows how geographic isolation and differing views about the hospitality of the land resulted in the U.S. government's decision to use the Marshall Islands as a proving ground.

It is hard to imagine any nation more remote and isolated than the Marshall Islands. The country lies in the midst of the vast Pacific Ocean, midway between Hawaii and Japan, and is part of the region known as Micronesia. Micronesia, or "small islands," which includes Guam and the Commonwealth of the Northern Marianas to the north, Palau to the west, Nauru and the Gilbert Islands to the south, the Federated States of Micronesia in the center, and the Marshall Islands to the east, closest to the United States. Micronesia extends over an area larger than the continental United States, but its total land area is similar in size to the state of Rhode Island.

The Marshall Islands contains some 1,225 individual islands. All of these islands are low-lying with an average elevation of just six or seven feet above sea level. Most of the islands are extremely narrow in width and both the ocean and lagoon are visible on either side of the islands. There are no mountains or rivers in the country. The abundant coconut trees and the large expanse of water surrounding the islands are what visitors tend to notice when they first arrive in the islands.

I remember clearly the day I arrived in the Marshall Islands for the first time with the rest of my Peace Corps group. When our five and a half hour plane ride from Hawaii first circled the main island and capital of the Marshall Islands, Majuro, I had never seen such tiny strips of land or such vibrant colors in the water. The ocean surrounding the islands is so dark that it seems almost black, and the shallow waters that cover the networks of coral reefs are a spectrum of vivid greens. When it was time for the airplane to land on the runway, it was difficult to see the island below us. For awhile it seemed like the plane was going to land on the water, but the land came back into sight as we got closer to touching down.

One man in our newly arrived Peace Corps group had never seen the ocean before. He was a farmer from Kansas, and the expanse of ocean made him extremely nervous. From his perspective, he was used to having land all around him, areas that can be farmed and controlled by humans. The potential for outbursts or storms from the ocean that was visible from wherever we went was too much for him to handle. After a few days, the farmer returned to Kansas.

For me, the reality of what I committed myself to for two years did not sink in until I was sent out to my posting. Each volunteer was assigned to a different island. When I took all my worldly possessions in a few cardboard boxes down to the boat dock, I saw that my ride to Mili Atoll was aboard what looked like a few pieces of plywood with an engine. It was a copra (dried coconut meat) boat on its way to pick up bags of copra from Mili. Nervously, I waved goodbye to my Peace Corps friends on the dock. The door closed behind me, and I was in a 10 × 10 room packed with people and cargo. Someone made room for me to sit, and I sat huddled in the same position through the 16-hour journey to Nallu, Mili. There was no bathroom on the boat, and no room to lie down or stretch out. How could I be so unfortunate to be assigned to an island without an airport, I thought. A few women tried to talk to me in Marshallese, but all I could remember from my summer language training was *"Enno bao birae ippa"* (fried chicken tastes good to me), or *"Kwoj etal nan ia?"* (where are you going?), which seemed obvious.

When the boat arrived in Nallu and the door opened for the first time since our departure, the captain of the boat yelled "Peace Corps!" The men on the boat made a quick procession to carry my boxes from the boat to the shore. (People never seem to mind wading through water and getting their blue jeans or entire bodies soaked.) I was the only passenger to get off at Nallu. I sat on the beach by myself with my boxes as the boat chugged away. While I was relieved to be off the boat, I looked around and realized I couldn't see a single house or person. Since there had been no windows on the boat, the shore where I sat was all I knew of my surroundings. I had no radio or no means of communicating with anyone. I couldn't ask the Peace Corps office in Majuro for help. I burst into tears and curled up into the fetal position. I remember thinking at the time that if I survived this experience then I could handle any situation the world could throw my way.

As I was sitting on the beach feeling sorry for myself, a young Marshallese girl came skipping along. She saw me sitting in the sand, shrieked, and ran in the other direction. I guess I was the first white person she had ever seen. The reason no people were around is because it was Sunday morning and the entire community was at church. In a few moments the little girl brought the whole town to me. I wiped away my tears when I saw them approaching. Two people made their way to the front of the staring pack and shook my hand. They said two words that I understood: "Mama" and "Papa." I followed them and the second procession of my belongings to a compound in the center of the island. My new Marshallese parents went into a hut and yelled a bunch of words I didn't understand to people I couldn't see. Next thing I knew a family was throwing all of its belongings outside, and my soggy boxes were put inside. My Mama and Papa gestured for me to go into the thatch hut. I did, and closed the door behind me. I lay down on the ground and peered out of a crack below the door to get a sense of the alien world I had just arrived in. I was too scared to move. I didn't know what to do.

Eventually my Marshallese parents came back to the hut. I couldn't understand a word they said to me. They used sign language to ask me if I wanted food. I nodded. They made motions for a bath. Someone filled a bucket with rainwater and escorted me to a big bush that served as my cover. Every time I moved scores of eyes observed me. I was as different to them as they were to me.

The family I lived with obviously saw my duress and rightly determined that I would never survive without them. I took every bit of food I brought from the capital to the family cooking house. I ate three meals a day with the family for two years. Initially, we got by on a lot of sign language and long silences. Through patient instruction on their part, I eventually learned the language and began to communicate with them. I spent at least five hours of every day just sitting and talking with the family. Even though my family in the United States is extremely close, no one has the time to sit and talk for so long each day. I had never spent so much time talking to the same people. Consequently, my relationship with the family grew quickly and deeply.

I never imagined that the best part of the Peace Corps would be the relationships; before I left for my assignment I had grandiose ideas that I would go and do good work that would make a lasting impact on a community. When I left the Peace Corps, I couldn't help feeling that I had gotten more than I received. I had met a whole village of friends and been the eleventh child in a wonderful family; my family taught me about an entirely new way of life. I learned to catch crabs for dinner under the rocks on the ocean side. I tried to cook breadfruit and weave mats like the women, but I always seemed to fail at these tasks. I snorkeled in the lagoon with sharks, and climbed coconut trees (when no one was looking since women don't usually do this) when I got thirsty. Yes, there were plenty of frustrating and lonely times, too, but what I will always remember most is how my host family took me in and took care of me. I felt a gratitude to my family and the Marshall Islands I had to pay back.

Thinking back to when I first arrived in the Marshall Islands, I realize that one of the reasons that outsiders feel so disoriented in the Marshall Islands is because there is so little land in a vast ocean. The Marshall Islands consists of just 70 square miles of land. This land extends across 750,000 square miles of ocean, a distance roughly the equivalent of the landmass of Mexico. Almost all of the islands are clustered in 29 coral atolls and five large, stand-alone coral islands that began to evolve approximately 70 million years ago (see Figure 1.1, a map of RMI). Anthropologist Robert C. Kiste describes a coral atoll as:

> composed of a number of islands . . . resting on a coral reef that typically encloses a
> lagoon. Some atolls have passages that allow entrance to the lagoon; others do not and are

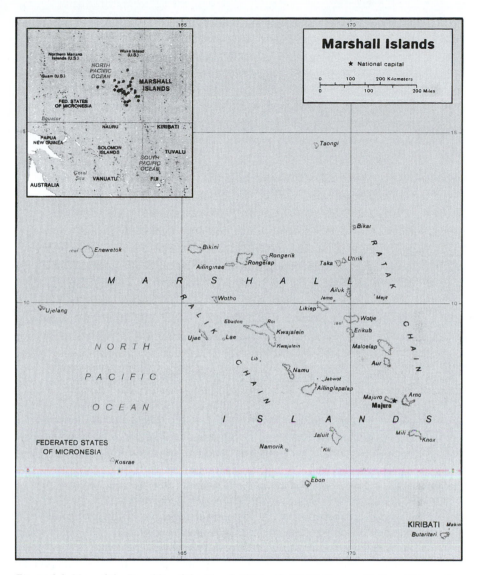

Figure 1.1 Map of the Republic of the Marshall Islands (RMI). Source: National Research Council (1994).

closed atolls. Atolls originated as fringing reefs around volcanic peaks that sank beneath the sea millions of years ago. As the peaks gradually submerged, coral growth continued to build upward, and reefs remained close to the ocean's surface. The islands themselves are a mixture of coral debris, sand, and humus. Being flat, or low elevation, and seldom reaching more than three to ten meters above sea level, they are extremely vulnerable to tropical storms (Kiste 1994:7).

These atolls and islands in the Marshall Islands extend down two parallel island chains: the *Ratak*, or sunrise chain to the east, and the *Ralik*, or sunset chain to the west.

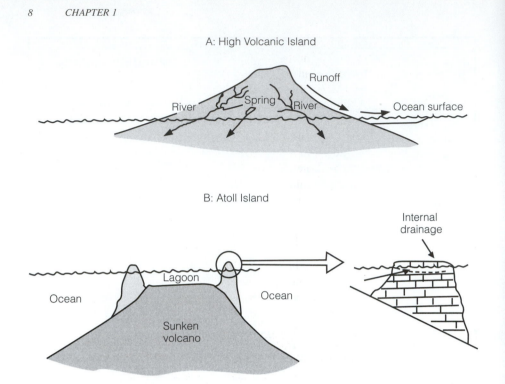

A: High Volcanic Island

Runoff

River   Spring   River   Ocean surface

B: Atoll Island

Internal
drainage

Lagoon

Ocean   Ocean

Sunken
volcano

Figure 1.2 Submerged volcanoes/atoll. Source: U.S. Department of Interior (1988:50).

The most well-known atolls in the Marshall Islands are Bikini and Enewetak, the ground-zero atolls for the U.S. nuclear testing program. Many U.S. servicemen spent time either on these atolls or on ships that patrolled the area during the testing program. Kwajalein Atoll, with the largest lagoon in the world, is also well known because today it houses the Ronald Reagan Ballistic Missile Test Site and plays a major role in U.S. government efforts to test a missile defense shield.

As discussed earlier, outsiders who travel to the Marshall Islands often describe the environment in terms of its limited land, its dry conditions, and the sparse resources available for human survival. The first anthropologists who worked in the Marshall Islands characterized the low-lying, dry atolls as having "[s]lender resources . . . [where p]ractically no soil covers the coral, and the inhospitable sand [that] will grow few plants" (Krieger 1943:21). In comparing the islands and atolls in the northern Pacific, early anthropologists characterized the drier coral atolls in the Marshall Islands as "present[ing] the greatest challenge to human occupancy" (Mason 1968:278). This is the view adopted by the U.S. government when it decided to test its weapons on land that no one supposedly cared about.

To the Marshallese, however, limited food and water resources, the seasonality of staple foods, droughts, and famines make survival challenging, but not impossible. Survival is contingent on specific and accurate knowledge of the local resource base. Instead of viewing their country as strips of dry land with scant resources, the way early anthropologists and outsiders did, the Marshallese view the surrounding seas and many islands as providing them with multiple opportunities to cultivate the resources necessary for survival.

The different perceptions about the habitability and viability of the Marshall Islands established before the nuclear testing program commenced would create discord between the Marshallese and the U.S. government both during and after the testing program. For the Marshallese, their nation was not a barren collection of sandbars that scarcely support human life. Instead, the diverse array of aquatic and terrestrial resources available to the Marshallese enables them to live sustainably in their environment. By cultivating resources from the land, sea, and sky, the Marshallese are able to adjust to seasonal and climatic variations, and ensure they do not deplete resources in any one location (Johnston and Barker 1999). For the U.S. government, the harsh and seemingly desolate environment was perfect for conducting military activities too dangerous or secretive to undertake in the United States.

EARLY MIGRATION

It is difficult to ascertain when the first settlers arrived in the Marshall Islands, and where they arrived from. Few material artifacts exist in Micronesia because most materials produced by the Marshallese were made from local resources that decompose and leave little evidence for archaeologists. Through the analysis of Pacific languages, researchers believe, however, that the first settlers of Micronesia were Pacific Island populations that migrated from Melanesia. The predominant theory of settlement of the Marshall Islands postulates that the initial settlers came from Southeast Asia, perhaps southeast China, approximately 5,000 years ago. Successive advancements in maritime and agricultural technology enabled people to migrate to what are now the Melanesian areas of the Solomon Islands, Vanuatu, and New Caledonia and then into the Central Pacific. Motivations for the migration and settlement across the Pacific included ecological pressures, quarreling families, and the desire of rival siblings from the families of chiefs to establish new blood lines and power bases on distant islands (Kirch 1984).

The linguistic record also supports the theory that the early settlers of Micronesia came from Melanesia, around the area of Vanuatu. Micronesian languages share traits from eastern Melanesian and Southeast Asian languages. This evidence, coupled with the greater antiquity of languages in western Micronesia, suggests a migration path across Micronesia from west to east (Kiste 1994).

SOCIAL AND POLITICAL STRUCTURE

Without question, land is the most important resource in the Marshall Islands. Not only does land provide the resources necessary for survival, but it also links people to their ancestors and their families, and provides the resources necessary to maintain the culture. Land is matrilineal: it is passed from generation to generation through the women. Anthropologists call systems in which women pass major resources to succeeding generations matrilineal systems. The Marshall Islands is a matrilineal society organized by its access to land and resources.

Traditionally, the oldest woman in a family passes on the land rights to other members of her family. When the oldest woman of one generation dies, the land rights pass to her brothers and sisters in order of their age, beginning with the eldest. When all the siblings of a generation die, the land passes through the next generation beginning with the children of the oldest woman in the previous generation.

Families in the Marshall Islands are large. Several generations of an extended family often reside on the same property either in a single house, or in neighboring houses. Traditionally, when a young woman marries it is expected that her husband will live with her on her mother's land. Similarly if a young boy in a family marries, he will be more likely to live on and help with the work on the land of his family's wife. Traditionally, the strength of land ownership remains with women, but urbanization and changes in land tenure have caused changes in family relations and power structures. Many families leave the outer islands for the services and opportunities in the urban areas (schools, hospitals, employment, etc.). The power of women is attenuated when family members move to the capital and have less of an interest in maintaining resources, or returning to live on their land. The relationship between land and family is also shifting as women increasingly invest a male member of their family with responsibility for managing the use rights of the land.

The Marshallese refer to their lineage or clan lines as *bwij*. Customary rules provide land use rights to members of a lineage:

> The lineage (*bwij*) members may live on and exploit the resources of the land parcel or, if they possess rights in more than one land parcel, as is usually the case, merely make copra on it and use its food resources such as: coconuts, breadfruit, arrow-root, pandanus, bananas, and taro. Pigs and chickens are kept and fish and shellfish are obtained from the adjacent marine areas (Tobin 1958:7–8).

Land is usually inherited in small parcels referred to as *wetos*. These land parcels are cross sections of land extending from the ocean to the lagoon (Figure 1.3). Most Marshallese construct their homes on the lagoon side of the land parcels to provide shelter from the wind and storms. Almost all land parcels have access to the ocean and lagoon. A village path usually runs down the center of an island, passing through each land parcel, and connecting the community.

Sometimes land holdings are broken into smaller portions. The boundaries (*kotan weto*) are often marked by local plants or prominent outcroppings in the land. To claim the right to use a land parcel, a person must know its boundaries and history. The power to recognize and validate land claims rests in the hands of customary authorities. Because land is critical to survival, "the Marshallese jealously guard their land rights and will not willingly part with them" (Tobin 1967:3).

Instead of a notion of individual property ownership, the Marshallese property rights system is premised on the notion that no single person owns the land. Marshallese culture and society revolve around a three-tier approach of reciprocal use rights for the *iroij*, *alab*, and *ri-jerbal* (Tobin 1953, 1958, Mason 1968, Kiste 1974). In western terms, the *iroij* are the chiefs who maintain authority over the clans and the land. The chiefs are responsible for taking care of their people, and the people, in turn, must provide food and labor to their respective chiefs. The land managers act as the managers for the chief with a day-to-day responsibility to ensure that the land is properly maintained and that everyone is provided for according to custom. The *ri-jerbal*, literally *ri*, or people, and *jerbal*, or work, are the workers. The Marshallese also refer to the *ri-jerbal* as the *kajor*, or strength of the clan. The workers have a symbiotic relationship with their chiefs and land managers; the workers provide the strength and support necessary to cultivate the land, and the chiefs and land managers ensure that the workers have access to the land and resources necessary for survival. In this arrangement, everyone benefits; the land would not be pro-

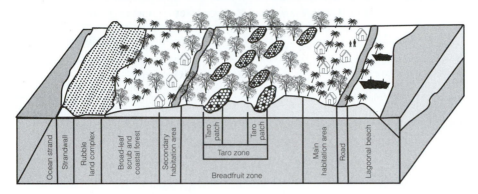

Figure 1.3 Diagram of a weto. From: Notes on the Occurrence, Utilization, and Importance of Polynesian Arrowroot in the Marshall Islands, Background Study No. 39, by Dirk Spennenmann. Majuro: Independent Nationwide Radiological Survey ©1992. Reprinted with permission.

ductive unless the workers maintained it. By the same token, the workers would not have the means to survive unless their chiefs and land managers extend use rights to the workers.

Maintenance of the property and resources is critical to ensuring the continued livelihood of everyone in the lineage or corporation, with rights to the property. In addition to caring for property and resources for the well-being of the existing generation, people with land rights work collectively to ensure that the lineage holdings will be productive for the succeeding generations that will inherit the land. In this regard, customary ownership of property and resources is based on sustainable interactions with the environment and responsible stewardship that will allow future generations to flourish. In a society that is organized on respect for the land, and the need to pass the land to future generations to ensure their survival, what complications result from the introduction of radiation into the local environment?

Like kinship, the political system is also based on land areas. Each of the major atolls and large islands in the Marshall Islands elects a senator to the *Nitijela*, or parliament. The parliament is a combination of the British and American systems of governance. The people choose their individual senators, and the senators decide among themselves which senator should be president. Once a president is selected, the president chooses members of the cabinet from the remaining senators. The president of the Marshall Islands in 2003 is Kessai H. Note. President Note is the third president of the Marshall Islands and the first president who is not a chief.

THE MARSHALLESE LANGUAGE AND ITS DIALECTS

Given the considerable distances between the atolls and islands, it is surprising that the Marshallese language varies little from place to place. Because of their navigational prowess, which is known throughout the Pacific region, the Marshallese historically navigated and traveled between the atolls and islands. This ability to routinely move across long distances was, undoubtedly, a factor in establishing a uniformity in the language.

TABLE 1.1   *RALIK* AND *RATAK* DIALECT VARIATION

	Ralik	Ratak	English Equivalent
Vowel variation of the word	*lok*	*lak*	directional, go toward
Selection of intervening vowels	*iaikuj*	*aekuj*	need or want
Longer words in the *Ralik* dialect	*iep*	*ep*	basket

Source: Byron Bender, *A Linguistic Analysis of Place Names of the Marshall Islands.* Unpublished Ph.D. dissertation, Indiana University. Available at the Alele Museum in Majuro or the Pacific Collection at the University of Hawaii, 1963.

All languages in the Pacific, including Marshallese, belong to the Austronesian language family, the largest of the language families. The Austronesian language family encompasses one-sixth of the world's languages and stretches from the edges of South America to Southeast Asia. The wide berth of this language family is a result of the extensive migration of populations, primarily by sea.

Similarities exist between the Marshallese language and other languages in Micronesia, particularly those from Pohnpei and Chuuk. Within the Marshallese language, there are two distinct dialects, the *Ralik* and the *Ratak* dialects that correspond to the two chains of islands that run north to south. The two dialects do not differ greatly, and speakers of the dialects have no problems understanding each other (Table 1.1). The first linguist to document the language, Byron Bender, notes some of the differences, primarily in the vowels, between the two dialects.

Traces still exist of a much older, traditional form of Marshallese language referred to now as *kajin etto,* or the "old language." Some of the Marshallese elders know the meanings of older words and phrases, and some elders can still recite chants (*roro*) in *kajin etto*. The meanings of most of these chants have been lost over the years, but the elders know enough of the words to understand whether they are reciting a chant to instruct listeners about navigation, war, or prayer to a shark god before fishing. The fact that the elders remember the meanings of some of the words, despite the fact that the old language is no longer functional and was never written, demonstrates the remarkable oral traditions of the Marshallese.

In 1998, an elderly woman from Rongelap Atoll, Kajim Abija, recited a chant for me. Unfortunately, I did not have a tape recorder at the time, but Kajim told me that although she did not know the exact meaning of the words, she knew that the chant instructs navigators to look for a particular pattern of waves that emerge when the sea bounces off of Kapijinamu reef, a large reef on Rongelap Atoll. Because the islands lie so close to the sea, navigators do not see the land until they have almost reached their destination. Therefore, they must rely on the wave and ocean currents to guide them to the islands. Marshallese navigators used charts made from sticks and shells to show them the location of the atolls and the major ocean currents.

In addition to the old language, evidence exists of an ancient, religious language used to show respect for sacred areas and the *iroij,* or chiefs. In all likelihood, the arrival of missionaries in the nineteenth century replaced the indigenous religion with Christianity. Little is known about the indigenous religion. There are indications, such as the chanting, that the Marshallese religion was devoted to the mythical characters that personify the natural world. There was a god of fish, *iroij rilik,* and a god of breadfruit, a major staple in the Marshallese diet, *jebro.*

Table 1.2   Marshallese Pronouns

kem	=	us, excluding anyone else in the area
kemro	=	the two of us
kemjeel	=	the three of us
kemean	=	the four of us
kemwoj	=	the five or more of us
kej	=	us, all inclusive
kejro	=	the two of us
kejeel	=	the three of us
kejean	=	the four of us
kejwoj	=	the five or more of us

Table 1.3   Marshallese Place Names

Atoll Names:

Rongelap	*ron* (hole, referring to the lagoon) + *lap* (large)	= [atoll with] large lagoon
Rongerik	*ron* (hole) + *rik* (small)	= [atoll with] small lagoon
Ailinginae	*ailin* (atoll) + *in* (in) + *ae* (current)	= atoll in the current

Island Names:

Eneaitok	*ene* (island) + *aitok* (long)	= long island
Enebarbar	*ene* (island) + *barbar* (rocky, lots of reef)	= island with lots of reef
Aeroken	*ae* (current) + *rok* (south) + *en* (away from speaker)	= distant island to the south

Weto Names:

Marren	*mar* (bushes) + *en* (away from speaker)	= distant [*weto*] with bushes
Monbako	*mon* (house) + *bako* (sharks)	= house of the sharks
Aibwej	*aibwej* (water)	= [*weto* with] water

Source: See Byron Bender, 1963. *A Linguistic Analysis of Place Names of the Marshall Islands*. Unpublished Ph.D. dissertation, Indiana University. Available at the Alele Museum in Majuro or the Pacific Collection at the University of Hawaii.

One of the first anthropologists to work in the Marshall Islands was Jack Tobin. Tobin documented evidence of a religion that protected and revered plant and animal life through the creation of nature preserves, and simultaneously recognized the unique role of lineage chiefs in protecting these sanctuaries. According to Tobin, the Marshallese had rituals that existed from "time immemorial" for approaching islands set aside for animals and birds. For example, elaborate rituals to *Lawi Jemo*, pisonia grandis, a large hardwood tree, or the *kanal* tree god accompanied annual food gathering trips to islands set aside as bird sanctuaries. Upon arrival, women hid under mats in the canoes for fear of bringing bad luck to food finding expeditions, such as fishing or bird and egg collection. For the men, it was taboo for them to speak ordinary Marshallese. Instead, they were required to use *laroij*, an esoteric language that would conceal the real names and protect the identities of the animals and the chiefs. Once an expedition arrived at the bird sanctuary island, people used special chants to request the strength necessary to haul their canoes up on the beach and waited for a signal from a tree that they were free to gather food. Tobin notes:

The chief was the first person to step ashore. Everyone assembled on the beach before proceeding inland and cut a leaf or coconut frond. With the chief leading the way toward *Lawi Jemo* (the *kanal* tree), they walked in single file, each individual carefully stepping in the footprints of the person in front of him so that only one set of footprints would appear, as if only one person had been there. Strict silence was observed on the way to worship *Lawi Jemo*. When the group reached the tree, each man placed his coconut leaf over a branch of the tree and then sat down in front of the tree and waited for a breeze to come and blow the leaf off. When this occurred, the *kebbwi in bwil* (ritual name for the chief on this occasion) would announce: *Wurin* (we are lucky) (Tobin 1958:51–52).

The same linguistic tendency to demonstrate respect by using pseudonyms remains today. Out of deference and respect, Marshallese often use nicknames or vague words that enable them to refer to an *iroij* without using proper names. This practice, also seen in other areas of the Pacific (such as Samoa, see Duranti 1991), uses politeness to acknowledge the higher status of the chiefs and the lower status of the speakers. In areas of land that are forbidden (*mo*) to Marshallese, such as a chief's land or medicinal areas, the Marshallese use nicknames or disguised names to refer to the animals, the trees, and the people. The extensive use of pronouns in the Marshallese language also enables people to use location specific pronouns to refer to people nearby without using their names, a custom that shows respect for people (Table 1.2).

Analysis of the Marshallese language also demonstrates the interconnectedness between people and the land, and the social significance of land and natural resources. In the Marshall Islands, each land holding has a unique name and history with which everyone with rights to the land is familiar. Atoll, island, land parcels, and reef names all remind people of the history and social significance of their property. For example, the names of land parcels are place names that describe the physical characteristics and why and how people inherited and use the land (Table 1.3). Examples of Marshallese place names that reflect the history and the importance of property are:

The Marshallese also give names to their reefs. The fact that people assign names to their reefs indicates that reefs are important reference points to the resource collection, navigation, and designation of property boundaries.

The next chapter details how colonial powers used the Marshallese land and its people to advance the interests of the controlling nations.

2/A Colonial History of the Marshall Islands

COLONIAL EXPANSION

Although Pacific island communities migrated and traveled to the Marshall Islands for thousands of years, it was not until just under 500 years ago that the western world learned of the islands' existence. The arrival of western visitors, or *ri-paelles* in Marshallese (literally, people with clothes) was anything but benign. Throughout Micronesia, western visitors disrupted, and indelibly changed, the islands:

> Early European explorers, missionaries, sea captains, traders, naval officers, and map makers gave names to these islands that commemorated their own sovereigns, ships, native lands, or themselves. Through these bestowals of names and accompanying acts of description, the otherness of the islands and their people was rendered in terms that were familiar, intelligible, and encouraging to those with an expansionist agenda. . . . [V]iolence, domination, exploitation, and racism would all characterize to varying degrees the tenures of each metropolitan power that governed Micronesia. . . . Each colonising nation would attempt to justify and enhance its rule through rituals of possession, denigrating descriptions of Micronesian societies, the usurpation of indigenous political authority, and the promotion of alien, disruptive systems of religion, education, and economy (Hanlon 1994:93).

Despite the damaging aspects of colonial domination, the colonial powers overlooked any inconveniences or hardships resulting from colonization because they believed they were bestowing all the benefits of civilization, including education, health care, and wage employment, on local Micronesian populations (Hezel 1995).

Spanish Rule

In 1594, the Treaty of Tordesillas gave Spain ownership of all the Micronesian islands. The first known contact between the Europeans and the Marshallese occurred in 1529, however, when Spanish explorer Alvaro de Saavedra went ashore on what appear to be islands on Bikini or Enewetak atolls. Despite the occasional visits by Spanish explorers in the sixteenth century, primarily to exchange goods for water and supplies necessary to support long voyages, the western world had no real contact with the Marshall Islands.

Centuries later, the strategic positioning of the Marshall Islands between Asia and the Americas made it an important resting and refueling stop for transpacific ships. As discussed later, this positioning was a critical asset to the defense interests of the U.S. government. In 1788, British captain John Marshall, the namesake of the nation, and Thomas Gilbert, whose name dons the neighboring Gilbert Islands, arrived. Marshall and Gilbert stopped in the islands during their voyage to transport convicts to Australia. After this voyage, the Marshall Islands began to appear on European maps.

In the mid-1850s, American Protestant missionaries arrived in the Marshall Islands. The missionaries were often accompanied by converted native Hawaiians, who more closely resembled the Marshallese than the Anglo-American missionaries did and who were instrumental in helping convince the Marshallese to embrace Christianity. The missionaries permanently altered traditional society as they "converted the Marshallese in great numbers, leaving them with an established church headed by ordained Marshallese ministers, a taste for formal education, and a sense of modesty in dress that was much like the missionaries' own" (Hezel 1995:45). Although some populations in the Marshall Islands initially resisted missionization, such as the people of Mili who fought and killed many missionaries, to this day approximately 99 percent of the Marshallese population remains Christian.

The missionization of the Marshall Islands was so complete that little evidence of the traditional religion remains, and few remember that it existed before contact with the missionaries. A century after the initial American missionaries arrived, the U.S. government would invoke the name of God as a means to persuade the Marshallese people of the importance of using their land for nuclear weapons tests.

German Rule

In addition to Christianity, German commercial interests in the Marshall Islands greatly impacted the nation. The most profound shift in the modern economy occurred during the German administration of the islands. By the 1870s and 1880s, German traders and the German Navy began large-scale trading operations in the Marshall Islands. Germany secured the exclusive use of the harbor at Jaluit Atoll and special trading privileges in the *Ralik* chain by concluding a "treaty" with a powerful *iroij* in 1878. In 1885, the Marshall Islands became a German protectorate.

German rule of the Marshall Islands was indirect. The chiefs retained their power and the Germans acted primarily as administrators of the islands. In this regard, the early colonizers further strengthened the power of the chiefs because the chiefs gained access to western goods and cash without relinquishing the traditional political structure to foreign occupants (Hezel 1995).

The early economy of the Marshallese was based on inter-island and inter-atoll exchange. Between the atolls, people exchanged food, such as preserved arrowroot and pandanus. Within island communities, people worked together and used their natural resources to survive sustainably from the environment.

The Germans' main objective in the Marshall Islands was the economic exploitation of copra, or dried coconut meat, a product used to make oils, soaps, and shampoos. German traders cleared breadfruit and food producing trees and encouraged the

Marshallese to plant coconut trees on every island. The Marshallese harvested the coconuts and provided copra to the Germans for export. Through the copra industry, the system of wage labor was introduced. Other than infrequent and informal exchange with ships, this was the first time the Marshall Islands became a participant in the world economy. Many Marshallese identify the era of German rule as the beginning of a shift from communal self-sufficiency and family to individual income generation. Today, copra remains the primary source of revenue for Marshallese residing on the outer islands (areas other than the two urban centers of Majuro and Ebeye).

Japanese Rule

During World War I, Japan captured the Marshall Islands from Germany and assumed authority for the islands. Japan's involvement in the Marshall Islands was much more direct than its predecessor. The Japanese had four specific goals with regard to its island territory: "economic development and exploitation, colonization for Japanese emigration, integration with Japan, and militarization" (U.S. Department of Interior 1987:336). By 1938, Japan considered the Marshall Islands a closed military area and restricted foreigners' movement in the territory. Marshallese describe the Japanese regime as strict, but effective: the Japanense built schools and roads, and provided formal education to the Marshallese.

With the onset of Word War II and the need to protect its island territory, the Japanese administration of the islands changed from civilian to military. Under Japanese military occupation, the Marshallese suffered greatly. The U.S. military cut off Japanese food shipments to the Japanese strongholds causing starvation for the Japanese and Marshallese residents of the islands. Starvation was particularly pronounced on the atolls of Mili, Maloelap, and Wotje that served as bases for Japanese troops. The Japanese gathered all existing food resources for their own use. Marshallese, who were starving from the meager rations they received from the Japanese, were hung, beaten, and even beheaded for attempting to steal food from the Japanese, by climbing trees at night in search of food, for example. At the time, food was severely rationed and it was forbidden for Marshallese to take a single coconut or other foods from their own trees.

In 1942, the Marshall Islands became a fierce battleground as the Allies began to attack Japanese forces in the Marshall Islands. Many Marshallese served as scouts to help the United States plan strategic attacks against the Japanese. The United States repeatedly bombed the islands and atolls where the Japanese positioned themselves. During the bombing, many Marshallese lost their lives and entire Marshallese villages burned (Figure 2.1). By 1944, the United States successfully defeated Japan and the allied forces seized control of the Marshall Islands.

U.S. NAVAL ADMINISTRATION OF THE MARSHALL ISLANDS

After seizing the Marshall Islands from the Japanese, the U.S. Navy immediately understood the geographic and strategic importance of the area. From a U.S. military perspective, the Marshall Islands was geographically isolated from Soviet and public eyes. During the height of the Cold War and the competition between the Americans and the Russians to develop and test nuclear weapons, the Marshall

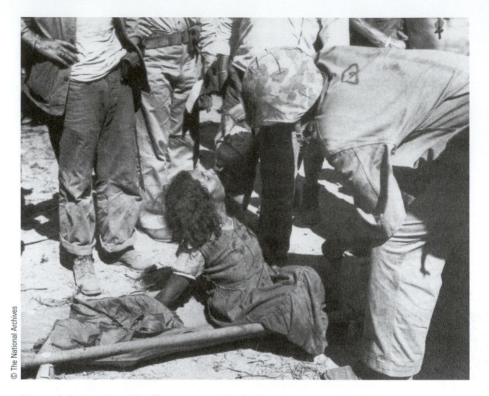

Figure 2.1 American GI offers water to Marshallese woman

Islands provided an ideal location to conduct top secret experiments while simultaneously ensuring tight control over everyone who entered the testing area.

In addition to its isolation, the Marshall Islands was thousands of miles away from the United States. By testing high-yield weapons in the Marshall Islands, the U.S. government could reduce radiation exposure for American citizens and allay criticism about continued testing and radiation hazards produced at the Nevada test site. The U.S. government would ultimately test 100 times more megatonnage in the Marshall Island than it did at the Nevada test site.

Shortly after the U.S. government claimed control of the Marshall Islands the battle in the Pacific drew to a close. The United States government dropped atomic bombs on the populations of Hiroshima and Nagasaki, Japan. Instantly, the heat of the bombs incinerated thousands of people and fire ravaged the cities. Many survivors suffered or died from radiation-related illnesses (see Chapter 9 for more discussion).

In August 1945 when the U.S. government dropped the bombs on Japan, the United States maintained that the atomic weapons were necessary to put an end to the war. Historians now know from recently declassified documents that the United States government did not have to drop the bombs on Hiroshima and Nagasaki to win the war because they knew the Japanese already planned to surrender (Alperovitz et al. 1996). By the same token, World War II and the Japanese enemy provided an opportunity for the United States to test its nuclear weapons for the first time on civilian populations. Until this time, the only test the U.S. government conducted was a test of the Trinity bomb in the Nevada desert to ensure that an atomic detonation was possible.

Despite the destructive capacity of the atomic bomb witnessed in Japan, the United States did not fully understand the effects of atomic bombs on human beings, infrastructure, or the environment. Although Hiroshima and Nagasaki answered some of these immediate questions about the destructiveness of nuclear bombs, the U.S. government needed to gain a better appreciation for its newest weapon. To answer these questions, the United States turned to its newly acquired territory, the Marshall Islands.

The geographic isolation and sparse population of the Marshall Islands, coupled with the tight control over entry and exit policies already in place, made it easy for the U.S. government to conduct top secret activities in the islands. In 1946, while the Marshall Islands were still in the possession of the U.S. Navy, the United States approached the people and leaders of Bikini Atoll to request permission to use their islands to test atomic weapons and their effects. President Harry Truman approved the tests.

The U.S. government invited photographers, journalists, and Hollywood film crews to Bikini to record U.S. Navy Commodore Ben H. Wyatt's request to the Bikinians. According to the accounts of Wyatt's interactions with the Bikinians:

> Church services had just ended when Wyatt arrived to meet with the people, who sat cross-legged on the ground under Bikini's coconut palms near their thatched-roof village. . . . The Navy reported[:] "It was an historic occasion, this impact of the accumulated scientific knowledge of centuries upon a primitive people, and it was staged with sincerity and poise."
>
> Wyatt knew how to appeal to the Bikinians. He drew upon the Bible, the common denominator between the Bikinians and the Americans, and delivered a short homily. According to Wyatt's own account, he "compared the Bikinians to the children of Israel whom the Lord saved from their common enemy and led into the Promised Land." He described the power of the atomic bomb and "the destruction it had wrought upon the enemy," and he told the people that the Americans "are trying to learn how to use it for the good of mankind and to end all world wars." The Navy had searched the entire world for the best place to test these powerful weapons, and Bikini was it. Wyatt then asked, "Would Juda and his people be willing to sacrifice their island for the welfare of all men?" (Weisgall 1994:107).

In response to Commodore Wyatt's request, Juda, a descendant of the bloodline that settled Bikini Atoll, indicated that, if the United States needed the islands, the Bikinians would let them use it. When Juda stated to Commodore Wyatt and the film cameras, *"Men otemjej rej ped ilo pein Anij,"* or "Everything is in God's hands," he expressed his faith in God to lead the Bikinians. The Marshallese credit American Protestant missionaries with bringing *meram,* or enlightenment to the islands by ending the warring and fighting between atoll populations and teaching the people to embrace the values in the Bible. Since the missionaries that came to the islands were Americans, the United States request for assistance to help promote world peace had credibility with the Marshallese. The Bikinians wanted to make a sacrifice that would help the United States and all of humankind. Futhermore, the Bikinians saw the United States as friends and allies after the U.S. liberation of the Marshall Islands from the brutal Japanese military regime. Honoring a request by the United States was one way to express appreciation for the U.S. actions in World War II (Almej 1999).

The United States government evacuated the Bikinians from their home islands in March 1946 in preparation for the first tests. Operation Crossroads, a name that reflects the historic juncture for the United States in the development of nuclear weapons, was the name given to the first and highly publicized series of weapons tests. Operation Crossroads consisted of two atomic tests, Test Able, an airdrop over Bikini on June 30, 1946, and Test Baker, an underwater test detonated in Bikini's lagoon on July 24, 1946. The U.S. government placed 95 vessels, including decommissioned American aircraft carriers, captured Japanese battleships, and a German cruiser in Bikini's lagoon before the tests. Researchers strapped pigs, rats, sheep, and goats to the vessels to see how they would withstand the blasts. Shot Able missed the target by a half mile and only sank a few ships. The Baker shot, detonated 90 feet below the water, sent a large plume of radioactive seawater into the air and sunk many ships (Figure 2.2). Observers of the tests from nearby ships could hear the faint cries of the animals on the distant ships (Welsome 1999:172). Hours after the tests, fifteen thousand American soldiers went back to Bikini's lagoon to survey the ships for damage and to hand scrub the ships in an effort to decontaminate them (Figure 2.3). The American soldier population was the first group exposed to dangerous levels of radiation from the testing program in the Marshall Islands.

During Operation Crossroads and each subsequent test series, the U.S. government's ability to secure the Marshall Islands ensured that only U.S. government scientists and researchers or contractors had access to the test sites or the highly confidential data about the effects of the tests. The few journalists that were allowed to witness the events had to have their stories approved by U.S. government officials before they were permitted to circulate them. Throughout the testing program, the U.S. government did not share even basic information, such as the number of tests, their yields, and the path of the fallout clouds for each test with the Marshallese people, the American public, or the international community (Barker 1997).

It was not until July 1947, a full year after Operation Crossroads, that the Marshall Islands officially became a trust territory of the United States. In the shuffling of national and political boundaries after World War II, the United Nations established 11 trust territories. The Trust Territory of the Pacific Islands (TTPI), that included the Marshall Islands, was the only trusteeship designated a "strategic" territory. As the administering authority, the United Nations required the United States to promote the health and well being of the citizens of the trust territory and to "protect the inhabitants [of the Trusteeship] against the loss of their lands and resources" (UN Trusteeship Council 1958).

Despite its promises to care for the people and their land, the United States determined that the strategic designation enabled the United States to use its territory for closed military operations. From 1946 to 1958, the U.S. government used its territory to detonate 67 atomic and thermonuclear weapons in the air, on the land, and in the seas surrounding the Marshall Islands. Some of these detonations completely vaporized islands, islands that no longer exist today; giant craters in the lagoons of Bikini and Enewetak atolls bear the scars marking the locations where islands once stood (Figure 2.4).

Eighteen of the tests detonated in the Marshall Islands were in the megaton range. Nearly 80 percent of all the atmospheric tests ever conducted by the United

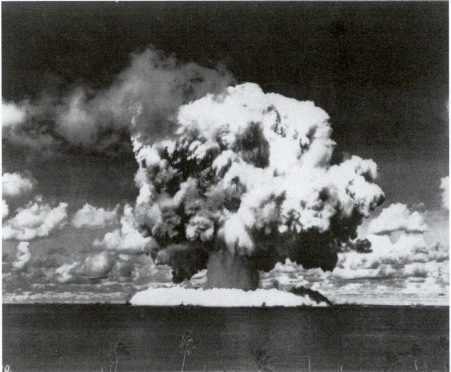

Figure 2.2 Baker shot sinking ships in Bikini's lagoon

States took place in the Marshall Islands. Thirty-three of the weapons tests in the Marshall Islands had greater yields than the largest atmospheric test conducted by the U.S. government in Nevada (O. deBrum 1999).

The power of the weapons tests completely pulverized six coral islands that no longer exist. The force of the explosions pulled the crushed coral of the vaporized islands and the surrounding water into the giant mushroom clouds that grew to 25 miles in diameter, in the case of the Bravo test. Crushed coral and water mixed with the radioactive particles released in the blast fell to the ground in the form of radioactive fallout. Scientists monitored the movement of radiation from the Marshall Islands as the atmosphere carried it to neighboring countries in the Pacific, and to every continent in the world.

On a local level, the force of the blasts obliterated lands and natural resources that the people depended on for survival. The radiation released from the tests exposed every atoll in the Marshall Islands to radiation. The levels of radiation were highest, however, in the northern atolls closest to the ground-zero locations. When radioactive ash fell on the islands where Marshallese people live, the people inhaled radiation into their lungs. In areas where fallout was severe, radioactive fallout stuck to the coconut oil people use on their skin and hair to keep them soft. Children played with and even ate what looked to them like snow. At no time did the U.S. government warn communities about the dangers of fallout, or instruct them about safety precautions should they experience fallout.

Figure 2.3 To decontaminate themselves, U.S. government workers scrub with Tide detergent

In addition to the direct inhalation or exposure to radiation, the Marshallese peo-ple ate and drank food and water tainted by radiation as the fallout contaminated resources and entered the food chain. Consequently, the health of the people was not only compromised by direct exposure to radiation, but also from radiation-related ill-nesses as a result of living on contaminated islands where radiation taints the water and food chain.

Although it is difficult to pinpoint exactly which health problems result from radiation exposure, it is clear that the introduction of radiation into the Marshallese environment results in numerous health care problems for the Marshallese, such as an array of cancers and thyroid diseases. Many of the northern most islands in the Marshall Islands remain too radioactive today for people to live or subsist directly from local foods. In addition to health problems from exposure to radiation, other populations, such as those that the U.S. government forced to leave their lands, expe-rience a different set of health problems linked to the testing program or nutrition and way of life. When the U.S. government displaced communities to areas where peo-ple could not cultivate local resources, it provided them with food subsidies, such as canned goods high in fat and sodium. Radioactive fallout exposed the Marshallese people and their environment to dangerous levels of radiation and consequently altered the health, economy, culture, nutrition, and well being of the islanders in the decades that followed.

As a precaution, the U.S. government initially evacuated Marshallese living downwind from the test sites for much smaller tests. When it came time to test the largest thermonuclear weapon ever conducted by the United States, the Bravo shot,

© The National Archives

Figure 2.4 Crater from a weapons test on Bikini Atoll

the U.S. government did not evacuate Marshallese communities despite knowledge that the winds could carry radioactive fallout from the test site and that the wind was blowing directly toward inhabited islands on the day of the test. The government of the Republic of the Marshall Islands (RMI) believes it was no accident that the U.S. government purposefully left the Marshallese people in harm's way and exposed people to radioactive fallout.

The Bravo shot was the equivalent of more than one-thousand Hiroshima-sized bombs and was designed to produce as much local fallout as possible for scientific purposes. By keeping fallout in the local area, researchers helped allay international criticism about the levels of worldwide contamination (Atomic Energy Commission 1954). I will explore the implications of the testing program for the Marshallese.

Despite efforts to produce as much local fallout as possible, radiation from the Bravo test spread throughout the world. One scientist located radioactivity in the thyroid glands of slaughtered steer that grazed on grass in Memphis, Tennessee. The scientist knew that radioactivity in the steers' thyroid came from fallout produced in the Marshall Islands. The monitoring of thousands of thyroid glands of slaughtered steer confirmed his hypothesis: "We knew in one week the entire country [U.S.] was contaminated. . . . Nobody believed you could contaminate the world from one spot" (Middlesworth in Welsome 1999:303). The Marshallese were not told about the effects of Bravo in their own nation, and certainly were not aware of its effects worldwide.

Fearing that their own world was becoming contaminated by the nuclear weapons tests, the Marshallese people attempted to petition the United Nations in 1954 and in 1957 to address the problems caused by the testing. Prior to petitioning the United Nations, the Marshallese voiced their concerns to the U.S. government administrators of the trust territory, but the U.S. government did not respond to their protests. The only other place the Marshallese could voice their concerns was the

United Nations. The 1957 petition expresses the Marshallese people's concern about damage to their health and the long-term implications of removal from their land:

> We, the Marshallese people feel that we must follow the dictates of our consciences to bring forth this urgent plea to the United Nations, which has pledged itself to safeguard the life, liberty, and the general well being of the people of the Trust Territory, of which the Marshallese people are a part. . . . The Marshallese people are not only fearful of the danger to their persons from these deadly weapons in case of another miscalculation, but they are also very concerned for the increasing number of people who are being removed from their land.
>
> . . . Land means a great deal to the Marshallese. It means more than just a place where you can plant your food crops and build your houses; or a place where you can bury your dead. It is the very life of the people. Take away their land and their spirit goes also. . . . (UN Trusteeship Council 1958).

William Lodge, the U.S. Ambassador to the United Nations, asked the Secretary General not to introduce the 1957 Marshallese petition to the United Nations until after the United States completed its last testing series in 1958 (Lodge 1958). The UN Secretary General agreed, and the United Nations considered the Marshallese petition four years after the Marshallese first used political channels to complain to the United Nations about the effects of the testing program. Although the Marshallese took the appropriate steps to protest the U.S. nuclear weapons testing program, as the colonial administrators of the Trusteeship, the U.S. government controlled all political developments by speaking for the Marshall Islands at the United Nations and elsewhere. The Marshallese were powerless to stop the destruction rendered against them and their islands.

As discussed in Chapters 6 and 7, the sense of powerlessness and the active resistance to U.S. government domination and control of the testing agenda is evident in the Marshallese language. The Marshallese language, as other languages, reflects the history of its speakers (Ngugi 1986). The abuses and radiation exposures imposed on the Marshallese by the U.S. government led to the selective victimization of the Marshallese people, a population that the U.S. government considered expendable and not as important as the pursuit of U.S. government strategic interests (Johnston 1994). This sense of victimization is evident in the language of the radiation populations who use their language to describe the events they witnessed and the changes to their health and environment they continue to experience. The victimization that people felt during the testing program, however, is giving way to a local desire of many people who were profoundly affected by radiation to take control of their lives and make conscious decisions about the type of life they want to build for their communities in a post-testing environment. In recent years, the Marshallese have become increasingly effective at learning how to influence U.S. government policy on radiological issues in the Marshall Islands by lobbying Congress and working directly with the executive branch.

THE ARRIVAL OF ANTHROPOLOGISTS

As an anthropologist working in the Marshall Islands, much of my work is influenced by the work of the anthropologists who preceded me. Good or bad, the communities where we work formulate opinions about anthropologists based on the actions and research of the collective group. Of course people will understand the differences between individual anthropologists, but there is an undeniable connection between the type of work that anthropologists do. Therefore, as anthropologists we have several obligations: first, and most importantly to the communities we work with, and secondly to our colleagues. In this section I will review the work of anthropologists working on issues related to the nuclear weapons testing and discuss the importance of applied anthropology as an empowerment mechanism for communities.

Anthropology during the Trust Territory

From the moment the U.S. government became interested in the Marshall Islands from a strategic perspective—even before the Marshall Islands became a part of the trust territory—the U.S. government employed anthropologists to learn more about the people and the culture in the area of interest. In 1943, anthropologist William Kreiger produced a war background study for the Smithsonian Institution that detailed local power structures and gave the U.S. military clear examples for the best means to work with and gain control over the people. Efforts to understand the psyche and social organization of the Marshallese helped American forces persuade Marshallese to join them in weakening the Japanese forces that held the islands during World War II.

After World War II, the U.S. government used anthropological research to demonstrate scientifically the primitivism of the people and to create a justification for the U.S. government's need to control and administrate the area. The U.S. government hired early anthropologists to the area, predominantly American, to justify the U.S. self-interest in the colonial process (Hanlon 1994).

The U.S. government employed numerous anthropologists in the Pacific region. Anthropologist Margaret Mead collaborated with the U.S. military and exerted a tremendous influence on anthropology in the region. Mead challenged antinuclear sentiments in the United States and believed that the westernization and militarization of the Pacific were the best avenues for modernizing the region (Gilliam and Foerstel 1992). The U.S. Army asked Mead to produce knowledge about the people and their culture for strategic purposes (*ibid:*127). In the vein of Mead's anthropology, early anthropologists in Micronesia helped produce studies that explained local power structures and the best means to gain the cooperation of local populations. This cooperation was essential to the U.S. government as it needed local assistance on a variety of military projects, including the construction of buildings and airfields.

Anthropologists in Micronesia worked with the U.S. military on two strategic initiatives: in the late 1940s, the United States Commercial Company conducted an economic survey to improve the Navy's ability to administer the islands (Mason 1989, Alcalay 1992); from 1947 to 1959, the navy sponsored a Coordinated Investigation of Micronesian Anthropology (CIMA), which spread 35 anthropologists throughout Micronesia to "compil[e] basic scientific information on the islands and to 'provide data relevant to the practical problems of administering the area and its peoples'" (Marshall and Nason in Alcalay 1992:185). The U.S. administrators assigned anthropologists to the district or local levels to serve "as intermediaries between the Micronesians and the [U.S. g]overnment" (Mason 1989:7). Because U.S. strategic interests in the Trusteeship centered on the U.S. nuclear weapons testing program, most anthropologists worked in the Marshall Islands.

After the United Nations placed the Marshall Islands under the administration of the U.S. government, one of the first anthropologists to arrive was Jack Tobin. Tobin prepared reports for the Office of the High Commissioner of the Trust Territory of the Pacific. In 1946, Tobin helped the U.S. Navy relocate the people from their home atoll of Bikini so the U.S. government could use the atoll for its first weapons tests. A year later, Tobin assisted with the relocation of the residents of Enewetak Atoll when the United States required a second ground-zero location for its weapons testing program. Tobin's work focused on the sociopolitical and land tenure problems resulting from displacement. The people of Bikini, for example, refused to recognize their paramount chief's rights to govern on Kili, the island where the community resettled, because the paramount chief did not own the land on Kili (Tobin 1953). As the Bikinians contested the authority of their chief during exile, Tobin reported to the U.S. administering authority that "the people have decided that they will stay under the U.S. government" (Tobin 1953:22). Because the U.S. government wanted the Micronesian people to cooperate with U.S. strategic interests, the administering authority was undoubtedly pleased to learn from Tobin that the Bikinians transferred the traditional care-taking role of their leaders to the U.S. government.

Alexander Spoehr and Leonard Mason were also among the first anthropologists on the ground in the Marshall Islands. Mason's research into the effect of displacement from the nuclear weapons testing alerted the High Commissioner of the trust territory about the near starvation of the Bikini community after the U.S. government relocated them to Rongerik Atoll for two years. Mason documented an accidental fire that destroyed critical food resources, and how the extended use of limited resources from a small area resulted in a critical food shortage. In an attempt to avert starvation, Mason noted that the desperate Bikinians destroyed all the plants on Rongerik, and chopped down coconut trees to eat the core, or heart of the palm (Mason 1948). It is also noteworthy that after their employment with the trust territory government ended, both Tobin and Mason remained deeply concerned for the well being of the Marshallese people for the duration of their professional careers.

Because Tobin and Mason worked for the trust territory government, the U.S. government used the information gathered in their reports for its own purposes. In this case, the primary purpose of the anthropological research was to exploit the Marshallese people and to pursue the U.S. government's strategic interests in the Marshall Islands. Although this information was not always used to assist local people, both Tobin and Mason became masters of the Marshallese language and developed deep ties with the local communities. Consequently, they became advocates for the local people. Mason's report about the near starvation of the Bikinians, for example, convinced the U.S. government to find an alternative location for the Bikinians during their exile.

After the U.S. nuclear weapons testing program ended in 1958, the U.S. government allowed anthropologists without affiliations to the U.S. government to enter the Marshall Islands. Byron Bender masterfully compiled a list of Marshallese place names and their meanings and became the first linguistic anthropologist to work in the Marshall Islands. Nancy Pollock studied nutrition on Namu Atoll. The only anthropologist to research an issue related to the nuclear weapons testing in the period before the trust territory ended was Robert Kiste.

Kiste's 1974 monograph, *The Bikinians: A Study in Forced Migration,* remains a classic for Pacific scholars. Kiste's research poignantly illustrates the powerlessness of the Bikinians in the face of the U.S. government's strategic and military interests, and the social, cultural, political, and economic problems that resulted when the U.S.

government removed a Marshallese community from its land. Kiste shaped peoples' understanding of the long-term problems—not just the immediate threats from radiation exposure—caused by the nuclear weapons testing program. Tobin, Mason, and Kiste helped lay the foundation for understanding the human consequences experienced by the populations displaced from the U.S. nuclear weapons testing program.

Anthropology in the Post-Trust Territory

As the relationship between the U.S. and RMI governments evolved from a trust territory to an independent relationship based on free association, so did anthropology in the Marshall Islands. Laurence Carucci, for example, spent several decades documenting the hardships and transitions of the Enewetak community as a result of their forced resettlement to Ujelang Atoll and the return of a portion of the community to Enewetak.[1] Carucci also researched the changes in Christmas rituals for the people of Enewetak as a result of the U.S. nuclear weapons testing program. Carucci's research includes descriptions of traditional Christmas dances incorporating themes about nuclear bombs or missiles, as well as changes to the traditional Christmas diet as a result of U.S. government food subsidies provided to the population. The communities of Bikini, Rongelap, Utrik, and Enewetak all receive U.S. government surplus food commodities because the foods on their atolls remain too contaminated for human consumption or because food supplies are limited in the areas where the U.S. government relocated the communities.

In the post-trust territory era, the Nuclear Claims Tribunal, established as part of the nuclear settlement of the Compact of Free Association, provided an unexpected and interesting venue for anthropological work. In the post-trust territory era, the role of anthropologists in the Marshall Islands has shifted away from conducting research for the U.S. government and increasingly toward applied anthropology. One unexpected employer of anthropologists is the Nuclear Claims Tribunal, the Tribunal established at the end of the trust territory as an alternative to the U.S. courts to consider claims arising from the testing program for personal injury and property damage. Lawrence Carucci, Nancy Pollock, Glenn Alcalay, Barbara Rose Johnston and I (as discussed in Chapter 5) all worked as anthropological consultants to the Tribunal. Carucci's participation in the first land claim before the Tribunal displayed the role anthropologists can play as cultural brokers. Carucci lived and worked with the Enewetak people for more than two decades and Carucci helped the Tribunal judges to understand the severe hardships encountered by the Enewetakese as a result of their displacement from their home islands, the problems they faced during their relocation, and current challenges that the community faces. Presently, a large portion of the Enewetak community returned to one island on the atoll after the U.S. government stripped it of all soil and trees in an effort to reduce residual contamination. The people of Enewetak started from scratch to rebuild their community, including intensive agricultural programs to restore the soil and to plant trees. Carucci, as well as the attorney for Enewetak, Davor Pevec, successfully

---

[1]The people from Enjebi Island of Enewetak Atoll have not resettled their home island due to high levels of residual radiological contamination. The portion of the Enewetak atoll that was resettled returned to an island scraped of the top level of soil, including the trees and plants, in an effort to reduce human radiation exposure. The resettled community also lives adjacent to a nuclear waste storage facility on Runit Island that contains the radiological debris and contaminated soil from the testing program.

persuaded the Tribunal to award $34 million to the community for the hardships it endured as a result of the testing program.[2]

In the case of all anthropologists working for the Tribunal, with exception of Nancy Pollock, the anthropologists worked for the local governments or the Public Advocate to help articulate the difficulties experienced by communities in the RMI as a result of the weapons testing program. Pollock served as a consultant to the Public Defender. As the titles suggest, the Public Advocate advocates for the interests of the claimants and assists them with their cases before the Tribunal, while the Public Defender of the fund protects the corpus of the Tribunal's funds by making sure the claimants are legitimate. Although it is difficult to understand how an anthropologist could undertake research intended to challenge the claims of radiation survivors, Pollock's participation in the Tribunal's deliberations allowed the Tribunal to conduct fair hearings and to fully consider the merit of the claims.

Similarly to Carucci, Glenn Alcalay translated his decades of work with the Utrik people into a powerful case of community damages presented to the Nuclear Claims Tribunal. Alcalay completed his testimony to the Tribunal in 2002, and like the Rongelap land claim case that Barbara Rose Johnston and I worked on, the Tribunal has yet to make a ruling on Utrik's case.

Out of all the anthropologists that researched issues related to the weapons testing program, Glenn Alcalay produced the most groundbreaking work. As a Peace Corps volunteer, Alcalay lived on Utrik for two years. He learned the language and the culture, and he developed a deep rapport with the people that is ongoing. The Peace Corps assigned Alcalay to Utrik during the time that the U.S. Department of Energy sent medical researchers from Brookhaven National Laboratory to study the effects of radiation exposure on human beings. Alcalay gained a firsthand understanding of the U.S. government's exploitation of the community for research purposes by observing the U.S. government's failure to translate information about medical procedures and their results to the community, or to obtain the consent of the people for the procedures. These experiences led Alcalay to become an advocate for the communities most affected by the testing program.

After returning to the United States, Alcalay successfully used political channels and the media to bring attention to the abusive power relationship between the U.S. government and the people of the Marshall Islands. Alcalay appeared before the United Nations and discussed the injustices he witnessed. Alcalay assisted major American television companies in putting together documentaries about the real consequences of the weapons testing program. Understanding the power of the media, Alcalay also published several articles about U.S. government's cover-up of information in the Marshall Islands. After receiving training as a medical anthropologist, Alcalay conducted his dissertation research on the incidence of women's reproductive health problems in the Marshall Islands. This was the first research that challenged U.S. government insistence that there are no second generation problems linked to radiation exposure in the Marshall Islands, and the first effort to systematically document the widespread extent of reproductive abnormalities in the Marshall Islands.

---

[2]Although the Tribunal judges made the award, the Tribunal does not have adequate funds to pay the Enewetakese their award.

MOVE TOWARD SELF-GOVERNANCE

U.S. colonial control of the Marshall Islands remained throughout the weapons testing period. After the testing program ended in 1958, Micronesians discussed plans to regain their autonomy. In 1965, representatives from all of the TTPI islands formed the Congress of Micronesia. The purpose of the Congress was to prepare for greater self-governance in the islands. By 1978, 48 delegates in the Marshall Islands gathered to write the nation's constitution. The Preamble of the Constitution reflects the perseverance of the Marshallese people, their pride in their island traditions, and their difficulties resulting from colonial control, war, and nuclear weapons testing:

> WE, THE PEOPLE OF THE MARSHALL ISLANDS . . . have reason to be proud of our forefathers who boldly ventured across the unknown waters of the vast Pacific Ocean many centuries ago, ably responding to the constant challenges of maintaining a bare existence on these tiny islands, in their noble quest to build their own distinctive society. This society has survived, and has withstood the test of time, the impact of other cultures, the devastation of war, and the high price paid for the purposes of international peace and security. All we have and are today as a people, we have received as a sacred heritage which we pledge ourselves to safeguard and maintain, valuing nothing more dearly than our rightful home on these islands (Preamble, Section 5.5).

On May 1, 1979, Marshallese citizens formed the government of the Marshall Islands, and the nation became self-governing although still under the auspices of the United States trusteeship. By 1982, the country changed its official name to the Republic of the Marshall Islands (RMI).

COMPACT OF FREE ASSOCIATION

After approximately 15 years of political status negotiations that involved two American presidents and their representatives and more than 30 hearings in both Houses of Congress, the RMI and the United States redefined their political relationship. Voters in the Marshall Islands approved the Compact of Free Association with the United States in 1983, but it was not until the U.S. Congress adopted the Compact as U.S. Public Law 99-239 in 1986 that the Compact came into effect.

The Compact represented a critical juncture for the Marshall Islands. The foremost achievement of the Compact was to terminate the trusteeship and to return the Marshall Islands to independence for the first time in more than four hundred years. Both the United States and the Marshall Islands understood that a trusteeship no longer served their best interests.

The Compact creates a new category of political affiliation between nations called free association. This unique relationship exists between the U.S. government and three of the nations to emerge from the TTPI: the RMI, the Federated States of Micronesia (FSM), and Palau.

The United States has a closer military relationship with the Marshall Islands than it does with either of the other two freely associated Micronesian states because of the U.S. Army's lease of Kwajalein Atoll. In fact, no other nation has a closer military alliance with the U.S. than the Marshall Islands, including NATO countries (Zackios 2001). The Marshall Islands entrusts its defense wholly to the United States. The United States also maintains plenary powers to exercise its own defense in the Marshall Islands' 750,000 square miles of land and ocean that is strategically situated between Asia and the United States. Marshallese citizens serve in every branch of the U.S. Armed Services. Under free association the Marshall Islands is not a colony or territory of the United States; it is fully self-governing and is a member state of the United Nations.

The arrangement recognizes that the RMI is fully independent and sovereign, with separate nationality and citizenship. Free association allows the RMI and the United States to remain aligned as strategic allies while simultaneously giving the RMI the right to exercise its own interests and provide Marshallese citizens with the right to enter, live, work, and go to school in the United States.

177 Agreement

In addition to terminating the trusteeship, the 177 Agreement (an agreement that refers to section 177 in the Compact, the section that addresses the consequences of the U.S. nuclear weapons testing program) is a critical component of the Compact. Under the 177 Agreement, "The Government of the United States accepts responsibility for compensation owing to citizens of the Marshall Islands . . . for loss of damage to property and person . . . resulting from the nuclear testing program. . . ." In response to its recognized responsibilities from the testing program, the U.S. government agrees to provide remedies to address associated damages and injuries. Under the 177 Agreement, the U.S. government provided the Marshall Islands with $150 million for all past, present, and future damages and injuries resulting from the nuclear weapons testing program. The $150 million amount was a political decision, not an amount based on actual damages and injuries (Hills 1999). I discuss this issue in greater detail in the next chapter.

Assistance for Radiological Problems beyond the 177 Agreement

Beyond the 177 Agreement, the Compact agrees to provide the people of Rongelap and Utrik with a medical care program operated by the U.S. Department of Energy. The U.S. government's determination of who is eligible to participate in the DOE medical program and which communities are affected by radiation gives a glimpse of the narrow terms of responsibility that the U.S. government accepts for radiation related problems.

The Compact rigidly imposes legal definitions of exposure that directly determine which Marshallese receive medical assistance for their radiation-related needs. In the section of the Compact pertaining to agreements between the Marshall Islands and the United States, the Compact provides "special medical care and logistical support" from the U.S. Department of Energy (DOE) for the population defined as "exposed" to radiation from the testing program (Section 103(h), P.L. 99-239). The Compact defines the group of people exposed to radiation as "the remaining 174 members of the population of Rongelap and Utirik who were exposed to radiation resulting from the 1954 United States thermonuclear 'Bravo' test" (*ibid*). When the Compact came into effect in 1986, only 174 people of the original 226 people exposed to radiation on Rongelap and Utrik atolls on March 1, 1954, remained alive. In 2003, less that 120 of those original survivors are alive and eligible to participate in the DOE medical program.

The DOE medical program was not a new creation under the Compact. In addition to extending the DOE medical monitoring program to the "exposed" population, the Compact also extends the program to include a control population of "unexposed" Marshallese. Immediately following the near lethal exposure of Marshallese from the Bravo test, the Atomic Energy Commission (AEC), the predecessor of DOE, sent a medical team to the Marshall Islands. As shown in Chapter 4, the people from Rongelap and Utrik were unknowingly enrolled in a top-secret medical study program to study the effects of radiation on human beings.

Beyond the medical program, the Compact also requires the U.S. Department of Energy to provide an environmental monitoring program in the areas with residual radiological contamination. For several decades, Lawrence Livermore National Laboratory (LLNL) in California has been DOE's contractor for the environmental monitoring program.

Kwajalein and Mutual Securities

The RMI's involvement in U.S. security matters was not limited to the Cold War. In fact, the RMI continues to play a critical role in supporting U.S. strategic interests. In this regard, the bilateral relationship between the RMI and the United States is based on a notion of mutual securities: the United States gains military security from the relationship and the RMI gains economic security in the form of financial assistance from the U.S. government. Specific provisions of the Compact attempt to foster economic development in the RMI, a condition necessary to support the security requirements of the U.S. From a Marshallese perspective, this arrangement works out only if the terms are fair for both sides. The Kwajalein landowners believe the United States benefits much more from the arrangement and are currently involved in negotiations with the United States to increase benefits for the people of Kwajalein.

Although separate from the Compact, the United States maintains a lease agreement for Kwajalein Atoll until 2016. Kwajalein Atoll has the world's largest lagoon that is the perfect location for the U.S. Army to test its missile defense capabilities. The U.S. Army uses the Ronald Reagan Ballistic Missile Defense Test Site on Kwajalein for the developmental testing of theater and strategic ballistic missiles and missile interceptors, to support NASA space operations, and to assist the U.S. space command with satellite tracking and surveillance.

Recent activities on Kwajalein Atoll amplify the RMI's strategic importance to the United States. On October 3, 1999, the U.S. government successfully located and destroyed a mock warhead for the first time. After the U.S. government launched a ballistic missile from Vandenberg Air Force Base in California, a "kill vehicle" sent from Kwajalein ignored a dummy target and struck the intended missile at 16,000 miles an hour, 1,400 miles away from Kwajalein. The U.S. Army conducted two additional tests successfully in 2001, and raised the Bush administration's interest in continuing development of a missile defense shield.[3]

On September 30, 2003, the economic provisions of the Compact of Free Association will terminate. While the economic security the RMI receives from the

---

[3]For additional information, see the U.S. Army's website: http://www.smdc.army.mil/KMR.html, and Wypijewski, Joann, "This Is Only a Test," *Harper's Magazine*, December 2001.

bilateral relationship ends, the U.S. government's rights to Kwajalein continue until 2016 because these rights were negotiated under a separate agreement from the Compact. The U.S. government has an interest in providing economic assistance beyond 2003 to ensure the stability of the Marshall Islands that U.S. defense interests depend on. For example, the operations on Kwajalein Atoll depend on the support of the Marshallese people, a local and healthy labor force, a stable government, and a strong bilateral relationship. In May 2003, the U.S. and RMI governments signed an agreement to renew economic provisions and extend lease rights for Kwajalein to 2066. The legislative branches of both governments must consider approve the agreement.

3/The U.S. Nuclear Weapons Testing Program

THE OFFICIAL U.S. GOVERNMENT
ACCOUNT OF THE EVENTS

As discussed in the previous chapter, the U.S. government successfully confined its responsibility for radiation-related damages to four communities in the Marshall Islands. At the time of the negotiations to terminate the trust territory relationship, the U.S. government had complete control of all scientific and medical information related to the testing program. The Marshallese did not have any scientists or doctors who were involved in or knowledgeable about the testing program. As a result, the U.S. government had complete power to define the range of damages and injuries resulting from the testing program.

In preparation for Compact negotiations and to develop a U.S. position about the consequences of the nuclear weapons testing program, the U.S. government conducted a radiological survey of the 14 northernmost atolls in the RMI. The study, undertaken in 1978, characterizes the northern atolls in terms of degrees of radiological contamination and the resulting risks for human populations that reside on the atolls. The 1978 survey is referred to in the Compact of Free Association as "represent[ing] the best effort of . . . [the U.S.] Government [to] accurately evaluate and describe radiological conditions in the Marshall Islands . . . and [it] can be used for the evaluation of the food chain and environment and estimating radiation-related health consequences of residing in the Northern Marshall Islands after 1978" (U.S. Public Law 99-239, 177 Agreement, Article VIII).

In the 1978 Department of Energy report, the authors assign a number to each of the 14 atoll areas in the study to indicate the levels of persistent radiation in 1978: a number one rating indicates "the least amount of radioactive atoms" and a number four rating represents "the largest amount of radioactive atoms" (Bair et al. 1982:9). In the survey, only the uninhabited areas of Bikini, Enewetak, and Rongelap receive ratings of four. The village area where the Rongelapese resettled in 1957 rates three, indicating "a larger amount of radiation" (*ibid:9*).

Using the 1978 survey as the basis of determining what areas in the Marshall Islands the U.S. government contaminated with radiation, U.S. government negotiators succeeded in codifying within the Compact an extremely narrow parameter for U.S. government responsibility. In the Compact and the 177 Agreement, discussion of the atolls affected by radiation is limited to four atolls: Bikini, Enewetak, Rongelap, and Utrik. Bikini and Enewetak atolls experienced severe radiological contamination as the ground-zero location for 66 of the 67 tests.[1] The U.S. government also acknowledged that fallout from the Bravo test in 1954 exposed residents of Rongelap and Utrik atolls; the U.S. government could not deny exposure to these atolls because the U.S. government evacuated its residents after Bravo and enrolled them in a program to study the effects of radiation on human beings. There is no discussion of any other atolls affected by radiation in the Compact or the 177 Agreement.

The drafting and approval process of the 177 Agreement proved to be highly contentious. Individuals in both the RMI and the United States argued that it was important to accept the 177 Agreement to prevent a delay in the termination of the trusteeship and to halt claims by individual Marshallese communities in U.S. courts. In the 177 Agreement, the U.S. government agreed to provide $150 million as a one-time settlement for all past, present, and future consequences of the testing program.

Under the 177 Agreement, the RMI had to abandon all claims in U.S. courts. As an alternative, the 177 Agreement established a Nuclear Claims Tribunal in the Marshall Islands to consider individual claims for personal injury and for property damages. The U.S. government provided the Tribunal with $45.75 million dollars to make its awards. In a January 2003 report by Governor Richard ("Dick") Thornburgh, the Attorney General for George Bush senior, Thornburgh concludes that this amount is manifestly inadequate to cover the scope of damages and injuries recognized by the Tribunal. The initial money given to the Tribunal by the U.S. government is not enough to pay for the personal injury claims, and there is no money available to pay for land damages despite the fact that the Tribunal made substantial awards for loss of property.

When the United States set aside $150 million for the 177 Agreement, it was expected that the RMI would establish a Fund that would generate $270 million over the 15 years of the Compact. Due to poor market performance and investment choices by the American company that managed the funds, the Fund did not perform as well as expected and the Fund generated less money for use under the terms of the 177 Agreement than anticipated. Furthermore, the number of claims anticipated far surpassed any initial estimation.

Through the Tribunal process, people from every atoll in the Marshall Islands, not just those in the northern area adjacent to the testing program, have successfully demonstrated to the Tribunal's judges that they contracted illnesses linked to radiation exposure, and presumed to be the result of the testing program. The Tribunal currently recognizes 35 illnesses as being linked to radiation exposure, such as a variety of cancers, thyroid diseases, and skin or bone marrow problems (see the appendix for a full accounting of radiological illnesses recognized by the Tribunal). People who contract one of these illnesses are eligible for an award if they were in the Marshall Islands during the testing program and can prove (usually in the form of a medical record) that they contracted a radiogenic illness. The size of these awards ranges from a low of $12,500 for certain thyroid disorders to $125,000 for

---

[1]The remaining tests took place on a barge in the ocean near Enewetak.

many of the cancers. If a person contracts more than one illness, he or she is eligible to receive compensation for any of the conditions recognized by the Tribunal as linked to radiation exposure. Once the Tribunal makes a personal injury award for an individual, the individual is also eligible to participate in a 177 Health Care Program.

In addition to establishing and funding the Nuclear Claims Tribunal, the 177 Agreement also provides:

- $2 million annually for 15 years to assist with health care services for the people of Enewetak, Bikini, Rongelap, and Utrik, and claimants of the Nuclear Claims Tribunal who contract a radiation-related illness (an amount that provides less than $12 per patient per month).
- $3 million for medical monitoring and surveillance (a one-time amount that has already been spent).
- $183 million in payments for claims from the testing program (allocated to the communities on a quarterly basis over the 15 years of the Compact).
  - $75 million to the people of Bikini
  - $48.75 million to the people of Enewetak
  - $37.5 million to the people of Rongelap
  - $22.5 million to the people of Utrik

Many of the communities most affected by the testing program, including the four atolls, felt betrayed by the RMI government's ultimate decision to accept the 177 Agreement because they viewed it as woefully inadequate to address the full scope of damages and injury. The national government determined, however, that it concluded the best deal it could given the circumstances and knowledge at the time. It was important to conclude the agreement so the trusteeship would end. To appease critics of the settlement, negotiators included a provision in the 177 Agreement, called the changed circumstances provision, that allows the RMI to petition Congress for additional assistance if it can produce new information about the damages and injuries from the testing program and if these new damages and injuries render the $150 million settlement manifestly inadequate.

LIMITATIONS IN U.S. GOVERNMENT RESPONSIBILITY

The 1978 survey discusses radiation levels at the time of the survey in 1978. It makes no mention of radiation levels during the 1940s and 1950s when radiation levels were highest and Marshallese populations lived in the survey areas. DOE's assertion of its power to confine the discussion of radiation exposure to narrow parameters enabled the DOE representative working on the Compact negotiations to effectively erase U.S. responsibility for acute exposures during earlier decades and to ignore the needs of any communities beyond those identified as areas of concern in the survey. Chapter 4 covers the implications for populations not adequately characterized in the 1978 survey.

By narrowing the number of atolls defined as affected by radiation to four, the U.S. government effectively limited its responsibilities for clean-up and medical problems resulting from radiation to a small area. Within the Marshall Islands, the four atoll communities defined by the United States as most affected by radiation understood the value of minimizing the number of atolls affected by the testing. The four-atoll designation created a political benefit to the four atoll communities by providing them with compensation and programs from the United States. If the U.S. government recognized more communities as affected by radiation, the four atoll communities would undoubtedly receive less of the U.S. government's assistance and compensation.

Once the four atoll communities received financial compensation from the United States, they were able to hire American lawyers to represent their interests. Through their American lawyers, the power and influence of these four atoll communities grew. To this day, the four atolls contract aggressive lawyers and lobbyists who look out for the best interests of the atoll communities on Capitol Hill. Meanwhile, the majority of the atoll populations exposed to radiation, yet never cared for or compensated by the U.S. government, do not have the financial or human resources to bring their concerns to the attention of U.S. policy makers. Most of these atolls depend on the RMI national government to assist them.

In addition to the divisions that the four-atoll designation caused between communities in the RMI, communities that were not included in the four-atoll designation have no programs to address residual radiation in their environment, or medical problems resulting from radiation exposure. The U.S. government maintains that the 1978 survey is the definitive scientific proof that other communities did not receive harmful exposure to radiation. In areas beyond the four atolls where people remember the radioactive ash that fell on their islands, people did not have scientific documents or knowledge to refute the 1978 survey or to validate the exposures they knew they received.

In addition to the exclusion of populations from care, clean-up, and compensation from the U.S. government, the definition of four atolls is problematic because it defines radiation contamination in terms of finite, geographical definitions of communities. The Compact discusses radiation exposure in terms of which people resided on four atolls during the testing program. This definition of atoll communities confines people to a single time and place and ignores the more fluid definition of community in the Marshall Islands. People move throughout the Marshall Islands constantly to visit family and areas where they have land rights. They may visit for a few days, weeks, or years. This constant movement of people provides the Marshallese people with multiple identities. The Compact's failure to account for land rights on multiple atolls and a constant movement of people in and out of the four atolls and other communities in the RMI results in a failure to provide for and compensate all people affected by the weapons testing program.

People residing on atolls in the southern area of the country may retain land rights on the four atolls. Although they were not residing on the most acutely affected atolls during the testing program, they are denied access to the land and the cultivation of its resources. Or, they may have lived on or worked in contaminated lands even if they were not present during the testing program. In another scenario, a Marshallese reverend and his family moved from Arno Atoll in the south of the Marshall Islands to live and work on Rongelap Atoll when the U.S. government initially resettled the community in a highly contaminated environment. They are not considered a part of the Rongelap community by the Compact, and they do not have land rights to the area. As a result, they are not entitled to the medical programs available to the Rongelapese despite the fact that they contracted cancers and other radiological problems after living on Rongelap when it was dangerously contaminated.

One of the most poignant examples of a group of people that is not from the four atolls but was exposed to high levels of radiation in those four atolls is the Marshallese clean-up workers. After the testing program ended, the United States attempted to clean up and restore Bikini and Enewetak atolls. The clean-up involved removing the top layer of soil and radiologically contaminated debris (pieces of metal, buildings, and other rubble from the structures erected for the testing program) from the atolls. The U.S. government contracted Marshallese workers to do the clean-up work. These workers, and sometimes their families, lived on the ground-zero atolls in the 1970s and 1980s when the atolls remained highly contaminated. Their jobs consisted of bulldozing radiological materials into the ocean, or in the case of Runit Island on Enewetak, into a large crater from one of the tests; the crater was then capped with cement and functions as a nuclear waste storage site (Figure 3.1). Ground-moving activities, particularly bulldozing, were dangerous to the workers because they released plutonium particles from the soil into the air that the workers breathed. Plutonium is most dangerous to human beings when it is inhaled.

Many Marshallese workers and their families that resided on Bikini and Enewetak became ill as a result of their exposure to radiation. Due to the restricted definitions of community and exposure in the Compact, the Marshallese test-site workers and their families are not eligible for medical monitoring or care. Frustrated by their inability to get medical care or compensation from the U.S. government, the workers created an organization called Marshall Islands Radiation Victims Association (MIRVA). To this day, MIRVA continues to fight to get assistance for its members; the U.S. government still fails to recognize the plight of the Marshallese workers. As discussed later in the book, there are many other categories of people exposed to radiation, but outside the purview of U.S. government assistance and recognition.

"Exposed" and "Unexposed"

In the same manner that the U.S. government used the 1978 survey to control the number of atolls defined as exposed to radiation, the U.S. government also maintained control of all information about the medical consequences of radiation exposure in the Marshall Islands. For years, medical practitioners conducted exams of the evacuated Rongelap and Utrik populations in English without the consent of the participants.

The U.S. government established a control group to compare the incidence of radiation-related illnesses between the small populations from Rongelap and Utrik that directly experienced the effects of the Bravo test on March 1, 1954, and a control group of "unexposed" Marshallese. Some members of the control population resided in the capitol, Majuro, and matched the Rongelapese and Utrikese by sex and age. Other members of the "unexposed" group were not present on Rongelap or Utrik in 1954, but joined the Rongelap community in 1958 when the U.S. government resettled them on their home atoll. The Rongelapese and members of the control group resettled a highly contaminated environment where they lived, ate, drank, worked, and played in an area with dangerous levels of residual radiation.

Over time, the "unexposed" control population exhibited the same types of illnesses, such as thyroid nodules, cancers, and reproductive abnormalities, as the legally exposed group of Rongelapese that experienced the Bravo test. From 1954

© The National Archives

Figure 3.1 Runit Dome on Enewetak

until 1998 when the DOE contractor changed, DOE summaries of its medical find-ings maintain that the health effects of radiation exposure in the Marshall Islands are minimal because the "unexposed" control group experience the same medical problems as the "exposed" population. In other words, DOE says that the medical problems experienced by the "exposed" population are nothing out of the ordinary since they also appear in a population that is "unexposed" to radiation (Conard 1965). Later in the book, I discuss the problems that populations face when they are exposed to radiation but denied medical care and assistance from the U.S. government.

RECENTLY DECLASSIFIED
U.S. GOVERNMENT DOCUMENTS

In the early 1990s, the U.S. media and the Congress became concerned about reports that the U.S. government conducted human radiation experiments during the Cold War. To investigate the allegations of experimentation and possible unethical conduct by the U.S. government, President Clinton created a White House Advisory Com-mittee on Human Radiation Experiments (ACHRE) in 1994. President Clinton directed ACHRE "to uncover the history of human radiation experiments and inten-tional environmental releases of radiation; to identify the ethical and scientific stan-dards for evaluation of these events; and to make recommendations to ensure that whatever wrongdoing may have occurred in the past cannot be repeated" (ACHRE 1995:1). In its search for information, ACHRE located and urged the U.S. govern-ment to declassify thousands of U.S. government documents related to human radi-ation experiments. President Clinton's Secretary of Energy, Hazel O'Leary, released the newly declassified documents from her agency to the public as part of an "open-ness initiative."

As a result of the openness initiative, the U.S. government literally handed over thousands of documents to the RMI government, documents seen by the Marshallese for the first time. The RMI government received information about the U.S. nuclear weapons testing program that the U.S. government did not share with the Marshallese during the testing program or during negotiations to determine the U.S. government's responsibility for the testing program. It was my job to sift through the boxes of documents that began to arrive at the doorstep of the RMI's embassy in Washington, DC.

The declassified documents demonstrate, without question, that the level of damages and injury from radiation was much more widespread than previously understood. The RMI government has conclusive documentary evidence that atolls previously considered "unexposed" to radiation, atolls such as Ailuk, Likiep, Wotho, Mejit, and Kwajalein, received dangerous levels of radiation. Furthermore, the documents show that the U.S. government was aware of the high exposures to these atolls during the testing program but did not provide the evacuation, clean-up, and medical care warranted by the exposure. In the case of Ailuk atoll, a recently declassified U.S. government document states that the U.S. government made a purposeful decision not to evacuate the people of Ailuk although they knew that the atoll received substantial fallout from Bravo:

> [b]ased upon the best estimate of the fallout time it was calculated that a dose . . . would reach 20 roentgens. Balancing the effort required to move the 400 inhabitants against the fact that such a dose would not be a medical problem it was decided not to evacuate the atoll (U.S. Air Force 1954).

Given that the people of Utrik received a dose of approximately 17 roentgens, it is clear that the U.S. government knew 20 roentgens would create medical problems for the community. Ground and air surveyors that went to Utrik after the Bravo test "[d]ecide[d] to evacuat[e] based upon the fact that estimated dose at time of earliest evacuation would be 13 r[oentgens]" (Deines 1991). The failure to evacuate Ailuk is also troubling because the Maximum Permissible Exposure (MPE) for a U.S. serviceman in the RMI at the time was 3.9 roentgens. Clearly a double standard was at work that led to a higher permissible exposure for Marshallese citizens. What is saddest about the Ailuk document, however, is that the U.S. government found it too much of an "effort" or burden to remove 400 people from a highly radioactive environment. The people of Ailuk could have been spared tremendous health, social, and environmental burdens if the U.S. government had evacuated the Ailukese from their contaminated environment after Bravo and provided them with medical care during the last five decades.

Some of the most startling information in the declassified documents pertains to the weather conditions before the Bravo test, the extent of exposure from the Bravo shot and other tests (such as top-secret medical studies conducted on the radiation survivors), and the resettlement of communities on highly contaminated lands.

Weather

In 1954, the U.S. government prepared to detonate its largest nuclear weapon ever tested, the Bravo shot. As part of test preparations, U.S. government researchers consulted meteorological data regarding wind direction and the potential radiological hazards that could result from Bravo. From recently declassified documents it is clear that some researchers predicted the winds would push Bravo's radioactive fallout toward inhabited atolls to the east and southeast of Bikini. Colonel Lulejian, a U.S. government meteorologist determined that "the [inhabited] islands of Rongerik, Rongelap, and Bikar are clearly in the fall-out area even when . . . a simple extrapolation is used" (Lulejian 1954). U.S. government documents also demonstrate that military commanders purposefully ignored or rejected predictions about exposure to inhabited atolls. After receiving one such report, the Commander of Joint Task Force 7, the military team responsible for carrying out the testing program, D. W. Clarkson, proposed to "treat the report the same as I would a report from any other member of my staff when I do not agree with him. In short, we will kill it and stick it in the file" (Clarkson 1953).

For smaller tests conducted before the Bravo shot, the U.S. government evacuated downwind communities when there was a concern about possible exposure to the islanders. Prior to the Bravo test, however, the U.S. government decided to exclude the people of Rongelap from the evacuation area. There were no precautionary evacuations before the Bravo test despite the fact that Bravo was purposefully designed to produce as much local fallout as possible both to reduce international criticism about worldwide fallout and to create a laboratory in the Marshall Islands to study the effects of radiation.

Just six hours prior to the Bravo test, U.S. government weather forecasters determined that the winds from the test site on Bikini Atoll were blowing in the direction of the inhabited atolls of Rongelap and Rongerik (House 1954). Despite this weather report and other predictions by meteorologists, Commander D. W. Clarkson proceeded with the detonation of the Bravo weapon. The giant mushroom cloud from Bravo extended upward more than 100,000 feet, and fallout from it eventually reached every continent in the world. As predicted by U.S. government meteorologists, the radioactive cloud spread over inhabited islands, where the dusty, gray fallout rained on Marshallese communities.

Exposure from Bravo

Once Bravo's radioactive cloud began to move downwind, Joint Task Force 7 ordered the evacuation of U.S. government weather forecasters stationed on Rongerik Atoll to monitor radiation levels from the test. Joint Task Force 7 also ordered the weather forecasters not to eat or drink anything, and to put long sleeve shirts on. Within hours after the fallout, the U.S. government sent airplanes to Rongerik Atoll to evacuate the weather forecasters.

Less than 20 miles from Rongerik, the Marshallese community on Rongelap was totally unprepared for the large fireball that rose in the sky, or for the radioactive fallout that rained down on them. A U.S. military ship anchored off of Rongelap during the Bravo test steamed away from the approaching fallout cloud without evacuating the residents of Rongelap.

The Rongelapese were exposed to near-lethal amounts of radiation from Bravo. According to a declassified U.S. government document:

> The individuals exposed on Rongelap and Ailinginae remained outdoors and had no access to shelter of any kind on the island. . . . [T]he heavy coconut oil hair dressing used

by the Marshallese tended to concentrate radioactivity in the hair . . . (Joint Task Force 7 1955:10–11).

The U.S. government waited more than two full days before evacuating the people from Rongelap and Utrik after their exposure to fallout from Bravo. The U.S. government took residents of the evacuated communities to the U.S. military facility on Kwajalein Atoll where American doctors examined them.

Project 4.1

On November 10, 1953, four months before the Bravo test, the headquarters of Joint Task Force 7 in Los Alamos distributed a document outlining the scientific tests to be performed in conjunction with the Bravo test. This document lists 48 scientific programs ranging from measuring the force of the winds produced by the blast to monitoring radiation in plankton throughout the Pacific Ocean. Also contained in this list of scientific studies was Project 4.1 entitled "Study of Response of Human Beings Exposed to Significant Beta and Gamma Radiation Due to Fall-Out from High Yield Weapons."

When the Bravo test exposed Marshallese populations downwind from Bikini Atoll on March 1, 1954, Project 4.1 came to fruition. The U.S. government issued a preliminary report on Project 4.1 on April 29, 1954; the title was modified, and was called the "Study of Response of Human Beings *Accidentally* Exposed to Significant Fall-Out Radiation" [emphasis added].

The RMI government brought the 1953 document that included Project 4.1 in the list of Bravo tests to the attention of the U.S. government (T. deBrum 1994). The RMI government asserted that the exposure of Marshallese to fallout from Bravo was premeditated. Project 4.1 took place during the same time period that the United States conducted human radiation experiments with its own citizens (see Chapter 9). The U.S. government responded by saying that someone in the U.S. government went back to the 1953 document after the Bravo incident to insert the Project 4.1 study. Many people in the Marshall Islands do not accept the U.S. government's explanation and maintain that the United States purposefully exposed Marshallese citizens to radiation.

Project 4.1 became an elaborate study that included the acutely exposed populations from Rongelap and Utrik, a control population from Majuro and Kwajalein that matched the demographics of the acutely exposed group, and the 28 U.S. weather forecasters exposed to radiation and immediately evacuated from Rongerik Atoll. Project 4.1 had a convenient range of exposures to study in its human population— studies that would continue for decades after the 1954 event. The U.S. government never asked people for permission to enroll them as study subjects in Project 4.1.

Initially, Project 4.1 doctors documented the loss of hair, burns, blood counts, and nausea resulting from the initial radiation exposure (Figures 3.2 and 3.3). Patients did not receive painkillers or medication for their burns that went down to the bone, in some cases. After documenting the immediate effects of exposure to radioactive fall-out, Project 4.1 doctors established a regular schedule for monitoring the health of the people enrolled in the study. A U.S. government weapons laboratory in New York, Brookhaven National Laboratory, assumed responsibility for Project 4.1.

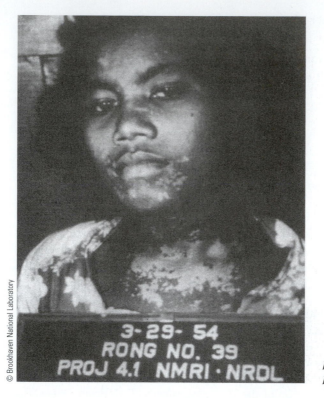

Figure 3.2 Photo of a
Project 4.1 test subject

Doctors routinely took blood, bone marrow, and urine samples from the patients. Researchers did not provide translators, and the Marshallese patients did not understand the procedures doctors subjected them to. From the Marshallese perspective, they knew they were sick and they assumed that the doctors were taking care of them. Over time, the patients complained to U.S. government officials that they felt like "guinea pigs." In some cases, communities protested the doctors' visits and refused to allow the doctors to examine them. U.S. government researchers used bribery or force to ensure that the doctors had access to the patients. The local police returned children who ran away from the doctors; during the trust territory the police force was under the authority of U.S. government administrators.

As discussed in Chapter 9, information about the effects of radiation exposure in the Marshall Islands was just one of multiple studies by the Atomic Energy Commission using human subjects to understand how radiation affects human beings.

Studies Involving Radioisotopes

Project 4.1 was not the only study to take place without the consent or knowledge of the Marshallese. President Clinton's Advisory Committee on Human Radiation Experiments acknowledged that the U.S. government undertook research projects that were of no benefit to the Marshallese and increased the radiation exposure level of individuals already exposed to substantial doses of radiation.

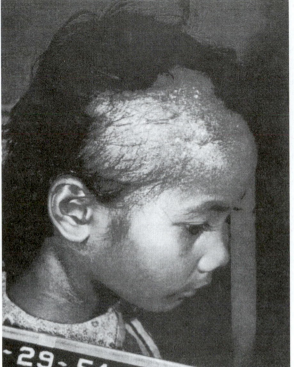

© Brookhaven National Laboratory

Figure 3.3a Photo of Project 4.1 test subject, Nerje Joseph, after the Bravo test

© Holly M. Barker

Figure 3.3b Photo of Nerje Joseph today, standing beside her photo as a girl

U.S. government researchers administered chromium-51, a radioactive substance, to people from the Rongelap community. Researchers used chromium-51 as a tracer to tag red blood cells and measure red blood cell mass. Researchers administered the substance to people from Rongelap who were not present for the Bravo incident in 1954, but resettled on Rongelap in 1957. The U.S. government maintained that chromium-51 would not present a risk to the test subjects because they were considered "unexposed" to radiation. This rationale failed to take into consideration the substantial exposure test subjects received from consuming contaminated foods and living in a radioactive environment (for an example of the health and reproductive problems experienced by this "unexposed" population that received chromium-51, see Catherine Jibas' testimony in Chapter 4).

In another experiment, U.S. government researchers exposed subjects to radiation when they administered a chelating agent (EDTA) to some individuals exposed to fallout from Bravo. The chelating agent was supposed to bond with radiation and help move radiation out of the body after internal exposure. In this case, however, the chelating agent was administered seven weeks after exposure and U.S. government researchers acknowledged that there was no therapeutic benefit for the test subjects. Consequently, the U.S. government knowingly increased the radiation burden of a population already acutely exposed for research purposes.

Resettlement of Communities

It is clear that Marshallese populations received high levels of external and internal radiation as a result of the radioactive fallout produced by the weapons tests. The fallout that landed on people's skin and hair produced external exposures to radiation. People also received internal exposure to radiation that they breathed into their lungs, or swallowed when they drank or ate contaminated food and water after the tests.

In addition to the exposure people received directly from the fallout, the declassified documents provide evidence of substantial exposure to radiation from the environment. The U.S. government exposed Marshallese people to environmental sources of radiation when it resettled populations on highly contaminated lands, and in some cases, when it failed to remove people from contaminated environments immediately after the weapons tests. The declassified documents also make it clear that the U.S. government understood that environmental sources of radiation posed a health threat to the people, particularly the communities that returned to the highly contaminated lands. The protracted exposure of the Marshallese occurred after people returned to the contaminated areas. The people of Utrik and Rongelap returned to an environment involving radioactivity from many detonations, not just the Bravo test. The people of Bikini and Enewetak atolls returned to a post-testing environment involving radioactivity from multiple tests (AEC 1956). The U.S. government's resettlement of people on contaminated islands resulted in the cumulative and continued exposure to radiation of thousands of people.

BIKINI   In the case of the people from Bikini, the U.S. government resettled a portion of the community on their home atoll in 1972. The U.S. government made the decision to resettle the Bikinians despite multiple warnings about the dangers of resettlement, including a memo from the Atomic Energy Commission stating that

"Bikini natives can never return to that atoll" (AEC 1952). The U.S. government was fully aware of the persistent radiation on Bikini when it resettled people on their home islands. Once the U.S. government resettled the community, it treated the people's exposure to radiation as an important scientific opportunity:

> Bikini may be the only global source of data on humans where intake via ingestion is thought to contribute the major fraction of plutonium body burden. . . . It is possibly the best available data for evaluating the transfer of plutonium across the gut wall after being incorporated into biological systems (Conard 1958).

After the Bikinian community returned, monitoring of the environment by the U.S. government revealed levels of radiation in the well water above U.S. maximum limits and "an 11-fold increase in the cesium-137 body burdens of the more than 100 people residing on the island" (Niedenthal 2001:12). According to the late senator of Bikini, Henchi Balos, the Bikinians absorbed more cesium than any known human population in the world (Balos 1995). In 1978, six years after the first resettlement of people on Bikini, the U.S. Department of Interior announced its decision to once again evacuate the community from its home island.

To date, the Bikinians still do not live on their own land. Most of the community lives on the small, single island of Kili—an island with rough lagoons that make fishing and the docking of boats extremely difficult.

RONGELAP   Like the people of Bikini, the U.S. government also resettled the people of Rongelap in an environment known to contain dangerous levels of radiation. The resettlement of the community was important to the U.S. government from a research perspective. As noted by the physician in charge of the medical research: because "[t]he habitation of these people on the island will afford most valuable ecological radiation data on human beings" (Conard 1958). Clearly the research potential of people exposed to radiation outweighed health concerns about the Rongelapese, whom the U.S. government viewed as less than human, but a step up from the mice used in laboratories. In an internal meeting, the Atomic Energy Commission discussed a unique research opportunity provided by the resettlement of the Rongelapese on contaminated land:

> Now data of this type has never been available. While it is true that these people do not live, I would say, the way Westerners do, civilized people, it is nevertheless also true that these people are more like us than the mice (AEC 1956).

From 1954, after the Bravo test, until 1957 the Rongelap community lived on the small island of Ejit on Majuro Atoll. During the three years that the community was absent from its homeland, the U.S. government conducted extensive studies of the radiation levels in the plants, animals, birds, and sea life at Rongelap. Researchers found that cesium and strontium levels were particularly high, and according to U.S. government documents, too high for human consumption: "Edible plants other than coconuts, such as pandanus, papaya, and squash, have been found to contain levels of Sr 90 which are above the tolerance level as defined in the Radiological Health handbook" (Applied Fisheries Laboratory 1955:32).

Researchers also found high levels of radiation in arrowroot, a staple food for the community, particularly in the 1950s. Arrowroot grows best in pits or depressions in the soil. Unfortunately, these depressions in the ground also accumulated radiation and were known to be "hot spots" of radiation before people were resettled. The arrowroot consumed by the resettled population grew in the most heavily contaminated soil.

Another food that had high concentrations of radiation was the coconut crab, a delicacy in the Marshall Islands. Coconut crabs eat the coconuts from the trees and thus bioaccumulate radiation. Radiation moves from the soil, to the plants that grow in them, to the animals that consume them, and finally to the human beings. By the time human beings consume animals that live in a contaminated environment, such as coconut crabs, the radiation levels are highly concentrated (Bair et al. 1982). More than a year after the Rongelapese resettled one of their home islands, the U.S. government informed the people that eating coconut crabs presented a health risk due to high levels of strontium 90. As one member of the Rongelap community told me: *"First they said we could eat crabs, and then they said to stop. What's the point when we already ate them?"* (Nerje Joseph 1999).

As discussed in Chapter 5, the community suffered from serious health problems as a direct result of its consumption of contaminated foods.[2] The U.S. government was aware of the illnesses experienced by the people as a result of their consumption of contaminated food and resettlement of an island with high levels of radiation.

Despite knowledge about the community's exposure to radiation, the U.S. government maintained that Rongelap was safe for human inhabitation. Fearing for the health and safety of their children, the Rongelap community members disagreed with the U.S. government and sought assistance from an international nongovernmental organization, Greenpeace, to evacuate them from their homeland. The decision was painful to make and came with severe consequences for the community (see Chapter 5).

It was not until the 1990s that the U.S. government officially recognized that Rongelap remains too contaminated for human habitation. The U.S. government authorized a trust fund for the community to begin restoration efforts. If the U.S. government acknowledges that Rongelap is currently unsafe for human inhabitation without remediation, surely it understands that the area was far too contaminated for the three decades that people lived on the atoll. Rongelap local government hired a contractor to reduce radiation levels on the island through a combination of soil removal and the use of potassium fertilizers (potassium reduces the uptake of cesium by the plants). The Rongelapese want to create an opportunity for people to return to their home island one day if that is what the community decides.

UTRIK   Unlike the people of Rongelap who spent three years away from their home atoll after the Bravo test, the U.S. government returned the people of Utrik to their islands just two months after the community's evacuation. Consequently, the U.S. government exposed the people of Utrik to significant amounts of environmental sources of radiation, including those with very short half-lives, in addition to the exposure to fallout they received from Bravo and other tests.

The U.S. government was keenly interested in studying how the Utrikese absorbed radiation from their environment. The ability to knowingly place human beings in a contaminated environment requires a certain mindset. U.S. government

---

[2]To read an extensive account of the damages to the land and natural resources of the Rongelap community see the 1999 and 2001 reports that coauthored with anthropologist Barbara Rose Johnston.

researchers viewed the Marshallese, with their brown skin and "traditional" lifestyle, as primitives—something less than human beings.

After their resettlement, community members came to understand that the U.S. government viewed them as research subjects. The Utrikese formerly protested the visits of U.S. government doctors and researchers. Like the Rongelapese, the U.S. government researchers offered bribes of money and material goods, such as baseball hats, to get the people to cooperate with their studies. Researchers were anxious to get data on human absorption of radiation from the environment.

ENEWETAK   In 1980, the U.S. government resettled the Enewetak community on the southern portion of Enewetak. Before the community returned, the advisory committee of U.S. government officials making recommendations about the resettlement of the community acknowledged that it could not assure that radiation doses from transuranics to future residents would not significantly exceed proposed EPA guidelines. The U.S. government also determined that U.S. radiation standards for cleanup should not apply to the Marshall Islands despite the fact that the country was a trust territory of the United States. This double standard permitted higher levels of radiation exposure for the people of Enewetak than for the American public:

> The Defense Nuclear Agency believes the radiation standards applicable to the general public are not appropriate for the small Enewetak population and that such use could establish an undesirable precedent for other situations of environmental contamination from nuclear explosives. . . . The DNA also recommended a risk-benefit analysis that they believe would justify the selection of higher radiation dose levels for the cleanup criteria (Conard 1958).

Neither the Enewetak community nor the Marshall Islands government was told about the full scope of radiological threats on Enewetak Atoll before the community resettled because negotiations were underway to end the trust territory relationship. The U.S. negotiators determined that it was not in the best interest of the U.S. negotiators to release information about radiological contamination on Enewetak because of the effect that such knowledge would have on the negotiations.

The resettlement of Enewetak was not complete. Not everyone from the Enewetak community returned to their home islands. The people of Enjebi Island have been unable to return to their home island because of residual contamination, and have no choice but to live on the island of Enewetak, the only resettled area on the atoll. It is not enough to return people to a portion of the land; people want to live on the islands that were once their home, not on an island that was home to other community members (Figure 3.4).

In their resettlement, the U.S. government placed the Enewetakese people near a two-mile wide nuclear storage facility (Figure 3.1). In the 1970s, the U.S. government tried to clean up Enewetak Atoll by bulldozing all of the contaminated debris—including all of the trees, grass, and top layer of soil—into a large crater left by one of the weapons tests. The U.S. government then put a cement cap over the radioactive debris and told the RMI government and the people of Enewetak that this was a temporary, but safe, nuclear storage facility.

To date, there is no U.S. government agency that has responsibility for monitoring and ensuring the integrity of the radioactive waste storage site on Enewetak. A similar nuclear storage site in the United States would require strict environmental

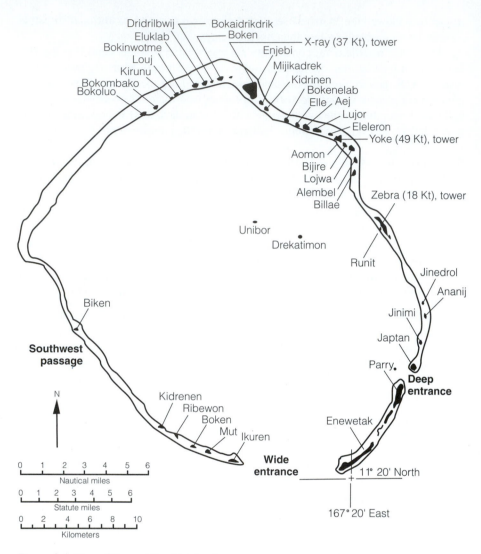

Figure 3.4 Map of Enewetak with island names

codes and quality assurance tests; once again, the U.S. government seems to apply a different safety standard for the Marshallese than its own citizens despite the fact that the Marshallese people were under the protection and care of the U.S. government at the time when the radiological contamination occurred. The people of Enewetak want assurances that they are not assuming greater health risks as a result of their resettlement. Recently, the leadership from Enewetak expressed concern about an increased incidence of birth abnormalities in the community.

During bilateral meetings with the U.S. Department of Energy and the U.S. Department of State, the resettled community and the RMI government repeatedly asked the U.S. government to take responsibility for properly managing the radioactive waste. The RMI government sent a diplomatic note to the U.S. State Department requesting that the executive branch assign an agency with responsibility for assuring the dome's integrity. The U.S. government has yet to respond to the RMI government's diplomatic note.

CONCLUSION

The U.S. government fails to take responsibility for a host of environmental and medical problems associated with the testing program. On the one hand, the language of the Compact indicates that the U.S. government will take responsibility for all past, present, and future damages and injuries resulting from the testing program, yet the laws governing U.S. assistance for problems related to the testing program remain extremely narrow and exclude thousands of people exposed to radiation from the testing program. Consequently, the U.S. government fails to act in good faith to honor its responsibilities to the RMI. As discussed in Chapter 8, the Marshallese must petition the U.S. Congress for the adequate medical care and environmental clean-up the people need and deserve.

4/Ethnography
and a Marshallese
Narrative of History

After the deluge of declassified documents from the U.S. Department of Energy, two leaders from the RMI government asked me to undertake research with some of the communities most affected by radiation, but not a part of the four-atoll designation. The leaders were Wilfred Kendall, who was the RMI's ambassador to the United States at the time as well as my boss, and Senator Tony deBrum. For his entire career, Senator deBrum has actively pursued and loudly protested the inconsistencies in U.S. government activities and reports related to the testing program. The information contained in the declassified documents provided the truth about the level of damages and exposures from the testing, a truth known to Senator deBrum and others for decades before the documents were declassified.

Ambassador Kendall and Senator deBrum wanted to see if the experiences of the radiation survivors in the Marshall Islands matched the new evidence to emerge from the declassified documents. In 1994, they asked me to meet with and interview radiation survivors from three atolls: Rongelap, Ailuk, and Likiep. My interviews with the Rongelapese were to determine whether people had a full appreciation for the range of medical and environmental problems detailed in the U.S. government documents. My interviews with the people of Ailuk and Likiep were to better understand the experiences people had with radiation in communities that the U.S. government does not recognize as affected by radiation—communities that were left to their own devices and had no external assistance to understand or cope with problems caused by radiation exposure.

In this chapter, I let the survivors speak for themselves; they share their experiences in their own words; they describe the events they experienced on March 1, 1954, the day the U.S. government detonated the Bravo test upwind from their home islands; they recall their evacuation from Rongelap and the humiliation of the decontamination process; they recount the birth defects experienced by their offspring, and their experiences with U.S. government doctors and scientists. Again, the damaging information contained in these U.S. government documents is not new to the Marshallese survivors of the nuclear weapons testing program; they remember the fallout; they remember the illnesses that followed; they remember how the U.S. government ignored them.

These testimonies are more powerful when they stand alone without inter-pretation. The witnesses whose remarks appear on the next several pages know exactly what they want to convey without any help from me. I will save my com-ments for the end of the chapter when I consider why these testimonies constitute a Marshallese narrative of history that is drastically different from the U.S. gov-ernment's version of these events. I discuss the methods I used to collect oral histo-ries from radiation survivors in Chapter 10, the chapter dealing with the role that anthropology plays in helping communities address problems related to the testing program.

It is also important to note that the testimonies in this chapter are just a fraction of the story of the Marshallese, a history rife with death, illness, and suffering ema-nating from the U.S. nuclear weapons testing program.

WITNESS TESTIMONIES: MARCH 1, 1954—THE DAY THE U.S. GOVERNMENT DETONATED THE BRAVO SHOT

Rongelap

I was living with my parents and some other family members on an islet across the reef from the main island where we had gone to make copra [dried coconut meat]. On that March morning, my father woke me while it was still pitch dark to cross the reef with some of my friends to the main island to buy some coffee, flour, and sugar.

There were four of us, three girls and a boy [named Hiroshi, see Figure 4.1]. Well, we were in the middle of the reef between the two islands when the whole of the western sky lit up. It seemed like it was afternoon, not early morning. The color went from bright white to deep red and then a mixture of both with some yellow. We jumped behind big rocks on the reef. We were too afraid to decide whether to run back to the small island or to run across the reef to the main island. . . .

It was Hiroshi who finally pushed us to run to the main island. Just as we reached the last sandbank, the air around us was split open by an awful noise. I cannot describe what it was like. It felt like the air was alive. We ran the last bit to the island. Everything was crazy. There was a man standing outside the first hut staring at the burning sky. A couple of us threw ourselves onto his legs, the others ran into his hut where they threw themselves onto his wife who was trying to come outside to see what was happening.

That afternoon, I found my hair was covered with a white powder-like substance. It had no smell and no taste when I tried tasting it.

Nearly all the people on Rongelap became violently ill. Most had painful headaches and extreme nausea and diarrhea. By the time of our evacuation to Kwajalein, all the parts of my body that had been exposed that morning blistered and my hair began to fall out in clumps. I just had to run my fingers through it and they would come out full of dust (Aruko Bobo, August 27, 1994).

Ailinginae
(the atoll next to Rongelap frequently used by the Rongelapese for short periods of residence, or for food gathering)

I was in my late 20s at the time of Bravo. I was on Ailinginae with my husband, who has since died. All the older people, like my husband, have died.

We lived on Rongelap, but we used to go to Ailinginae to gather food. We were on Ailinginae when the bomb dropped. We saw a light. It [the light] was to help find submarines my husband said [laughs]. Then the powder [fallout] fell on the lagoon side. We were looking for birds when the powder fell. The old man told the children not to play on the lagoon side. I was supposed to take care of the kids, but we all were so sick it was like we were passed out.

When they came to take us away from the island later, our clothes had powder on them. We saw the powder and we thought it was something to reduce the poison from the bomb. We were happy because we said we wouldn't get as much poison. . . .

I stayed with the kids. We saw the boats coming and we wondered why the huge boat came. We had no idea what was happening. . . . Some people hid from the Americans inside the cement water catchments because they thought they were coming because there was a war, not that people were coming to evacuate them. We didn't understand yet about bombs.

On Ailinginae, they didn't stop us from eating and drinking after the powder fell. We blew the powder off of our food and ate it. We couldn't take care of each other, even the kids, because we were all sick. We ate sprouted coconut because we were really nauseous,[1] and when we ate, we got even more nauseous (Dorothy Emos, March 18, 1999).

Ailuk

In the year 1954, I was 10 years old. My knowledge of what was happening around me was limited. When the bomb exploded and the earth rumbled, I looked up and saw the sky turn into strange reddish colors. At that time we children didn't take anything seriously. The adults were the ones who were excited. They led us into thinking it was Armageddon. Then we became scared. I didn't even know what a bomb was until I actually heard the explosion, felt the earth shaking and saw half of the sky turn red (Jalel John, September 5, 1994).

The atmosphere was foggy. It was like some dust falling from the sky on the lagoon and on the land (Lontak Jili, September 3, 1994).

Likiep

We woke up in great terror, not understanding what was happening. Many thought they were witnessing the end of the world. A short while after the sky lit up an indescribable sound shook the island. It was so great that it seemed as if the island would split into a million pieces. Standing outside, the intensity of the sound almost knocked me over. Some concluded that maybe the "Big War" that foreigners kept telling us would happen between the United States and Russia had finally begun. . . .

After what seemed like ages, the noise subsided and then we heard a different kind of noise, a whooshing sound that seemed to travel at tree-top level. People rolled around on the ground crying and clutching their children to their chests. Even the dogs and other animals were howling and yelling. Then suddenly, there was total silence—no sound except the sound of people crying, dogs barking, and waves breaking on the ocean side of the island. We picked ourselves up from the ground, amazed we were still

---

[1]The Marshallese often eat sprouted coconut, known as *iu*, for upset stomachs.

alive (Kalemen Gideon, Marshallese doctor on Likiep during the testing program, September 2, 1994).

I remember the white powder-like substance that covered the whole island (Joe Saul, August 22, 1994).

WITNESS TESTIMONIES: EVACUATION AND THE DECONTAMINATION PROCESS

Rongelap

When the U.S. government evacuated people on March 3, 1954, the ship first evacuated the people from Rongelap Atoll. After everyone from Rongelap was on board the ship went to Ailinginae to evacuate the residents. The American personnel on the ship told all the people from Ailinginae to take all their clothes off. Men and women—fathers and daughters, mothers and sons, and relatives that it was extremely taboo to disrobe in front of—were forced to stand naked together while the ship's personnel hosed the people down with water. The evacuees from Rongelap had been through the same process and had already dressed by the time the people from Ailinginae were told to disrobe.

Still today some people find it inappropriate [in Marshallese custom] for women to show their thighs, especially near their male relatives, but in the 1950s it was extremely taboo for women to show their thighs, let alone their entire naked bodies, particularly around male relatives. Both men and women were trying to cover themselves with a small towel given to each person and with their hands, but they could not hide their nakedness from one another. We didn't understand at the time why we had to do this.

After the Rongelapese were evacuated to Kwajalein, U.S. government doctors required the Rongelapese to bathe in the lagoon three times a day in an effort to reduce their exposure to radiation. These daily baths went on for three months.

Each day the Rongelapese women rode in a bus from the camp where the Rongelapese were staying to the lagoon where they bathed. The women were instructed to wear just their underwear and a T-shirt on the bus ride to and from the lagoon. The Navy clothes didn't fit the women properly and they couldn't conceal their bodies properly. To make matters worse, we were accompanied by two male relatives who were supposed to translate.

When the bus arrived at the lagoon, the women were told to stand at the water's edge and take their clothes off. The two men translated. They were related to most of the women there. In the Marshallese culture there are strict guidelines directing behavior between male and female relatives. We were crying in shame at having to be indecently clothed in front of our male relatives, and we did our best to conceal ourselves with our hands (Lijohn Eknilang, March 28, 2001).

WITNESS TESTIMONIES: BIRTH DEFECTS

Rongelap

I was not on Rongelap for the Bravo test, but I returned with everyone in 1957. . . .

It was around this time that I had my first pregnancy. My baby had a very high fever when he was delivered, and the attending health assistant conveyed his doubts as to whether my son would survive the night. He was so dehydrated from the fever that his skin actually peeled as I clasped him to me to nurse. The only thing we knew to do was to wrap him in wet towels. And so it was that I held him to my body throughout the night, changing the towels and willing him to fight for his life. He lost the fight just as dawn broke.

My second son, born in 1960, was delivered live but missing the whole back of his skull—as if it had been sawed off. So the back part of the brain and the spinal cord were fully exposed. After a week, the spinal cord became detached and he, too, developed a high fever and died the following day. Aside from the cranial deformity, my son was also missing both testicles and penis. He passed water through a stump-like apparatus measuring less than an inch. The doctors who examined him told me that he would not survive. And sure enough, he was dead within a week. . . . You know, it was heartbreaking having to nurse my son, all the while taking care his brain didn't fall into my lap. For in spite of his severe handicaps, he was healthy in every respect. It was good he died because I do not think he would have wanted to live a life as something less than human. . . . If it were not for the bomb testing, I would not have had to watch helplessly as two of my children were taken from me (Catherine Jibas, August 23, 1994).

There is a boy, actually a young man now, whose head is so large that his body is unable to support it and his only means of getting around is to crawl backwards dragging his head along—like the movements of a coconut or hermit crab. . . .

What is there to think about? We never had any of these illnesses, these grotesque deformities—these grape-like things that do not resemble human beings at all. And you ask me what I think. I think that if it were not for the United States and their desire to be stronger than Russia, we, the people of Rongelap, would not have to turn our heads in shame for fear of being considered freaks of nature (Aruko Bobo 1994).

Ailuk

Two [of my children] died. One of them was born defective. It didn't look like a human. It looked just like the inside of a giant clam (Jalel John 1994).

Four [of my] children were born prematurely. . . . One of them died after his first birthday. Another was stillborn. . . . I have yet to see any doctor (Rine Sneid, September 5, 1994).

Likiep

After the testing, she [my wife] got pregnant. When the baby was born, it had two heads. . . . Two heads. Two heads. One was on top of the other. . . . There was one head that was smaller than the other head. . . . It breathed for just a short time when it was born. Maybe an hour, only some minutes. It was alive, but it wasn't doing so well (Anonymous, August 14, 1994).

Some babies that were born resembled bunches of grapes. Another was said to have a horn-like protrusion on its forehead making it look like the image of Satan we see in books (Seiko Joniber, September 1, 1994).

Other children born during this time did not have any noticeable deficiencies, and yet lacked the ability to understand anything. Others were incapable of any motor activity although they seemed to comprehend their surroundings. Some of the children in the second category survived for a number of years although as nothing more than human vegetables or adults with the minds of toddlers (Agnes deBrum, August 14, 1994).

I was terribly, terribly upset. I cannot explain exactly what my feelings were except remembering the horror and compassion I felt for the women. I wondered to myself it those monsters the women gave birth to felt any pain or had any of the human qualities we all share. I suspected black magic and wondered what those women may have done to offend someone to such a degree that the spell cast on them was so terrible (Ersa deBrum, August 19, 1994).

WITNESS TESTIMONIES: OTHER MEDICAL AND ENVIRONMENTAL PROBLEMS

Rongelap

Hiroshi [died as a young boy], who had been severely affected by the fallout, had deep burns covering large areas of his body and suffered hair loss. His body was burned to such an extent that the bones in his feet were exposed and visible to the naked eye (William Allen August 22, 1994) (Figure 4.1).

Ailuk

There are a lot of sudden changes that we never experienced before the nuclear testings. It's happening to trees and even animals and people, too. Take a cat. A cat could give birth to a single kitten with what seems like two bodies combined. We might say a "twin" with one body. Eight legs and eight paws (Kenji Takia, September 5, 1994).

Some of the fish that we used to eat now give us fish poisoning. We cannot eat them anymore. . . . Pigs also have defective bodies. Some have twisted legs. . . . Sometimes the fieldtrip [supply] ships wouldn't come for a long time so we had to kill them and eat them. What could we do? We were hungry and we needed something to eat (Jalel John 1994).

A few years later [after the testing], a lot of strange things occurred on our small islands that affected our food crops. One of them was arrowroot. It died away from then up until now as I speak. It's completely gone. We are very sad because it was one of our main food sources. . . . Furthermore, I can use the example of the coconut tree. A single tree could bear coconuts with different colors—some orange while others are green and other colors. It was very strange to us. As for the animals, take pigs for example, some pigs were born with their sexual organs in the wrong places. . . . This never happened prior to the nuclear explosions. (Dikjen Jilon, September 2, 1994).

Likiep

Do you know that I had a major operation on my head? Yes, a tumor. . . . I underwent surgery to have it removed. I think they also removed fragments of my skull along with the tumor. . . . A brain tumor from the bombs, they say. . . . I found out I had epilepsy. . . . [M]y doctor explained to me that people who undergo head surgery such as mine stand a very good chance of developing epilepsy. . . . I first became aware of the symptoms when I would wake up with a very painful mouth and discover that I had chewed the insides to shreds . . . (Anonymous 1994).

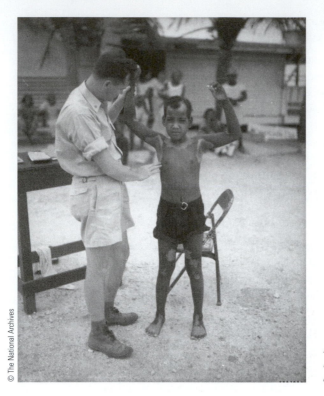

Figure 4.1 Hiroshi raising his hands to display burns to an American doctor

We were astonished to find that arrowroot had been destroyed, along with such things as breadfruit, coconut trees, and pandanus. We assumed that whatever caused this was poisonous because it was able to not only destroy vegetation at ground level, but also it was able to cause damage to things growing in the soil. (Alion Alik, August 14, 1994).

WITNESS TESTIMONIES: INTERACTIONS WITH U.S. GOVERNMENT MEDICAL PROVIDERS AND SCIENTISTS

Rongelap

The health assistant who delivered the [abnormal] child sent a message to Kwajalein and I am certain these doctors came so they could see for themselves a live "bomb baby." In fact, they flew in the very same day the message was sent. . . . They did a complete physical, took blood samples, and took the baby outside so they could take lots and lots of photographs.

DOE [U.S. Department of Energy] ignored us. They did not want to admit the Rongelapese were contaminated. Or, they did not want the world to know about us so they could go on with their radiation studies without any outside interference. So they ignored what we told them—saying that Rongelap was not contaminated and our health problems were unrelated to radiation. . . . [W]e don't believe them now (Catherine Jibas 1994).

What can we say? Nothing—we don't know anything. We don't know a thing about medical care. . . . [W]e don't know what procedures they did to us. What did they see? They just told us to go see a doctor, and then they tell us everything is okay. But us, we don't know, we don't know about medicine. We don't know how to examine the human body like they do (Ellyn Boaz, August 26, 1994).

Ailuk

If the U.S. [government] insisted that poison did not effect Ailuk, then how would they consider Utrik effected when the distance from Ailuk to the center of the explosion is approximately the same as Utrik? Nobody answered my questions. They were obviously hiding the true fact that this island was actually affected by the nuclear testing. Even though we knew and felt that Ailuk was poisoned, we couldn't do anything because we were being ignored all along. Not a shred of information was released to us. My other concern is this: after all these years of suffering, why is this issue of Ailuk's contamination now being discussed when it should have been done a long, long time ago?

. . . Why didn't they notify us of what they were going to do beforehand so we could protect ourselves? . . . They treated us like guinea pigs for their experiments. . . . There was a ship that visited us twice. They took blood samples from the people. They told us they will examine our blood samples in the labs and inform us of the results. To this day, not a shred of information about any results has been released to us. They took so much blood from every person. . . .

The USS *Wheeling* brought some scientists to show us maps and charts of the route of the nuclear fallout as it was carried downwind. The movements of the fallout was so funny to us because the lines actually zigzagged between Likiep, Ailuk, and the other atolls. I actually saw the charts and we were wondering how the radioactive poison could navigate itself between these islands without touching them! They thought we were a bunch of idiots!. . . I told them in nasty words, because I was mad, I told them why didn't they do their experiments in their own country. In America there are deserts, there is so much unused public land. Instead, they chose some small islands to poison and kill the people. I was furious.

They didn't listen to us. They said it was nothing to worry about. Every word we said was ignored (Tempo Alfred, September 8, 1994).

Likiep

When I asked [the scientists] if the sudden disappearance of the arrowroot plant on Likiep had anything to do with the bomb tests, they assured me that it was all a part of the earth's cycle where one time there is plenty of one plant to be followed by a period where there is none. I was naïve at the time and happily went off to tell my equally naïve friends and family of the cycle of plants the scientists told me about (Kramer deBrum, August 19, 1994).

[F]rom discussions I had with numerous people . . . [t]hey all wanted to know why they were not being told anything at all when it was their life's blood that the DOE doctors were taking to conduct their tests and experiments. Therefore, they questioned whether the doctors were truly concerned for their well being or just for the success of their damned experiments (Kalemen Gideon, September 2, 1994).

A MARSHALLESE NARRATIVE OF HISTORY

On March 1, 1954, the U.S. government unleashed the Bravo test on Bikini Atoll. It is clear from the accounts on Rongelap, Ailinginae, Likiep, and Ailuk that the Bravo event caught the people completely by surprise. The Marshallese people living

downwind had no idea that a test was taking place, nor that they should take protective measures afterwards (as the U.S. weather forecasters on Rongerik did). Prior to
this day, the people had never heard of radiation, and they certainly did not understand its detrimental effects on human beings or the environment.

What emerges poignantly from the testimonies of the radiation survivors is
the intense suffering and disruption of every aspect of life caused by the weapons
testing. The U.S. government documents reveal that the testing exposed atolls where
people live. But, those documents do not give a sense of what it was like to be on
those islands, to experience the nuclear tests firsthand, and to live for decades with
the consequences of radiological contamination. The oral histories bring the voices
of the Marshallese into the picture; they create portraits that capture a history of the
nuclear weapons testing program from a Marshallese perspective—a perspective that
varies greatly from the U.S. government documents that see the Marshallese only as
numbers or research vehicles.

Instead of numbers and geographic locations, a Marshallese history of the
nuclear weapons testing includes descriptions of the fear and chaos that descended
on the villages that experienced the Bravo test. The Marshallese history includes the
immediate onslaught of nausea and flu-like symptoms, and burns deep enough to
expose the bone of people on Rongelap. The Marshallese history also includes the
humiliation of the decontamination process and the flagrant disregard for
Marshallese as people or their customs during emergency washings to reduce radiation levels on the skin and hair of the people. It is a history of being lied to and
ignored by the U.S. government.

In the more than 200 interviews I conducted over the years, the Marshallese version of history is also full of death and illness. Every family that lived on these
islands knows what it is like to lose family members from radiological illnesses. No
families have been spared. In a Marshallese version of history names are given to the
countless grandmothers and grandfathers, mothers and fathers, aunts and uncles,
cousins, children, and babies that died prematurely as a result of the weapons testing.
Hundreds and hundreds of these stories exist.

The Marshallese history of the testing program includes the detrimental health
and environmental problems resulting from living and reproducing in a contaminated
environment. The people living downwind from the testing area have a firsthand
understanding of the problems radiation causes when it enters the food chain. Neither
plants, people, nor animals could escape the insidious effects of radiation exposure.
Pets, livestock, plants, trees, and newborn children embodied the disruptive forces of
radiation.

It is also clear from the oral histories that the suffering people experienced as a
result of their exposure to radiation is compounded by a feeling of complete exploitation. The radiation survivors know that their country, their islands, and they themselves have been part of a giant U.S. government laboratory. The continued denial
and cover-up of the full extent of damage and injuries by the U.S. government only
exacerbates the anger and resentment expressed by the survivors. The United States
must acknowledge its wrongs and take full responsibility for the consequences of the
testing program before meaningful healing can take place.

It is also important to note that the testimonies do not differentiate between
groups of people as either "exposed" or "unexposed" the way the U.S. government
does. If two women from Rongelap give birth to deformed children and one woman

was on Rongelap in 1954 for the Bravo test, and one was resettled on the contaminated atoll in 1957, the community considers both of them "exposed" because they exhibit the physical characteristics of radiation exposure. To the contrary, the U.S. government does not consider the woman who painfully described the deaths of her children, including the one with no back on his head to hold his brains in, "exposed" to radiation, and therefore eligible for U.S. medical assistance. Nor does it consider any of the children born on contaminated lands to parents exposed to fallout in need of medical care, nor the entire populations of Likiep and Ailuk. Unlike the U.S. version of history, the oral histories and a Marshallese narrative of history capture the birth defects, health problems, and changes to the environment that ensued.

CONCLUSION

In the Marshallese narrative of history, it is the experiences of individuals that determines if they are *baam* (bombed), and affected by the radiation, not the atoll of residence on a particular day as the Compact prescribes. The life histories and life stories of the people most affected by the weapons testing describe the suffering of the Marshallese people, a fact that is absent from any of the U.S. government accounts of the effects of the testing program. U.S. government documents do not discuss the pain involved in losing a child, mother, father, sister, or brother. They do not discuss the pain involved in battling cancer and other serious medical conditions. The Marshallese narratives put faces on the injuries and damages caused by the testing program. The testing program achieved nuclear superiority for the United States, but it achieved it at a cost of great suffering to the Marshallese people as evident from their testimonies. The oral histories force us to come to terms with the human costs of U.S. nuclear superiority.

5/Alienation
from the Land
The Rongelap Experience

IMPORTANCE OF GEOGRAPHY

In 1946, more than a year before the United States became the official administrating power of the Marshall Islands, the U.S. Navy approached the people and leaders of Bikini Atoll to request permission to use their islands to test atomic weapons and their effects.

It was understandable that the Bikinians agreed to vacate their land so the U.S. government could conduct its weapons tests. The U.S. government told the Bikinians their move would be temporary. They did not have televisions or newspapers to provide images from Hiroshima or Nagasaki, and, like most people in the world at the time they did not have an appreciation for the destructive capacity of the weapons.

In this chapter, I assess the human environmental impacts of the testing program by examining the consequences for one community, Rongelap. The testing program denied the Rongelapese use of their lands and resources. Persistent and dangerous levels of radiation in the environment eventually forced them into exile. I abstracted portions of the Rongelap discussion from two reports that I coauthored with environmental anthropologist Barbara Rose Johnston in October 1999, and September 2001 for the Public Advocate of the Nuclear Claims Tribunal, Bill Graham.[1] Dr. Johnston and I made an excellent and complementary team; Barbara's training in environmental science and anthropology brought important understandings to my ethnographic data collected in the Marshall Islands. As a result, our joint analysis allowed us to consider the broader consequences of environmental contamination for a community. In Chapter 9, I will discuss the methods we used to ensure that our research project was collaborative and participatory at every stage.

---

[1]The two reports are on file at the Nuclear Claims Tribunal in Majuro: Johnston, Barbara Rose and Holly M. Barker. Assessing the Human Environmental Impact of Damage from Radioactive Contamination, Denied Use, and Exile for the People of Rongelap, Rongerik and Ailinginae Atolls: Anthropological Assistance to the Rongelap Land Valuation/Property Damage Claim. October 3, 1999. Johnston, Barbara Rose and Holly M. Barker. Hardships and Consequential Damages from Radioactive Contamination, Denied Use, Exile, Human Subject Experimentation Experienced by the People of Rongelap, Rongerik, and Ailinginae Atolls. September 17, 2001.

The Public Advocate for the Nuclear Claims Tribunal, William ("Bill") Graham, asked Barbara and me to undertake our research to determine what it means from a Marshallese perspective, and more specifically, a Rongelapese perspective to have land contaminated by radiation, to be denied the use of land and its resources, and to be forced to live in exile as a result of radiological contamination. Our reports document and describe Marshallese notions of land value, damage, and loss. We used this information to support the Rongelap people's claim for property damage to the Nuclear Claims Tribunal. As discussed earlier, the Tribunal contemplates claims for both personal injury (medical problems linked to the testing program) and land damage. Rongelap's land claim includes the atolls of Rongelap, Ailinginae, and Rongerik since the people of Rongelap cultivated, inhabited, and survived from all three atolls.

IMPORTANCE OF LAND

To understand the implications of contaminating Rongelap and denying the people access to their resources and lands, it is important to understand the importance of land in the Marshall Islands. Land is not just a place to live and grow food; land in the Marshall Islands is the essence of life. In a country with only 70 square miles of land, land is the most valued commodity. Much of Marshallese life, culture, and people's sense of identity comes from the land:

> Land gives you the meaning of life and the role of each individual in society (Mike Kabua, March 4, 1999).

> The people here have tenaciously held onto land. The resource people treasure most is land. Land speaks of your being, essence, reason for living. You relate to the world in terms of land. . . . Land provides for your present, future, and future needs. . . . You cannot put enough value on land. How do you put a value on something that people consider as a living thing that is part of your soul? (Wilfred Kendall, March 3, 1999).

> Without the land all shatters. Land binds us. I was really happy on Rongerik because it's my place. I grew up there (Mwenadrik Kebenli, March 16, 1999).

In another interview, a Rongelapese youth equated the loss of land with suicide. From his perspective, loss of land is akin to a violent death (Malal Anjain 1999).

Historically, attachment to the land was rooted in the indigenous religion of the Marshallese before Christianity replaced it, as discussed earlier in the data gathered by Jack Tobin.

Observations by Tobin demonstrate a conscious effort to minimize human impact on an ecologically fragile and important environment. The Marshallese respect for the environment and its resources is evident in Tobin's data as well since the Marshallese people asked and waited for permission from a tree to enter an area.

As demonstrated by the relationship between the chief and the people in Tobin's passage, Marshallese culture and society is tightly structured by its land rights. There are three different tiers of society, each with distinct land and resource use rights. As discussed in Chapter 1, the three tiers or classifications of people are the *iroij* (chiefs), *alap,* (managers of the land), and the *ri-jerbal* (workers). Land rights exclusively define a person's designation into one of the three social categories:

> We have different customs than the Americans. They won't say there are three-tier of land rights, but for us there are. We protect the land. This is our inheritance from our grandfathers and grandmothers (Dorothy Emos, March 18, 1999).

Emos notes that the Marshallese expend much energy in the protection and upkeep of their land. The fluid system of land rights and access to resources provides an effective means of ensuring that the land is cared for and remains productive, and that everyone has access to the resources necessary for survival. In the case of the *iroij*, they are not expected to work and maintain the land, which is the job of the *alap* and *ri-jerbal*. Instead, their main job of the *iroij* is to care for the people. The *iroij* gives other people access and permission to use the resources on his or her land so they can survive. In exchange, the *alap* and *ri-jerbal* provide gifts to the *iroij* of food or money that they earn from selling copra. The *iroij* often distribute these goods, particularly gifts of food, to needy people on other parcels of land.

The Marshallese socially construct rights to use critical resources, typically determined according to maternal relationships and legitimized by the community's common understanding of a complex system of inheritance and use rights. Rights to use land typically involve the right to occupy an area, but do not include rights to freely use any of the resources without permission. In exchange for the right to occupy and live from the land, workers provide the labor to maintain the land and keep it productive (care for trees and plants, clearing underbrush, maintenance of food and livestock). The chief can revoke the privilege to use an area if workers do not adhere to stewardship principles that ensure the long-term vitality of the land and its resources.

> The *iroij* have people work on and clean the land. People get to use the resources on the land and the *iroij* benefit from having the land maintained and productive (Wilfred Kendall, March 5, 1999).

In addition to establishing social hierarchy, the land and its resources provide the means to sustain customary practices. Access to natural resources is a critical component of every important social event such as the one-year birthday of a child (*kemem*), funerals, and visits by the *iroij*. For these occasions, people are expected to provide gifts of food, to weave mats, to make necklaces from shells and flowers. Visits by *iroij* require access to special foods that are reserved only for the *iroij*, such as certain species of fish and turtle. At funerals community members place white rocks around graves as a sign of purity. Without access to natural resources, the basic social relations of society cannot continue. As shown later in this chapter, the contamination of the land and the inability of people to work on and live from their land alters the entire social fabric of the community.

From a Marshallese perspective, their terrestrial land is a sacred part of, not separate, from the seas and the skies. The Marshallese people have survived for centuries on what outsiders see as barren stretches of land by drawing on their intricate knowledge of the land, sea, and sky, and their resources. Their land is not the harsh area with limited resources that outsiders see. For those who inherit the knowledge of many generations, the islands are a place rich with crops, plants, and animals:

> The islands in the northern islands, like Rongelap, they were the garden islands. Everyone knew they were the best place to grow arrowroot, pandanus . . . there were whole islands covered with birds, and turtles (Lijohn Eknilang, March 4, 1999).

> I was born in 1917 on Rongerik. We came together and made food. We stored food. So many kinds of food. Every type was there. There was water. We ate arrowroot, preserved breadfruit, pandanus, coconut, fish, crab, foods from the reef like octopus, clam, and small fish. There's an island, Jipedbao [literally, the place of birds], with lots of birds. There were also turtles on the islands. We would sail overnight in the outrigger canoe to Rongelap. We would take food to Rongelap. We always exchanged food (Mwenadrik Kebenli 1999).

In order to survive in the Marshall Islands, people need not only access to critical resources, such as food and materials to build houses and boats, but also the knowledge necessary to use and exploit resources in sustainable ways. Each atoll environment is slightly different. The people who lived on Rongelap, Rongerik, and Ailinginae possess specific information about the location of critical resources. The Rongelapese can identify sources of fresh water, clam beds, reefs that are good for catching lobsters, beaches with the best shells for making handicrafts, areas where turtles lay eggs, and bird habitats. They also know where to locate the plants they need to make medicine. Families pass down knowledge about medicine. Marshallese consider this knowledge about the medicinal qualities of plants rare, highly valued, and powerful.

Because it is vital to describe the precise location of critical resources, the Rongelapese gave names to distinguishable areas of the land and reef. A reef that serves as an important food collection area or an important navigational point has a name.

The Marshallese also give names to terrestrial and marine property as a way to explain the history of each holding. Atoll, island, and *weto* (see Chapter 1) names remind the Rongelapese of the history, and the social and environmental significance of the property. *Weto* names, for example, are place names that describe physical characteristics of the land and sea and how people inherited and use the land (see Table 1.3 in Chapter 1).

In addition to knowing the location of precious resources, the Rongelapese also know how to use their resources sustainably to ensure that resources remain available in the future. By having access to three different atolls, the community had a flexible, fluid means of gathering resources. Multiple cultivation options ensure that people do not deplete resources, and that the community can adjust to seasonal and climatic changes:

> We know to only fish for two days in one spot and then move. With the coconut crab, we didn't used to take the females and we didn't take too many from one place. We never took small crabs or pregnant crabs. As for the turtles and birds, we never took all the eggs (George Anjain, March 3, 1999).

> We broke the wings of some birds (so they would stay and make more birds). We ate the younger birds so the adult birds could make more birds. We only ate them during the birthing season (Mijua Job, March 10, 1999).

Since coral atolls have limited amounts of food and water, the sharing of resources is critical for community survival and essential for life. The Rongelapese worked together to harvest and prepare food, and shared water and food resources with family and neighbors:

Because of its critical importance, water was shared perhaps more than any other resource. It was understood that if you have a good well, people could come and ask to use it, or just take it (Wilfred Kendall, March 2, 1999).

On Monluel *weto* there was a big fence with chickens in it. The birds belonged to the family, but people would ask for them. When there were many birds sometimes they would hand out a bird to each family (Mijua Job, March 10, 1999).

People got together to harvest arrowroot, breadfruit, and other foods to preserve them. We salted, dried, or grated pandanus for preservation (Lijohn Eknilang, March 3, 1999).

DAMAGE, INJURY, AND LOSS

In a society organized around respect for the land and the need to pass healthy, productive land to future generations to ensure survival, what complications result from the introduction of radiation into the local environment?

The U.S. nuclear weapons testing program created health problems and environmental hazards that will last for decades and generations to come. In the case of Rongelap, the testing program destroyed the community's means to sustain a self-sufficient way of life. The introduction of radiation into the environment not only damaged the health and viability of the natural resources and those who depended on them for survival, but it also denied the Rongelapese the means to live self-sufficiently. The social, cultural, economic, political, and psychological consequences of this damage and loss are complex and profound.

A community does not have the means to traditional subsistence in the Marshall Islands if the U.S. government moves them to an area where the people have no rights to the land and the resources. On Rongelap, Rongerik, and Ailinginae, the people had access to the resources they needed to ensure their survival. Local materials provided the people with food, shelter, transportation, toys, medicine, and tools. People did not purchase many provisions other than kerosene, tin roofing, lamps, cigarettes, matches, thread and needles, sugar, rice, and flour. Many of these items could be obtained by trading or selling dried coconut meat (copra).

MOVEMENTS OF THE COMMUNITY

The U.S. government forced the entire community of Rongelap to move four different times. The Rongelap community decided to move themselves one additional time. If you think about the difficulties of moving a single person or a family from one location to another or from one house to another, imagine the challenges involved in moving an entire community five separate times (see Table 5.1).

HUMAN ENVIRONMENTAL INTERACTIONS

As we discussed in Chapter 3, the U.S. government resettled the people of Rongelap in an environment known to contain dangerous levels of radiation. The U.S. government was aware of the high radiation levels because of the research it had done on the presence of radiation in the plants, animals, and soil on Rongelap. When the people returned to Rongelap in 1957, the U.S. government used the island as a laboratory to better understand the movements of radiation from the environment to human beings. The health problems and environmental hazards that were the subject of U.S.

TABLE 5.1   RELOCATIONS OF THE RONGELAP COMMUNITY

May 1946

The U.S. government relocated the people of Rongelap and nearby Wotho to Lae Atoll for several months as a preventative measure to protect the community from downwind fallout. Lae is an extremely small atoll with limited space and resources. On Lae, the Rongelapese lived in canvas tents. Food supplies from the U.S. government were inadequate (Isao Eknilang, October 31, 2001).

March 3, 1954

The U.S. government waited more than two days after the Bravo test before evacuating the people from Rongelap to Kwajalein despite knowledge that radiological contamination was severe.

June 1954

After U.S. government doctors monitored and reported on the immediate effects of human radiation exposure, the U.S. government moved the people of Rongelap to Ejit Island on Majuro Atoll. The U.S. government told the community it could not return to Rongelap because the islands were too dangerous for human habitation. On Ejit, the people experienced a polio epidemic and subsisted primarily from canned goods (Norio Kebenli, October 31, 2001).

July 1957

The U.S. government told the Rongelapese that it was safe for them to return to the island of Rongelap on Rongelap Atoll. Rongerik, Ailinginae, and the rest of the islands on Rongelap were off limits.

May 1985

Fearing for the health and safety of the community and future generations, the Rongelap community disagreed with U.S. government assertions that Rongelap was safe for human habitation. With great sadness, the community went into self-exile. Rongelap's *iroij,* the Kabua family, agreed to let the community use the uninhabited island of Mejatto on Kwajalein Atoll. The community is now dispersed to different locations within the Marshall Islands and the United States.

government research efforts created significant problems for the Rongelap community that will last for decades to come.

After the Bravo test exposed the Rongelapese to radioactive fallout, the U.S. government's medical researcher, Dr. Eugene Cronkite, declared that the Rongelapese

> should be exposed to no further radiation, external or internal, with the exception of essential diagnostic and therapeutic X-rays for at least 12 years. If allowance is made for unknown effects of surface dose and internal deposition there probably should be no exposure for [the] rest of [their] natural lives (Cronkite 1954).

Despite this recommendation that the Rongelapese should not receive further radiation for 12 years, U.S. government researchers routinely observed increased body burdens for radiation in the resettled community that ingested radiation from the food, water, and soil on Rongelap.

U.S. government scientists measured the levels of plutonium evident in the urine samples of the resettled Rongelapese. The samples showed extremely high levels of plutonium. In fact, the plutonium levels were so high that researchers thought their samples could have come from the environment, not from human beings. This suggests that the Rongelapese ingested so much plutonium from their surroundings that they achieved equilibrium with the plutonium levels on the island. Based on their findings, U.S. government researchers acknowledged in the *Journal of Health Physics* that "the body burden of Rongelap people exceeded allowable levels" (Franke 1989:7). By 1989, four years after the Rongelapese left the island for fear of their safety, U.S. government scientists reported that the "soil on Rongelap Island contains about 430 times more transuranics (plutonium and americium) than the average transuranic levels for the Northern hemisphere (Franke 1989:3).

According to physicians, the health consequences of exposure to environmental sources of radiation are profound for the Rongelapese. Immediately after the Bravo detonation, both U.S. government doctors and the Rongelapese worried about the health of the children who were born and raised on Rongelap and exposed to fallout from the weapons tests (Bugher 1959). Children have smaller bodies than adults so if an adult and a child receive similar levels of radiation exposure, the same amount of radiation will have a much more adverse impact on the child. Many children born on Rongelap had severe deformities; these children died quickly after their births. Many other women experienced high levels of spontaneous abortions and stillbirths (Bertell 1989:3). In the Rongelapese children that survived, U.S. government doctors noted severe growth retardation and developmental delays (Conard 1965).

The Rongelapese that were not on the atoll for the Bravo test but resettled on Rongelap Island in 1957 displayed medical problems similar to those who received high doses of radiation exposure from Bravo. One doctor found that two-thirds of the adult men and three-quarters of the adult women who resettled the island in 1957 had medical problems (Bertell 1989:1). The higher incidence of medical problems among women is noteworthy given the reproductive illnesses repeatedly described by the Rongelapese women.

In comparison to the United States, cancer mortality rates in the Marshall Islands are much higher. Research conducted by Neal Palafox, a doctor with more than a decade of experience in the Marshall Islands, found that cervical cancer mortality in Marshallese women is sixtyfold higher than the United States[2], breast and gastrointestinal cancer rates are fivefold, and lung cancer is threefold. In men, the liver cancer mortality rate is thirtyfold incidence levels in the United States.

While U.S. government doctors seemed to focus exclusively on the thyroid gland and the levels of radiation present in urine, the Rongelapese experienced a full array of medical problems (including reproductive abnormalities discussed in Chapter 6) that were not present in the community before the nuclear testing:

> We had no problem with our food before the testing. Afterwards, arrowroot and the plants gave us blisters in our mouths. I also think the problems with our throats (thyroid) are from the poison. After we went back [to Rongelap in 1957], new fish gave us fish poisoning, such as red snapper. Rongelap's lagoon was affected. I got fish poisoning twice after returning. . . . (John Anjain, March 16, 1999).

[2]The results of studies from the Radiation Effects Research Foundation in Japan do not show a link between uterine/cervical cancer and radiation exposure. Consequently, the Nuclear Claims Tribunal in Majuro does not provide compensation for people who contract these cancers.

I returned to Rongelap . . . in 1957 [after being away during the Bravo test], and I saw friends and relatives who were afflicted with illnesses unknown to us. Their eyesight deteriorated, their bodies were covered with burn marks, and people were weak and sick all the time (Catherine Jibas, August 23, 1994).

We saw coconut trees that had two heads, some three. We saw they weren't good for us to eat. We understood there were differences [in the land] because we grew up there and we knew. . . . It's really sad. Now we go to doctors. Many have thyroid problems. Some don't. Some have had operations twice. Some three times. We take medicine to help our thyroids. One pill every day. Don't forget one day—keep taking it, keep taking it. Sometimes I forget, but I'm not supposed to miss a single day. . . . Sometimes my throat really hurts, all the way down the esophagus. There are times when my head goes numb, my leg, my hand (Dorothy Emos, March 18, 1999).

People died of radiation but we had no doctors or charts to prove that is was radiation. . . . I have scars on my hands now. No medicine will take them away, Marshallese or American. They itch and they are bothersome. My thyroid is gone. I have to take medication every day. When I take too much medication I have too much energy—I can't sleep. I walk around and around, but I can't tire myself out to rest. When I don't take enough, I gain weight and get lethargic (Nerje Joseph, March 8, 1999).

EXPERIENCES IN EXILE

Despite assurances by the United States government that Rongelap was safe, the Rongelapese believed that their health and safety was compromised after 1957 by living in an environment contaminated by radiation. As the Rongelapese describe, the food tainted with radiation gave people blisters in their mouths and made them sick. The people also believe that their environmental exposure led to the premature deaths, and severe deformities in their offspring.

Believing their lives to be in danger from continued exposure to the radiation in their environment, the senator of Rongelap at the time (who died from bone cancer), Jeton Anjain, led the RMI *Nitijela* (or parliament) to pass a unanimous resolution asking the U.S. government to relocate the Rongelapese. The U.S. government ignored this request and maintained that Rongelap was safe despite extensive information to the contrary. The U.S. Department of Energy told the Rongelapese that there was "no justification" for their self-evacuation (Anjain 1989:14). The Rongelapese turned to Greenpeace, an nongovernmental environmental organization, for help. Greenpeace dispatched the *Rainbow Warrior* to Rongelap Island in May, 1985 to assist the Rongelapese with their evacuation.

Environmental contamination from the nuclear weapons testing program forced the Rongelapese to abandon all that was familiar and owned by them. They had no option but to live on other people's land. The Rongelapese moved to Mejatto Island, a small island on the western side of Kwajalein Atoll. Eventually the community dispersed to the two urban centers of Majuro, and Ebeye, and to other locations. The social, economic, and environmental problems the community experience in their exile are some of the consequential damages directly linked to the U.S. nuclear weapons testing program.

LOSS OF SELF-SUFFICIENCY

The nuclear weapons testing program destroyed the means to sustain a self-sufficient way of life for the people of Rongelap. While approximately one-half of the Marshallese population subsists from agricultural production (RMI Government 1999), the weapons testing program alienated 100 percent of the Rongelapese population from the land and resources they need for survival. This loss of access affects diet, health, and household economy and severely inhibits the Rongelapese ability to produce or reproduce cultural knowledge about the local environment—knowledge that is essential to the survival and long-term well being of the community. The disbursement of the community into several residence areas means that the Rongelapese are now a fractured community rather than a community where everyone once worked together. Each of the different areas where the community now lives provides challenges for the Rongelapese that they did not experience on their own land.

Life on Mejatto

Approximately 350 people moved from Rongelap to Mejatto in 1985. Mejatto is a small island approximately one mile long. It is situated on the western end of Kwajalein Atoll, approximately 60 miles from Ebeye Island. Mejatto has no airstrip and its residents rely on small boats to travel to Ebeye. After their move, the people did not own motorboats or have money to pay for gas to make the more than 10-hour trip over rough waters.

Mejatto was an uninhabited island before the Rongelapese arrived. As a result, no cultivation had taken place on the island and little traditional food was available. The people planted pandanus, breadfruit, and coconut, but it took five years before they would produce food (Greenpeace 1986). Furthermore, there were no houses on the island and many people had to sleep outside in the rain for weeks before the Rongelapese could build adequate shelter (Ken Kedi, March 1, 1999).

The islands surrounding Mejatto had food, but the Rongelapese were reluctant to gather food because they had no rights or permission to use these islands. Dangerous tides and rocky reefs around Mejatto made it difficult for the Rongelapese men to fish or to pass on knowledge about fishing to the younger generation.

On Mejatto, the Rongelapese longed for their home islands:

> I didn't want to leave Rongelap in 1985, but the elders did, so I went. Because Rongelap was no good, I left. But I didn't like Mejatto. It is pretty difficult to fish on Mejatto. Wind prevents people from fishing. On Rongelap, there were many choices—many ways to fish and many places to fish. . . . Kids on Mejatto don't know how to sail an outrigger canoe. It's too low to launch there. On Mejatto it's hard to sail and hard to teach. On Mejatto there is lots of American food. There's more food—local food—on Rongelap. There was nothing at all on Mejatto in the beginning. Now it's better because we planted food. Mejatto is bad because it's hard to get back and forth. It's dangerous on all the small islands. Some people have disappeared, some drowned. It's hard to move about (Boney Boaz, March 17, 1999).

> Mejatto is really different from Rongelap. Mejatto is really small. There are scarce resources, such as fish and grown foods. In Mejatto people fish only two to three times a week, but on Rongelap people fished everyday. People depend on USDA and imported

foods. It's like a camp. People are not healthy. They have bad diets, diseases, and the health services are inadequate. It's expensive for me to visit Mejatto [because of travel and foods I have to bring]. . . . It is too rough to fish in Mejatto, and there are too many sharks. People die in the current around Mejatto (Johnsay Riklon, February 28, 1999).

Life on Ebeye and Majuro

Since all social relationships in the Marshall Islands evolve from land rights, the community lost its structure and hierarchy when it moved to Mejatto. The Rongelapese do not own the land on Mejatto. On Mejatto, people do not have the same interest in maintaining land that they do not own or that they do not have rights to. Furthermore, the social structure on Rongelap, based entirely on land rights to their home islands, does not transfer to another area. People with the title and prestige of a land manager (*alap*) on Rongelap lose their authority on Mejatto. This left the Rongelapese on Mejatto with no structure for the community. Many Rongelapese left Mejatto, and the community dispersed into several locations, particularly the two urban areas in the Marshall Islands.

Consider the role of individuals in a society defined by the environment. There are three tiers of rights. These rights are reciprocal. . . . Community life comes from the land. The movement of people from their land changes all of this: people are no longer connected to the land, or anything. When people are not on their land with its social ranks they cannot perform what is expected of them. This makes them feel insecure. Land is a privilege and it tells you who you are in the community. . . . Moving away really messes up things. Going to new land, new area, you don't know what land belongs to who (Wilfred Kendall, March 2, 1999).

The community is scattered and splintered with no base. There are many different categories of Rongelapese now—those who have lived there, those who have not, teenagers, etc. (Johnsay Riklon, 1999).

Throughout the world, a global trend of urbanization creates challenges for all communities. This is no different for the Marshall Islands where urbanization is on the rise. People from the outer islands come to the two urban centers of Ebeye and Majuro to further their education and to seek wage jobs. With most populations in the RMI, the shifts to urban areas happens slowly, however. For example, a family from Mili Atoll may send one son to the public high school in Majuro since there is no schooling beyond eighth grade available on Mili. The son may live with extended family while attending school. If the son is fortunate enough to get a wage-earning job after high school, the family may send another person to Majuro to live with the son and search for a job. The trend continues slowly.

For the people of Rongelap, the shift to the urban areas came abruptly with no gradual transition and no preparation. On Rongelap, the people could earn a living through subsistence. In the urban areas, the skills they have to work the land are not the skills required to obtain a wage-earning job. Members of the community complain that many Rongelapese who used to work hard on their own land are now largely idle. They do not have the right to cultivate any of the resources around the houses they now rent on other people's land. People in the community, as well as researchers, acknowledge that suicide, malnutrition, alcoholism, smoking, and lack of physical exercise are problems for the community (Palafox 2002b).

Housing is a major problem for the community. Ebeye Island, the urban area closest to Mejatto where many from the exiled community relocated, is one of the most densely populated areas in the world. Approximately 15,000 people live on a tiny island that is just one-tenth of a square mile (Figure 5.1). Scarcely any trees exist on the island, and there are almost no open areas for children to play, with the exception of the dump (Figure 5.2). While Majuro has a larger land mass, the poorest areas of the island where most of the Rongelapese live is extremely crowded as well. On both Majuro and Ebeye, water, electricity, education, and health are difficult for families to obtain. Unlike Rongelap, the community must purchase all of its needs. The Rongelapese feel frustrated by many of the problems they experience in their urban environments:

> On Ebeye . . . we buy things. We don't have pandanus leaves to make sleeping mats. I lie on the tile. We need money for everything. When it runs out, there is no food. Our things to cook with break. I still haven't eaten breakfast today (11:15 a.m.). There's no medicine. There's no vehicle to go and get birds to eat. They are far away. . . . My children grew up on Ebeye. They just hang around (Mwenadrik Kebenli 1999).

> What is life like now? It's filled with sickness. It was better on the island (Rongelap). I came to Ebeye because my kids have to go to school. Food is hard when you don't live on your own land. It is also hard to find enough money to pay for school tuition (Jerkan Jenwor, March 17, 1999).

> Now we stay at one of the . . . houses at Dump Town (the section of Ebeye bordering the dump). Six of our kids are married. There are lots of grandchildren. There are thirty-some people in three rooms. You would laugh if you could see us sleeping—everyone together. I really need a house. My husband is retired but he still works because no one else has jobs (Timako Kolnij, March 18, 1999).

> My father died. There are five people in my family now. No one in the family works. . . . I want to go to college, but it will be tough on the people at my house because no one works (Malal Anjain, March 19, 1999).

BURIAL

A major concern of the Rongelapese community in its exile is that the community cannot be near or tend to the graves of its ancestors nor can the community bury the deceased on their families' land. Tending to and being near the graves of family members is important in the Marshallese culture. In the areas where the displaced Rongelapese now live, they have no connection to their ancestors.

In 1999, I accompanied members of the Rongelap community back to their home island. The people took a quick excursion to Rongelap to review efforts to reduce the radiation on the island and in the plants and foods people need to survive if they decide to resettle the island. When our airplane touched down on Rongelap, an elderly woman in the group got off the plane and proceeded immediately to the burial area. She called out: *"yokwe kom"* or "hello to all of you," and walked between the gravestones to see her family members. It was clear that she had been thinking of them, and wanting to be close to them, but her exile makes it impossible for her to do so (Figure 5.4).

For the Marshallese it is important to bury deceased family members on their land so that they will rest peacefully in a place that belongs to them. The importance

Figure 5.1 Modern day Ebeye

Figure 5.2 Ebeye's Dump Town

of land and dying on your own land is captured in the first national anthem of the Marshall Islands (translated by Lijohn Eknilang; reprinted by permission):

Ij iokwe lok aelon ko ao	I love my islands
Ijo iar lotak ie	Here where I was born
Melan ko ie im ial ko	The beautiful surroundings and joining together with friends
Ijamin ilok jen e	I don't want to leave here
Bwe ijo jiku emool	Because this is my true place
In ao lamoren indeo	It's my inheritance forever
Emman lok mae inaaj mij ie	It's best for me to die here

For as long as the community remains in exile, the Rongelapese will feel deep regret and sadness because of their inability to bury their deceased family members on their own land. The people cannot afford to rent the large boats required to ship bodies to Rongelap for burial.

Another aspect of burial that is difficult for the community in its exile is the lack of space for burial. On Majuro, and particularly on Ebeye, there is not enough room to bury people. Furthermore, the Rongelapese must ask for permission from people to bury their family members on other people's land. Families that own the land housing graveyards often deny permission because of severe overcrowding in the cemeteries (Figure 5.3):

> We shouldn't have to ask to be buried. Here on Ebeye it's too crowded to bury. We have to look for places to bury our dead. I want to go back to Rongelap to die. Now they're starting to cremate on Ebeye because there's no place to bury now. They told us it's too full to bury—the cemetery is full. Burial areas are overcrowded, but cremation is against our custom and religion (Lijohn Eknilang, March 3, 1999).

STIGMA/PSYCHOLOGICAL PROBLEMS

"The Bombed People"

Stigmatization, fear, and health problems cause profound problems for individuals, families, and communities in the Marshall Islands. After the Bravo test exposed the Rongelapese to radiation and the U.S. government evacuated the community to Kwajalein, the U.S. government kept the community in a highly secure area where only U.S. government representatives could come and go. Family members living on Ebeye Island at the time heard that their relatives had become ill for unexplained reasons, but they were not allowed to see their relatives and they did not understand that people were exposed to radiation, or that radiation is dangerous to the human body.

For many years after the Bravo incident, the Rongelapese say that many of their family members did not want to see them, or touch them for fear that they would get contaminated in their presence:

© Holly M. Barker

Figure 5.3 Cemetery on Rongelap, April 1999

© Holly M. Barker

Figure 5.4 Cemetery on Ebeye, April 1999

> We were very isolated on Kwajalein. Our relatives on Ebeye were afraid of their own family members—they were afraid to visit us for fear they would get radiation from us (Isao Eknilang, June 13, 2001).

> This was the first time in the history of our community that brothers and sisters, uncles and aunts, and relatives turned their back on one another. This created a deep divide in our community (Almira Matayoshi, October 29, 2001).

> When we would walk down the street in Majuro or somewhere people would look at us and point and say *"Ebaam,* (he's bombed) stay away from him!" (Norio Kebenli, October 29, 2001).

> The two hardest things for us to talk about are the divisions in our families caused by the bomb, and what happened to our bodies. The Rongelapese who weren't exposed wouldn't admit they were Rongelapese (for fear of stigmatization from the rest of the country). This is awful because we are family, and this is the worst kind of damage to have splits in the family (Almira Matayoshi, June 13, 2001).

After experiencing extreme illness and displacement because of the weapons testing program, the community experienced further indignities from other Marshallese who were scared by, and did not understand that the effects of radiation exposure were not contagious.

Fear of Radiation

The Rongelapese have found that radiation is a difficult threat to protect themselves from because they cannot see, hear, taste, or feel it. They relied on U.S. government scientists to tell them whether or not radiation was present in their environment. When the community moved back to Rongelap in 1957, the U.S. government assured them that it was safe to return and they would not be harmed by radiation in the environment. As discussed previously in this chapter, the people got blisters in their mouths and got ill from eating many of their local foods that contained radiation, yet the U.S. government maintained there was no danger. At one point, the U.S. government told the Rongelapese not to eat coconut crabs because the radiation levels were too high in the crabs, but the Rongelapese had already eaten many crabs before receiving this directive. The U.S. government's failure to disclose the true radiological content of the foodstuffs on Rongelap—information that became available only after the community put itself into exile—exacerbated the community's fears about radiation.

> Psychologically, you stop believing in everything around you. Your feeling of safety no longer exists when the radiation-contaminated medicine and food around you is no good, restricted, or makes you worry (Lijohn Eknilang, March 3, 1999).

> I won't go back. The radiation won't go away (Nerje Joseph, 1999).

SOCIAL CONSEQUENCES OF LOSS OF LAND

The multiple and far-ranging consequences of the testing program do not affect the Rongelap community uniformly. Men and women suffer different burdens. The youth and the elderly are also affected differently. Furthermore, persistent radiation affects the *iroij, alaps,* and *ri-jerbal* in unique ways.

Women

As discussed in Chapter 1, land passes down through families matrilineally. Because land is of central importance to the Marshallese, this tradition provides women with power and respect. Now that the community cannot live on its land because of the radiation, children do not grow up with knowledge about the land they will inherit or an appreciation for its importance. As a result, the resettlement of the community attenuates the power of women.

In their exile women do not have the rights to use the plant materials they need to make handicrafts. On Rongelap, women generated an income from their handicraft production. In their exile, the Rongelapese women cannot teach their daughters the skills they learned from their mothers:

> On Rongelap, young girls like me learned to make preserved pandanus and food from pandanus. We cooked it in the underground oven. We also made sitting mats, sleeping mats, and baskets. Our grandmothers taught us. We prepared shells for handicrafts. We got the pandanus leaves for the women (Timako Kolnij, 1999).

Men

Marshallese men are expected to provide food for their families. On Rongelap, the men had a range of fishing and food-gathering techniques that ensured they could provide for their families. The Rongelapese men are proud of the fishing, sailing, and navigational skills they developed and used on Rongelap, Rongerik, and Ailinginae. Many Rongelapese men indicated in interviews that they feel inadequate and compromised as men because they can no longer provide for their families. They lack the educational and occupational skills necessary to obtain wage-earning jobs. Several Rongelapese men told me they believe that suicide is increasing among young Rongelapese men because of low self-esteem:

> We have lost our knowledge, our ability, our moral standing, and self-esteem in the community. What we were taught is no longer practical. To be a good fisherman, you have to know where to fish on an island. A lot has been lost, not just our land (Ken Kedi, March 1, 1999).

Elderly

The older members of the Rongelap community, those who were children during the testing program, endure great hardship. The Bravo test exposed them to near lethal amounts of radioactive fallout: they suffer from a range of health problems, they watch friends and children die, the community relocated many times, they remain displaced from their land, they are anxious about death away from their homeland and proper burial ground, they find it difficult to obtain their basic needs (food and shelter), and they worry about the future of their children and community. Furthermore, the elders lack the traditional respect they used to receive on their own land—respect that comes from knowledge about how to survive from the land, a knowledge that was of critical importance on Rongelap but is useless in the eyes of the youth raised in exile:

> Elders lose their authority when the community is on someone else's land because they can't use the threat of kicking people off their land to get work done for them or to get

respect. There is no fear of punishment in the younger generation. Authority comes from land (Lijohn Eknilang, March 2, 1999).

On Rongelap, the care that the elderly received reflected the respect that the community accorded them. Family members always took care of the elderly. In their exile, many family members do not have the money or resources to properly care for the elderly. As a result, many of the elderly Rongelapese are sick, often hungry, and dependent on younger family members to care for them. The elderly also feel concerned that if they die no one will pass on information about Rongelap that is critical to future survival and proper stewardship of the islands.

> The elders mostly want to return to Rongelap because they know no other way of life (James Matayoshi, March 1, 1999).

> Most elders died. They died wanting to go back. My great grandfather, Talekerab, said he wouldn't leave the island when it was time to evacuate. After they took him off he started fasting and demanded to go back. Everyday he would chant, sing, and talk of the good old days. He would ask: "Why are we here [in Mejatto]?" He said he wouldn't eat until he went back. He died (Ken Kedi 1999).

Youth

A generation of Rongelapese born after the testing program face their own set of problems. According to the Greenpeace team that helped evacuate the Rongelapese to Mejatto, teenage boys had a particularly difficult time with the transition:

> They have little to do. . . . They sleep, talk story, play guitar and softball, and now and then go fishing or help with community jobs. . . . They are in between cultures, exposed to the American way of life through TV and videos and the consumer goodies available in Majuro and Ebeye. . . . Outer island life is very different and does not prepare people for the materially orientated imported lifestyle (Greenpeace 1986:3).

Rongelapese adults worry about the fate of their youth who do not have a connection to any land in a nation that values nothing more dearly. They also worry that the youth will not be able to exercise their property rights in the future because they do not know the history of their land, or even what land belongs to their family. The youth also have worries of their own. They worry because there are few opportunities available to them in the urban areas. They also worry about resettlement decisions that the adults may make in the future.

> When I was a young boy on Rongelap, I started to fish when I was about eight years old. I knew how to make copra and do all kinds of work. Eight to twelve years of age are important years for learning. When you leave home, there is no role for the kids. They used to work and contribute, but not anymore (Jerkan Jenwor, 1999).

> Rongelapese youth can't climb trees, but they are familiar with Coca-Cola. Youth used to keep busy and fit doing work in their environment, such as making copra. They can't do that in the urban areas, however, and they are unfit as a result. The types of current activities Rongelapese take part in are gathering, smoking, talking, making yeast (a locally made alcoholic beverage). Suicide seems to be increasing, especially on Mejatto (Ken Kedi 1999).

> Kids from Rongelap that live in Majuro are not involved in the Rongelap community. There aren't many community activities for them to get involved in. I don't think they feel

Rongelapese. They don't know their relatives. Their friends are kids from other atoll communities. I doubt these kids will want to go back to Rongelap (Johnsay Riklon 1999).

Iroij and Social Structure

When the Rongelapese determined that they could no longer live on their land, the land on Rongelap, Rongerik, and Ailinginae that the community managed and maintained for the *iroij* were no longer looked after. Consequently, the land is no longer productive and the *iroij* of Rongelap, Rongerik, and Ailinginae do not receive a portion of the earnings people generated from copra, or gifts of food that *iroij* use to distribute to needy people under his or her care. The power of the *iroij* diminishes by his or her inability to assist others as is customary, or to benefit from the money and resources generated from the land.

> Without people occupying the land, there is no *iroij*. The word *iroij* means many people and comes from the words *"er" "woj."* What's the point of being an *iroij* without any land? . . . When the bomb exploded, the culture was gone, too. It is impossible for people to act in their proper roles. Our social roles are something you use everyday, 24 hours a day. You have to use it everyday or you lose it (Mike Kabua, March 2, 1999).

From the perspective of the *alaps* who oversee the *iroij's* land and the *ri-jerbal* who provide the labor for the *iroij's* land, the displaced community feels sad that they cannot show their respect for their *iroij* in customary ways. Traditionally, people felt much pride when they could provide their *iroij* with gifts of food and maintain the *iroij's* property for him or her. The Rongelapese also feel great sorrow because they gave foods tainted with radiation to the *iroij* after they were resettled on their land in 1957 (George Anjain, March 3, 1999). Customarily, the people had no choice and had to provide the *iroij* with food during visits to the island. They did not want the *iroij* to consume contaminated foods but custom required that they give local foods to the *iroij*. By the same token, the *iroij* could not refuse a gift of respect and tradition from the people, and the *iroij* had to accept contaminated foods from the people (Mike Kabua, March 2, 1999).

> *Iroij* visits to Rongelap after 1957 were difficult. The people were required to give food to their *iroij* even when the food was contaminated, such as coconut crabs, because of the cultural importance. People didn't want to give contaminated food to the *iroij,* but they had to. By the same token, the *iroij* didn't want to accept the contaminated food, but had to. The *iroij* was scared of eating coconut crab, but it is so important to give coconut crab to the *iroij* that the *iroij* could kick people off the land for not giving it to him. The people were also afraid the *iroij* would reject the food (Mike Kabua, March 2, 1999). (See Figure 5.5.)

Once radiation entered the food chain that the Rongelapese depend on for survival, all of the community's interactions with their land and their resources changed. The weapons testing tainted the foods that sustained the community for hundreds of years and caused illness and death in the population. The community had no choice but to leave. In their exile, the Rongelapese do not have access to the land and resources they need to provide for their families. The weapons testing program dramatically altered the social fabric of the Rongelapese, and robbed them of their self-reliance that enabled them to provide for themselves.

© Holly M. Barker

Figure 5.5 Iroij Mike Kabua

CONCLUSION

After contamination forced the Rongelapese to leave their home islands, the community dispersed. Most community members moved to the urban areas of Ebeye and Majuro where they live in extremely crowded, unsanitary, and impoverished conditions. Because radiological contamination alienated the Rongelapese from their home islands, the people no longer have the ability to produce or reproduce cultural knowledge about their local environment—knowledge that is essential to the survival and long-term well-being of the community. The longer people are off of their home islands, the more difficult it is for them to exercise their land rights and ensure that future generations receive the land rights they are entitled to.

6/Language
and the
Testing Program

As discussed in Chapter 1, what makes the Marshallese language interesting is its surprising uniformity despite the isolation of and distance between different atoll populations in the more than 1,000 miles of ocean that separates the farthest populations.

Within the two major dialects are a number of minor dialects (Bender 1978). Some of the atolls situated closer to other island groups—such as Mili to the southeast that is close to Kiribati, and Enewetak and Ujelang to the northwest that are close to Kosrae and Pohnpei—borrowed words from their neighbors. For example, the people from Mili often use the Kiribati word for giant clam, *kabajua,* although the Marshallese word for the giant clam is *kapwor.*

Analysis of the Marshallese language requires the researcher to examine not only the grammar, rules, and sounds used by speakers, but also to understand the signals and context of the meaning conveyed by speakers. Joking, for instance, and particularly double entendres with hidden sexual meaning are a national pastime in the Marshall Islands (Bender 1978). The Marshallese love to laugh and joke, but a speaker must also understand the strict linguistic taboos in the language. Joking about sex or sexual topics is a favorite topic in some mixed groups, but is strictly forbidden in other groups. A speaker must be familiar with the relationships between everyone in a group before making any jokes about sex. Most taboos in a group occur between closely related men and women, but the taboo can extend between men in a group as well (Bender 1978). It is extremely difficult for non-Marshallese to know the relationships between all people in a group and wise for outsiders to take their cues from others in a group.

One of the best ways to determine how the Marshallese perceive the events and experiences related to the U.S. nuclear weapons testing program is through the analysis of language. The Marshallese language reflects the lived experiences of a population exposed to radiation. The language embodies the history of the exposed population and the social and cultural changes resulting from the introduction of radiation into their world.

RADIATION AND A COLONIAL LANGUAGE OF CONTROL

The United States government, the English language, and nuclear weapons came to the Marshallese people at the same time. When the United States began its nuclear weapons testing program in the Marshall Islands, the Marshallese people had no word for "radiation," nor any need to have such a word in their language. As the administrating authority of the trust territory, the United States government used its language, English, to explain the ideologies of its scientists and its institutions and to explain the consequences of nuclear weapons.

Throughout the world, colonizers exert total control over their territories, including linguistic control (Romaine 1994). In the Marshall Islands, the language of the United States became the language of the trust territory. The U.S. government conveyed its rules of governance, policies, and descriptions of U.S. activities to the Marshallese in English. The first documented occasion where the U.S. government discussed nuclear weapons and defense ideology with the Marshallese occurred on Bikini Atoll in 1946, as discussed in the first chapter, when Commander Wyatt asked the Bikinians for permission to use their land for the testing program. The film, *Radio Bikini*, includes footage of Commander Wyatt when he turned to the Marshallese translator, dressed in U.S. military clothes and cap, and said: "Now James, tell them [the assembled Bikinians] please that the United States government now wants to turn this great destructive power into something for the benefit of mankind and that these experiments here at Bikini are the first step in that direction" (Wyatt in O'Rourke 1985). As instructed, the Marshallese translator turned to the Bikinians and said in Marshallese:

> *Ej ba kio United States an Amedka rekonan bwe armej en kojerbal men eo ekajor en ukot nan men eo emman im jiban.*

Because the Marshallese language was yet to evolve to a level where it could adequately communicate concepts related to nuclear weapons, James simply stated:

> He said the United States of America they want people to use something strong and turn it into something good and helpful.

Every time I show that footage to bilingual audiences they laugh uproariously at the scene. They find the message and the attempt to translate it comical. From this footage, it is clear that the U.S. government and the English language failed to communicate even the basic purposes and rationale for the weapons testing program to the Marshallese. The focus of Commander Wyatt was on the strategic interests of the United States, not on the damage and injury caused by the weapons tests that the Marshallese soon discovered firsthand.

United States government officials used scientific, political, and legal language to describe the activities and consequences of the nuclear weapons testing program. The U.S. government carefully constructed the language it used to protect American defense ideology and support the necessity of testing nuclear weapons. U.S. government efforts to explain the consequences of radiation exposure to the Marshallese grossly minimize the injury and damages.

As discussed in Chapter 3, during the 1970s when the U.S. and RMI governments negotiated the terms of an agreement to terminate the trust territory relationship, the U.S. government undertook a study of the 14 northern most atolls in the Marshall Islands to explain radiological contamination issues to the Marshallese.

The U.S. Department of Energy traveled throughout the islands to provide copies of this survey, translated into Marshallese, to the population. It was the only nation-wide attempt to educate people about the consequences of the nuclear weapons testing program. The published survey explains to the Marshallese how radiation can affect the human body:

> People might consider that radioactive atoms are kinds of poison. However, radioactive atoms are different from poisons because radiation comes from them. The way radiation acts and the way poison acts are different because usually when poisonous things (like bleach, kerosene, battery fluid) enter a person's body, his body is quickly harmed—it can be within a few minutes or days. But if harm were to come from the amount of radiation in the atolls of the northern part of the Marshall Islands today, it would take a long time for it to being to appear—it could be after many years. Remember that there is radiation that has always been in and part of the world and there is radiation that comes from atomic bombs. All of these radiations can cause harm (Bair et al. 1982:23).

It is clear from this passage that the purpose of the U.S. government's survey was to blur the lines between natural sources of radiation that cause harm and radiation unleashed by the weapons testing. Just when DOE introduces the concept of radiation from weapons tests doing harm, the authors include the cautionary "remember" to remind people that they cannot be sure which type of radiation causes injuries. This single word, "remember," also shows the paternalistic and patronizing tone of DOE that treats the Marshallese like small children—children that must be taught the truth about radiation, a truth constructed by the U.S. government. The U.S. Department of Energy also used its survey to tell the Marshallese population that radiation exposure, miscarriages, and birth defects occur naturally and are not necessarily the result of radiation exposure (Bair et al. 1982:27) (Figure 6.1). These comparisons fail to distinguish between radiation produced from nuclear explosions and other, less harmful types of radiation.

Virtually all information about the effects of the weapons testing program that the U.S. government presented concludes that the Marshallese have no reason to feel concerned about their exposure. In 1998, Dr. William Robison, a DOE contractor, summarized 25 years of his environmental work in the RMI at a government-to-government meeting. I recorded my impressions of Dr. Robison's presentation in my fieldnotes:

> DOE proceeded to show that *background* levels of radiation in the RMI are lower than the U.S. and Europe. The conclusion was that radiation in the RMI is lower than other places in the world and people shouldn't be concerned about their environment. . . . The U.S. ambassador [to the RMI] was present at the meeting, indicating that the summary of data presented at the meeting is of importance to the U.S. . . . It made me angry that DOE controls all the information and the presentation of the data. The information was presented so nicely and scientifically that it made it difficult to refute. It was also, I think, a bit intimidating for community members to challenge [U.S.] scientists and political representatives. . . . It was misleading to talk about background radiation when there was no discussion of imposed, manmade radiation (Barker 1998:46–50).

Can Animals and Plants Receive Harm from Radiation?

Sometimes radiation can cause harm to animals like it can to people. However, the amount of radiation must be very much larger to food-bearing plants and other plants than to animals for there to be harm to plants such as breadfruit, coconuts, pandanus, taro, and arrowroot. This means that plants would only be harmed if they received an exceedingly large amount of radiation. Because the amounts of radiation are small in the Marshalls today, scientists do not believe that there will be harm to animals and plants.

Figure 6.1 Page from U.S. DOE book showing reproductive abnormalities the Marshallese could expect

In most cases it is not the data or the environmental scientists themselves that are problematic, but the conclusions and interpretations that the U.S. government draws from the data.

LANGUAGE AS RESISTANCE

It is through the examination of the language used by the Marshallese that anthropologists begin to understand the lived experiences of people exposed to radiation. The language of Marshallese populations exposed to radiation contains elements of U.S. government attempts to explain what radiation is and what it does. Ultimately, the radiation populations demonstrate their disdain for the U.S. government's explanations about radiation exposure by rejecting and transforming the language presented and imposed by U.S. government representatives, such as DOE representatives. The Marshallese create their own radiation language to convey their experiences resulting from the testing program that the U.S. government's language and politics will not accommodate. Through the radiation language, Marshallese convey notions of blame, powerlessness, and injury that speakers of English, such as U.S. government representatives, are not privy to.

Linguistic evidence demonstrates that the Marshallese resist attempts by the U.S. government to set parameters on their experiences with radiation. This resistance is evident in the language that the Marshallese continue to create in order to explain and discuss the aftermath of the U.S. testing program among themselves. Although the Marshallese radiation language contains links to the English language, the words have entirely different meanings. This does not represent a creolization or pidginization of the English language where English language creeps in and replaces a local language, but the evolution of a completely separate language with different meanings. During instances where speakers borrow an English word to explain their situation, the Marshallese radiation language remains the predominant vehicle for conveying the speakers' sense of powerlessness, for describing horrific medical ailments, and for assigning cause to their sufferings. This is particularly true for women whose discourse regarding reproductive abnormalities indicates that they continue to suffer the adverse affects of radiation exposure silently, and differently from their male counterparts. Yet, even among Marshallese women, linguistic evidence indicates that their experiences and illnesses vary due to both the degree of medical attention they receive, and their atoll of birth.

Loan Words

When analyzing the linguistic data from interviews with Marshallese exposed to radiation, I found speakers borrow English words pertaining to radiation science. While an analysis of language cannot rely on the details of grammar alone, an initial look at English loan words that the Marshallese borrow to convey their experiences with radiation does provide important clues about the radiation language and a useful context to investigate grammar use. An examination of loan words provides a launching point for discussing alternative language used by radiation populations.

Before I examined the linguistic data, I predicted that the Marshallese would draw heavily from the English language and that speakers would develop a pidgin English discourse. By isolating the loan words used in three lengthy interviews[1] (Table 6.1), I learned that my expectation was wrong. In fact, the scant number of English words borrowed by radiation survivors indicates that the speakers convey the majority of their experiences through a unique, highly situational, and localized radiation language that they construct almost entirely with Marshallese words. Furthermore, the paltry number of English words demonstrates that the radiation survivors claim the weapons testing event as their own—an event that the U.S. government does not have the right to define. The use of the Marshallese language to define

---

[1]Because the information in these three interviews is extremely personal, and forbidden to discuss in many Marshallese contexts, I changed the names of all the informants to protect their identities.

TABLE 6.1   ENGLISH LOAN WORDS USED DURING THREE INTERVIEWS

Kita	Jakori	Ertilang	English Equivalent
paijin	*paijin*	*paijin*	poison
tokta	*tokta*	*tokta*	doctor, noun and verb
kiraap	*kiraap*	*kiraap*	grape (molar pregnancy)
	book	*book*	book
	baam	*baam*	bomb
	paota	*paota*	powder (fallout)
	kanjir	*kanjir*	cancer
	tumur	*tumur*	tumor
	aujpito	*aujpitol*	hospital
	kilam	*kilam*	claim (for compensation)

the event also proves that the radiation survivors actively resist U.S. government representations of their experiences and the use of English, scientific discourse used to make those representations.

There are only three English loan words common to all three women: *paijin* (poison), *tokta* (doctor), and *kiraap* (grape). Despite the fact that these women represent both the "exposed" and "unexposed" categories created by the U.S. government, all three describe similar experiences: the *paijin* that dramatically altered the health of the people, the animals, and the land; the *toktas* who did not explain the women's ailments to them, and whose motives the women question; and the horrifying *kiraap* pregnancies that Marshallese women did not experience until after the weapons testing. Language shows a commonality of experiences with radiation between the legally "exposed" population and the undocumented radiation populations the U.S. government maintains are "unexposed" to radiation. As a result of this linguistic evidence, it is clear that experiences with radiation are not limited to the narrow constructions discussed by U.S. government representatives.

The word that Marshallese frequently use to describe toxins introduced into their environment, like radiation, is "poison." A person suffers from the effects of radiation exposure is also considered "poisoned." The Marshallese term used to describe the effects of local toxins that produce illness or death, such as fish poisoning, is *kadek,* a word that translates most closely to the English word "drunk." The effects of fish poisoning cause loss of control of the body much like excessive drunkenness, but these effects require a different term than poison, thereby demonstrating that the Marshallese consider poison from radiation as very different from fish or other sources of poison.

Another word used by all three of the women is "grapes." "Grapes" is the name that Marshallese women use to describe hydatidiform, or molar pregnancies. During molar pregnancies, the mitosis that begins shortly after conception continues only for a short time. At some point, instead of continuing to divide, the cells become enlarged and grow to the size of golf balls. The large strands of golf ball-sized growths attach themselves to the uterus. In many cases, there are dangers associated with these pregnancies, such as cancer from the roots of the growths that remain imbedded in the uterus, extremely high fevers, or the inability of women to abort the cell masses. According to the women I interviewed, women with this illness have all the symptoms of pregnancy, and the enlarged size of the uterus makes them think they are in the advanced stages of their pregnancy. Marshallese women report that they spontaneously abort their failed pregnancies after approximately three months although they appear nine months pregnant when they expel the "grapes." These accounts from the Marshallese women parallel descriptions of hydatidiform pregnancies in the United States but the incidence rate for this condition is extremely rare, perhaps one in 1,500 pregnancies and occurs when there are chromosomal abnormalities in the female ova (Plumbo 1999).

Beyond the three common words used by the women, such as grapes, the remaining seven words in Table 6.1 are common to the experiences of all three women even if they did not use the words in their interviews. For example, Kita's husband, Kino, used the words *baam* and *paota* to describe their shared experiences after the Bravo test, but I did not include these words in Table 6.1 because it was not Kita who spoke them. Furthermore, when I reviewed the taped interviews I realized that I introduced these words to the conversation before Kino used them. Therefore, I cannot conclusively determine whether Kino used the English words because I introduced them first, or because he wanted to make his Marshallese as simple as possible for me as a native English speaker. It is also interesting to note that both Kita and Jakori use the phrase *"men eo"* or "the thing" to refer to the bomb as if they could not find a word to describe the weapon that irreversibly changed their lives.

In addition to the English words that the women use in common, each of them has distinct patterns of borrowing. These words are not simply borrowed by the Marshallese women, but, like all loan words, the speakers modify them to fit the phonology and syntax of the Marshallese language. The differences in word selection correspond to the women's atoll of residence, and degree of contact with medical doctors and scientists. For example, some of the English words that Kita borrows and adapts to the Marshallese language enable her to make distinctions between different types of U.S. government representatives who came to her island after the testing began. Kita distinguishes between *ri-tokta,* literally "person who is a medical doctor," the *ri-etale paijin,* "person who studies/examines the poison (or radiation in the environment)," and most specifically, the *tokta en paijinro,* "the radiation doctors." In the same interview, Kita's husband also makes reference to Marshallese doctors, *takto ro i-Majol,* and to American doctors. The distinctions made by Kita and her husband are socially and historically important. The linguistic evidence demonstrates that non-English-speaking residents of a remote outer island distinguish doctors concerned with their well being from doctors or researchers interested in studying the effects of radiation on human beings and the environment. This pattern of borrowing English provides clues about the emergence of a distinct Marshallese radiation language; the Marshallese language makes important distinctions between doctors and scientists that the English language and the U.S. government representatives failed to or did not want to convey to the Marshallese.

While Kita and her husband's contact with U.S. doctors is limited to their observation of researchers who visited their islands, Ertilang is intimately familiar with U.S. government representatives. Similar to Kita and Kino, English loan words serve as a starting point for understanding Ertilang's familiarity with U.S. government researchers. As a resident of Rongelap, the inhabited atoll that received the highest doses of radiation after the Bravo incident, Ertilang identifies herself and her fellow Rongelapese as *ri-paijin,* the "poisoned (or irradiated) people." Ertilang's long history of medical ailments and participation in Project 4.1 made Ertilang familiar with U.S. government medical institutions, procedures, and physicians. Ertilang distinguishes between AEC and DOE doctors. This distinction demonstrates how language reflects historical influences: Ertilang identifies changes in U.S. government institutions, noting that the Atomic Energy Commission ("AEC") was the predecessor of the U.S. Department of Energy ("DOE"). Ertilang also identifies specific DOE contractors, such as doctors from Brookhaven National Laboratory ("Brookhaven").

In addition to demonstrating her knowledge about the different contractors and officials who had an interest in her medical conditions, English loan words help Ertilang supplement her radiation language. The use of the word "thyroid" is particularly indicative of Ertilang's frequent interactions with U.S. medical personnel since Kita, who is not familiar with English medical terms, refers to thyroid illness as *buj buru,* or swollen throat. Ertilang's familiarity with specific medical procedures or ailments results, in part, from her numerous trips to the United States where researchers and doctors performed medical procedures on her. She traveled to California; Cleveland, Ohio; Maryland; New York; and Washington, DC, for medical procedures. All of the facilities named by Ertilang are either U.S. military hospitals or locations where U.S. government researchers conducted human radiation experiments. Ertilang did not understand what the procedures were for, nor did U.S. government doctors record any medical procedures in her personal medical charts. To this day, Ertilang's medical records remain blank for the first decades following her exposure.

Like Kita and Ertilang, English loan words reflect how Jakori explains and understands her medical experiences. During the U.S. nuclear weapons testing program, Jakori lived on the main island of Likiep Atoll. As with the other two women, Jakori remembers the *paota* (powder), or radioactive fallout that arrived after the ground-shaking detonation and bloody red sky that hundreds of Marshallese witnessed on the morning of March 1, 1954. After completing grammar school on Likiep, Jakori moved to the capital, Majuro. Jakori is the only one of the three women to attend high school, to learn English, and to hold a wage-earning job. These experiences allow Jakori to converse in the language of her former colonial administrator.

Years after the tests when Jakori began to experience reproductive problems related to her radiation exposure, she was not eligible for U.S.-sponsored medical care for radiation survivors. Jakori went to Majuro public hospital where local physicians were unfamiliar with radiation-related illnesses (U.S. government physicians working with the radiation survivors operated independently from the local health care facilities). In her interview, Jakori describes her near-death experience in Majuro hospital. The English words Jakori borrows help her explain the trauma she experienced and recall the doctors' explanations about her illness.

Although Jakori uses many more English words than her counterparts, she still wanted me to interview her in Marshallese. I found this interesting because Jakori has the English skills to discuss her experiences in a purely English form. Jakori's insistence on the use of Marshallese further indicates that the radiation survivors claim the events in the Marshall Islands as their own. The Marshallese language shows that the people actively resist the accounting of events and consequences from the U.S. government, and the ability of English to convey adequately the damage and injuries experienced by the Marshallese people. The radiation survivors found their own way of describing their experiences, modifying information received from the

U.S. government to more adequately convey the lived experiences of the people, and ultimately to state the events in Marshallese terms.

In addition to Jakori, I found further evidence of English concealment over my years of interactions with the Marshallese. Even people who know me extremely well, and are not shy or insecure with me, often conceal their English language skills from me. Concealing English language skills could reflect modesty, or even pleasure at seeing an outsider speak Marshallese. But, I believe the concealment shows that the Marshallese resist acculturation through language choice. When I first arrived in the country and could not speak Marshallese, many people hid their English language skills from me and allowed me to stumble through or sit out conversations until I learned the local language. In the case of Jakori, whom I consider a friend, she knows I am aware of her English language skills. Jakori, and many other Marshallese prefer, and often demand, that speakers use Marshallese to discuss certain topics, such as radiation issues. This resistance technique allows the Marshallese to construct freely their social realities in the Marshallese language without fear that Americans will tell them their perceptions or experiences are not valid, or radiation related.

Insisting on the use of language, in this case the Marshallese language, provides the Marshallese with a "vernacular for in-group communication" (Mufwene 1994:84). Controlling the language of expression also allows women to talk quietly among themselves about the pain and social humiliation involved in giving birth to abnormal children. Also, it is often inappropriate to display anger publicly in the Marshall Islands, particularly if the speaker expresses anger directly rather than conveying his or her anger to a third party. From my experience, the only Americans who take the time and energy to learn the Marshallese language are those who become involved with the community and have concern for the well being of the Marshallese (such as Peace Corps or Jesuit volunteers, or Americans who marry into the community). Therefore, radiation survivors control who gets to hear their direct outbursts of anger by sharing their thoughts with those who speak their language. This allows the speakers to express their thoughts privately without violating customary practices for expressing anger. Anyone who hears the speakers using the Marshallese language to ascribe blame and to convey anger toward the United States will likely sympathize with the speakers' emotions.

A tendency to avoid direct confrontation does not mean that the Marshallese do not directly express their anger to the U.S. government, however. On numerous occasions, local government representatives share their anger with the U.S. government directly and loudly. Expressions of deep anger usually emerge during bilateral meetings between the communities most affected by the weapons testing, and the U.S. government, particularly the Department of Energy. At these meetings, speakers find it appropriate and necessary to share their frustrations and anger with the U.S. government. Although Marshallese leaders still get angry during these bilateral meetings, in recent years the leaders have come to realize that they can better address their problems with the U.S. government by figuring out how solving problems is in the best interest of both the atolls and the U.S. government. It is understandable that the Marshallese feel angry at the United States government for its failure to respond appropriately to the problems it caused, but experienced leaders have come to realize that working with U.S. government officials is the only way to make progress.

During my interview with Jakori, the vast majority of our time was spent discussing her *kiraap* (grapes) pregnancy. Jakori's extensive focus on this topic demonstrates the importance of her reproductive episode as the primary means to convey the consequences of her radiation exposure. Jakori uses many English words to explain her ordeal. Many of these words came from a medical book that her attending doctors showed to her while she was in the hospital. The doctors used the book to help explain Jakori's condition to her. The use of English terms in the passage below, even if mixed with Marshallese, such as *"ilukun skin im bones wot"* (I was only skin and bones), demonstrates the level of Jakori's competence with the English language. Clearly, she has the skills to relate the entire experience in English if she chose. Jakori and I sat in a private room with a closed door during the interview; no one could overhear our conversation so she was free to choose whichever language she wanted to tell me about her experiences. From her language choice, it is clear that delivering "grape" babies is a Marshallese event that Jakori had to explain in Marshallese.

In the following passage, Jakori describes the suffering she experienced during the delivery of "grapes." I highlight in bold the English loan words used by Jakori:

*Jilu wot ao allon ak reba **nine months** jonan ao kilep. . . . Rej ba imeloklok jete ao allon na iba ijjab. . . . Anbwinu elukkun bwil im rej boktok **water** molo im ijojo ilo **tub** eo jen jibon nan bon. Jonan ao lukun bwil, lukun bwil wot im bwil, im aolep raan rej **fill** juon **tub** ituru im ne ejako an molo **tub** eo ij etal nan **tub** eo juon. Im eliktata eo kio ilukun in mojono ijab mona kinke ibban menono im kojela **saliva** ejab bojrak an wotlok jen lonu . . . [I]lukun **lose weight** im ij **eighty pounds** im ej [tokta eo] ba na ilukun **skin** im **bones** wot.*

I was only three months pregnant but they said I was nine months because of my large size. . . . They said I forgot how many months pregnant I was but I said I didn't [forget]. . . . My body was so hot that they brought me cold water and I sat in a tub from morning to night. I was so incredibly hot, extremely hot, so hot that every day they filled a tub near me and when that tub was no longer cold I transferred to another tub. At the end of this time I was so weak that I could not eat because I could not breathe and you know the saliva it did not stop pouring from my mouth. . . . I really lost weight—I was eighty pounds and he [the doctor] said I was only skin and bones.

*Eliktata ij kolotak, rej kwalok kiraap ko im rej jolok jikin ninnin eo ao. Im tokta eo ear kolotake na ej ba **first time** ej **deliver** kon naninmej eo im ej boktok juon **book** kileplep im ej lale men ko ilowan lojieu im ejba: "Lojiem ebaam im men ko ilo lojiem rej ainwot bin kan ilo **bowling**. Men ko rej ainwot **shaped like that.**" Im aikwoj en kareok jikin ninnin eo ao bwe imaron **cancer** im emman lok ne ej jolok aolepen. . . .*

Finally, I gave birth and the doctors showed me the grapes and then they gave me a hysterectomy. And the doctor who attended my birth said it was the first time he had delivered this kind of illness and he brought me a huge book to see [pictures of] the things inside my stomach and he said: "Your stomach is bombed [irradiated] and the things in your stomach are like bowling pins. Those things are shaped like that." And [he] had to clean my reproductive system out because I might get cancer and it's better if he removes everything. . . .

In this passage it is clear that Jakori's use of English words to describe her experiences increases when she is paraphrasing the English that her doctor used to explain her illness to her. Most of the English words belong to the doctor; Jakori employs far fewer English words when using her own words to describe her experiences. When she does use English words, she uses words like "tub" because bathtubs did not exist in the Marshall Islands until outsiders brought them in. Like the word "radiation," the Marshallese did not need a word for "tub" before colonial times.

After examining my interviews, I wanted to make sure that speakers did not use more English words because they know I am an English speaker. I examined some of the interviews conducted by my students at the Nuclear Institute of the College of the Marshall Islands. These interviews capture dialogue between two or more native Marshallese speakers. In the following passage from an interview conducted by three of my students, the speakers use almost no English loan words to describe the events witnessed on March 1, 1954. One of the interviewers uses the English word "color" to ask the subject about the sky after the Bravo detonation. The subject uses the word "lights" to describe the changes to the sky.

In this interview, conducted, transcribed, and translated by Edma Tartios, Raymond Johnson, and Mary Silk, the interviewers ask Samos Relang to explain his experiences immediately after the Bravo event. Samos lived on Mejit Atoll, an atoll outside of the U.S. boundary defining radiation exposure in the Marshall Islands. His experiences were so unfamiliar and bizarre to him that he thought outsiders were recapturing the islands as they did in World War II.

Edma Tartios: *Ekar wor ta ear walok ilo ien eo elkin kar tore eo kom kar lo meram eo?*

Samos Relang: *Aet. Ekwe, ij ron ainikien inurnur eo, ekar mokta walok meram eo ke ej marok wot. Ejjanin lukun raan. Etal im lak lukun jade lok raan, jibbon, ejjanin tak al. Ewor jiljino jimatan. Ke ej bokolok, etobtob mejatoto eo im iar reiarlok im lale ne ilolo wa. Ke ij ron inurnur ejjanin bokolok men eo. Inurnur wot.*

ET: *Ewi wewen an inurnur?*

SR: *Einwot ne inurnur jorur. Na ij lomnak rej bake wot turin en eo. Ak ilak lale ejjelok jabdewot. Im elap ao bwilon—enaj ta? Ak ij lomnak ewor ijen rar buki.*

Raymond Johnson: *Kom jaje ke Bikini?*

SR: *Kom jaje.*

Mary Silk: *Ak meram mokta? Ewi wewen jokjok in meram eo?*

SR: *Meram mokta, einwot meram in **light** kane. Einwot meram in al ne etton joran tak.*

MS: *Kain color rot eo an?*

SR: *Einwot eburoro.*

Edma Tartios: What happened out on that island [of Mejit] during the time that you saw the light [from the Bravo detonation]?

Samos Relang: Yes. Well, I heard a rumbling sound. It began before the light appeared when it was still dark. It still wasn't daytime yet. When it got closer to daybreak, morning, the sun hadn't come up yet. At the time that it [the bomb] exploded, everything was hazy looking to me and I looked to the lagoon to see if I could spot a boat. That's because I heard the rumbling before the thing exploded. Just rumbling.

ET: What was the rumbling like?

SR: It was like the rumbling of thunder. Me, I thought they captured part of one of those islands over there. But when I looked out I couldn't see a single thing. And I was really surprised—what could it be? But I really thought they captured some place.

Raymond Johnson: None of you knew it was Bikini [where the Bravo detonation took place]?

SR: We didn't know.

Mary Silk: The light came first? Describe the characteristics of the light.

SR: The light came first, it was like the brightness of lights. It was like the brightness of the sun before it is about to rise.

MS: What was the **color** of it?

SR: It was red.

Interview reprinted with permission.

When Samos does inject the English word "lights" into the conversation, he uses the word as a noun. He refers to "lights," as in the lights that a light bulb or electrical light fixture produces. He uses the Marshallese word for light, or brightness (*meram*) three times in his two-sentence description of the lights:

> *Meram mokta, einwot meram in **light** kane. Einwot meram in al ne etton jo rantak.*

> The light came first, it was like the brightness of lights. It was like the brightness of the sun before it is about to rise.

The speaker demonstrates a preference for the Marshallese term for light or brightness to describe what he saw. The English word for lights only comes into play when Samos needs to compare what he saw to an object (light fixtures) that outsiders brought to the Marshall Islands.

In another interview conducted, transcribed, and translated by students at the College of the Marshall Islands, Bienthy Ned and Dorothy Simeon, the students interviewed a man who is extremely comfortable with the English language. The students interviewed John Milne, the president of the Marshall Islands Radiation Victims Association (MIRVA). John describes the illnesses faced by Marshallese workers exposed to radiation, including those employed by the U.S. Department of Energy to clean up the test site areas after the testing program ended. Like many populations discussed in this book, the workers constitute another category of Marshallese citizens injured by the testing program yet out of the scope of specialized U.S. government medical care, assistance, or acknowledgment for their exposure to radiation (reprinted here with permission):

> **John Milne:** *Na ij kar bed ilo **group** ko an dri-kal ilo **nineteen seventies** ko lok nan jen ba jen **nineteen seventy** eo nan **nineteen seventy-four**. Group eo ear ton komane **resettle program** eo ilo Bikini einwot dri-kal.*

> **Bienthy Ned:** *Kio elon ke boj—ewor ke men en kwoj enjake, oktak ko, boj naninmej?*

> **JM:** *Aet . . .*

> **BN:** *Kio armij rein mottam ke, ak ewor ke boj aer naninmej in kwalok boj lale reboj naninmej ke?*

> **JM:** *Aet. **Majority** in armij rain ilo **group** kein, aolepen **group** kein rualitok kenono kaki. Rar mij lok kin **cancer**, jet kein **leukemia**, jet kein **prostate cancer** . . . im bwijin kein cancer eo me jej watoki rainin ke rej jen **radiation**. **Problem** eo in elon wot ian armej rein rej mij kinke ejjelok, jikin en me remaron rej etal im **check-up** e enbwinier im ekatak kake naninmej kan aer. Im ejjab menin wot, ak armij rein relok mij ejjab lukun alikar kinke*

*ejjelok **autopsy facility** ilo **hospital** eo ad rainin nan etale naninmej kein mae **pathologist** ro me ewor kabeel ko ibbeir nan etale naninmij kein. Im men eo ekabiromojmoj in bwe jejela ke aolepen Majol in **epaijin.** Im elaptata **group** in armij rein en ej **target** e lok er im ejjelok wewein ko im remaron in etal nan ialan jiban . . .*

BN: *Kio kajitok eo juon ikar konan ba ne dri jerbal rekein mona einwot mona ko kijed make, einwot **local food**?*

JM: *Aet. Bar juon in men. Ike jekar etal nan jokan ejjelok juon **restriction** ikijien mona ko—**restricted** jen mona kein ion im kein ien. Boj **group** eo me na ikar **represent** e. Ak me na ij **represent** e dri-kal ro. Ejjelok juon men **DOE/AEC** kar ba mokta. Im kien eo an **trust territory** ba ke emo mona kein ion im kein ien. Tokelik jej kab jela ke emo mona jet dein mona einwot boj baru, oror bob, idaak ni. Ak men ko kim kar mona bwe etto an itok **field-trip** im to an itok **supply** ko am ilo ailin en jej mona mona in ailin kein kinke ejjelok juon men jemaron mona . . . Ak dren, aiboj ko kim ar etal im idaak ke, aiboj lal, ak aiboj jiment. Aiboj jiment ko rar etoon ke men kein rar bed iumwin **test bomb** ko maantak mae ien ko kemij kojerbali . . . Einwot jelak etal, jet ke ien ailin eo ejjelok dren bwe eka wot an dret. Ne ej maat koban aiboj ko ak **water catchment** ko kubwij aiboj lal ko im idaak dren. Ejjelok ar checki ak kim ar wonmanlok wot im ejjelok juon armij ear ba bojrak.*

John Milne: Me, I was in the group of the builders in the nineteen seventies, let's say from nineteen seventy to nineteen seventy-four. The group was sent as builders for the Bikini resettlement program.

Bienthy Ned: Now are there—just are there any things you feel, anything different, have you been sick?

JM: Yes . . .

BN: Now about your friends, do some of them have illnesses that show that they are sick [from radiation]?

JM: Yes. The majority of people in this group, from each of the eight groups (of different classifications of workers) talk about this. They have died off from cancer, some kinds of leukemia, some kinds of prostate cancer . . . and many other types of cancer that appear these days are from radiation. The problem is that there are many people that die but they don't know that they had illnesses. When it gets to the time that they're weak, they die because there is nothing, nowhere, not even one place they can go to get a check-up for their bodies and to learn about their illnesses. And this isn't the only thing; when these people die it isn't clear [what the cause of death is] because there still is no autopsy facility at our hospital to study illnesses of this type that pathologists know about from studying these sicknesses. And this is really saddening because we know that all of the Marshall Islands is poisoned. And most of these groups of people were targeted but can't do anything and there are no avenues open to them for assistance. . . .

BN: Now my next question: I wanted to ask about the workers is if they ate our [Marshallese] foods, what we call local foods?

JM: Yes. That is another thing. The places where we were sent [to work] there were no restrictions about the foods—restrictions about eating this or that. That's how it was with the group I was a part of, the group that built structures. There was never a thing that DOE/AEC told us in the beginning. Yet the government during the trust territory said that it was forbidden to eat this and that kinds of food. Afterwards, we learned that it was forbidden to eat some kinds of food like [coconut] crabs, pandanus, or drinking coconuts. The things we ate from the island we had to because it would take so long for the fieldtrip ships to come and bring supplies to the islands out there and we ate the local foods because there was nothing else we could have eaten. And the water, the water we drank, well water, water stored in cement. The water from the cement was dirty because it had been there earlier below the test bombs until the time that we used it. . . . Now when we look back, sometimes there was no water on those islands because of the droughts. If there was no more water in the water catchment we dug for well water and drank that water. Nobody checked us so we continued and not one person told us to stop.

John injects many English words into his speech, and he clearly models his knowledge of the English language to the students. But, examining the English words used by Mr. Milne shows that his use of English words is more complex than mere proficiency of English and the borrowing of its words. Table 6.2 divides the English words John Milne used into different categories.

The first category of words in Table 6.2 lists the English words John used that Marshallese speakers commonly use. Marshallese words exist for the words group, but Marshallese frequently use the English alternatives. The words "hospital," "fieldtrip," and "cement" are all nouns for objects that did not exist in the Marshall Islands before outsiders came. Fieldtrip is the word for the ships that take supplies and passengers from the capital to the outer atolls and islands.

The second category of words in Table 6.2 lists the English words John used that demonstrate his competence with the English language. For words such as autopsy facility and pathologist there are no Marshallese equivalent and it makes sense that he would borrow these words. Marshallese equivalents exist for the rest of the words in this category, yet I find his use of the word "targeted" notable. John uses the word to express his belief that the U.S. government targeted the Marshallese people to receive exposure to radiation and then left them with no avenues for assistance. Although he does not come right out in his interview and say that the U.S. government purposefully exposed the Marshallese to radiation the use of the word "targeted" shows he believes the U.S. government planned to expose the Marshallese to radiation.

In the final category of words in Table 6.2, the English words John used are part of the radiation language in the Marshall Islands. As a worker exposed to radiation during the clean-up of Bikini Atoll, John is part of a group exposed to environmental sources of radiation from the weapons testing program. The illnesses that he and the other workers experienced required them to become proficient with the radiation language to convey their experiences. I included the word "restriction" in the category of the radiation language and not the list of words showing English proficiency because from time to time the AEC and DOE would place restrictions on the consumption of highly contaminated foods, such as coconut crabs. In the case of the Marshallese workers who helped the U.S. government reduce levels of contamination on the ground-zero locations, such as Bikini where John worked, the U.S. government did not restrict the workers from eating any of the local foods despite knowledge of severe contamination of the ecosystem. This is an example where one exposed population borrows a term used by other radiation populations; the Marshallese workers borrow the word "restriction" from the downwinders. John's speech shows that the creation of a Marshallese radiation language is not just an example of English invasion of the language. Instead, it is a purposeful use and modification of English terms to explain a Marshallese understanding of events related to the weapons testing program.

TABLE 6.2   ENGLISH WORDS USED BY JOHN MILNE

English words commonly used in the Marshall Islands:
group, problem, hospital, fieldtrip, cement

Borrowed English words that show English proficiency:
water catchment, majority, 1970s, autopsy facility, pathologists, supplies, targeted

Words that convey experience with radiation exposure:
cancer/prostate cancer, leukemia, resettlement program, poisoned restriction/restricted, DOE/AEC, trust territory, test bombs, check-up/checked

Songs of Resistance

The Marshallese people love to sing. Song is an integral part of all important community gatherings, such as funerals, birthday parties, visits by an *iroij*, and public ceremonies. The Marshallese language, and for that matter the history of the country from the Marshallese perspective, is predominantly oral. Historians at the Alele Museum in the Marshall Islands are in the process of recording and documenting the history of the country according to Marshallese stories (*bwebwenatos*) and chants (*roro*). The Marshallese *roro* are usually four to six lines in length, and chanted in a deep, rhythmic tone with a sharp rise in intonation at the end (Tobin 2002:8).

Songs are the modern manifestation of the old chants. Frequently, songs come from communities and are not credited to any one individual. Many of these modern community songs, like the old chants, impart the listener with information about the community. For example, two songs from the Rongelap community reflect people's experiences with radiation and directly challenge the adequacy and purpose of the U.S. government's response to the radiological problems it created for the Rongelapese.

LoRauut, no author
Collected and translated by Abacca Anjain-Maddison,
and reprinted here with permission.

Rube im kalikar ialin jen Robert non LoRauut
Bunrokean ko ion to lien wot LoMejenma
Bun-nineaan ko ion tol lanin im raan dron
Jen na ubon im ban ke kim jo ro-koean non LaUkukot
Oh LoTalim ej jutak wot
Jekdron bwe LaBija ej watch raan im bon

Mr. Urine

Show the way from [Dr.] Robert [Conard's] examination room to Mr. Urine [Collector]
Over the hill to the right is Mr. Eyes [who gets so close to the patients he can almost kiss them]
Over the hill to the left is Mr. Call Numbers and Names and Assistants (to escort patients to the examination rooms).
From the chest to the back is examined by Mr. Spin Around [patients were on rotating equipment].
Oh, Mr. Touch [and Examine Internal and External Parts] is at ease while
Mr. X-ray watches day and night.

LoRauut is uniquely Marshallese and very difficult to translate. The meaning of the lines extend beyond the literal translation of the song. I could not understand the meaning of this song by myself. The senator of Rongelap, Abacca Anjain-Maddison, with her knowledge and experience of radiation-related health matters helped me understand the intense emotions captured in the community's song. As I will discuss in the methodology chapter, the information that Senator Anjain-Maddison brought to my attention is a perfect example of why it is imperative for anthropologists to work with local research partners, and how this partnering benefits their research.

LoRauut captures the obvious humor of the Marshallese people who take an absurd situation, such as the discomfort of being shuttled from doctor to doctor without knowing what the doctors are doing, and turning this strange and difficult situation into an experience to laugh about. It is important to note, however, that the humor evident in this song in no way conveys that the people's experiences with these doctors were easy or lighthearted. Just the opposite; the Rongelapese created a humorous song as a way to release their pain, and to recognize the common experiences of people in the community. Urine collection, for instance, was difficult for the Rongelapese because customarily it is forbidden for men and women to urinate in the company of each other.[2]

LoRauut reflects the dehumanizing and culturally inappropriate handling of the Rongelapese by the U.S. government doctors. In this song, the doctors create a feeling of discomfort by getting too close to the patients, they subject the patients to procedures the people do not understand (the spinning), they examine every square inch of the patients, both inside and out, and they reduce the Rongelapese to a number. During my interviews and work with the Rongelapese, the people expressed great sensitivity about the AEC and DOE's dehumanizing of the people. After their exposure to Bravo when the U.S. government enrolled them in the medical research program, the U.S. government issued ID cards to the people and referred to them as numbers, not as people. Many people also said that the doctors examine them as if they are body parts, not human beings; to the Rongelapese, the doctors were interested in them as thyroids, or as cataracts, but not as people. Again, the Rongelapese do not find these experiences humorous, but creating a song that makes people laugh about their experiences provides a means to acknowledge publicly the abuses rendered against them by the U.S. government and to talk about highly sensitive subjects in a culturally appropriate manner.

Similarly to *LoRauut,* another song by the Rongelap community, the 177 Song,[3] provides a glimpse of the emotional burdens of the radiation survivors. As with the interviews, the song borrows English radiation words and changes the meaning of the words to reject and resist their prescribed meanings. The English words, in their modified form, convey uniquely Marshallese experiences of pain, illness, and despair as a result of the U.S. nuclear weapons testing program:

---

[2]When I asked my Marshallese mother who I lived with during Peace Corps why this is true she said it is because men and women expose their reproductive organs when they urinate and men and women must be kept separate so no inappropriate sexual contact ensues.

[3]Again, a song without an individual author, a song for and by the community.

Al in 177, no author
Provided by the women of Rongelap

I: *Naat inaaj ella lok jen entan kein ko ijaje kio*
Komaron ke juon ao ri-jinet im ao marin ko? (repeat)
Chorus: *Ne ij ped ilo ao radiation en bwe imojino kon tyroit im ao jojolair,*
Konan eo in bwe in wiwa wot ion juon ao jikin aeneman.
*Im jab na wot ak ro ilo **nomba** en **177.*** (repeat)
II: *Aolepen lomnak e ao ij liwoj rej nan kom kio*
Kon wewin ko ij lo ilo an raan jabe kein ad. (repeat)

177 Song

I: When will I be released from my sufferings that I still now do not understand?
Would you guide me and give me strength? (repeat)
Chorus: I am irradiated because I am weak from thyroid disease and despair,[4]
I only want to live in peace.
This is not only my wish but all those who belong to the number 177. (repeat)
II: All these thoughts of mine I give to you.
These are the experiences I see in these days that don't belong to us. (repeat)

It is clear from the first verse of the song that the Rongelapese still do not understand the causes of their suffering or when it will end. Frustrated, ostensibly from the U.S. government's lack of adequate answers, the Rongelapese appeal to God for assistance. The chorus shows that radiation not only causes thyroid disease as the U.S. government acknowledges, but it also causes despair. Radiation is no longer simply the poison produced by nuclear weapons, but the use of the word "radiation" signifies a loss of health and quality of life. The repeating section of the chorus makes fun of the U.S. government's categorization of radiation victims; the reference to "number 177" refers to the group of people from Bikini, Enewetak, Rongelap, and Utrik eligible to participate in a medical program extended to the Marshall Islands under Section 177 of the Compact of Free Association.[5] The song highlights the real desire of the radiation communities—to live in peace. In the final verse, the song underscores how detached the people of Rongelap feel from their lives. Radiation caused the people to relinquish control over the course of their lives. No longer can the people determine what they eat or where they will live. They will contract illnesses that will change the course of their lives.

---

[4]As an exercise with my class at the College of the Marshall Islands, I asked students to translate the Rongelap song so they could think about the difficulties involved in expressing Marshallese experiences with the problems resulting from the testing program. The students said it was hardest to translate the line: "Ne ij ped io ao radiation en bwe imojino kon tyroit im ao jojoloair." Variations of their translations to this line include: "I've been effected by radiation exposure," "When I live irradiated that I'm weak because of my thyroid and I'm lost," "When I'm in radiation, my body goes weak because of my thyroid and loneliness," "I am irradiated because I suffer from thyroid problems and I am deprived of my life," and "I'm affected by radiation that weakens my thyroid and makes me feel alone."

[5]U.S. government funding for this program ended in September, 2001.

CONCLUSION

The Marshallese learned English words about radiation from U.S. government scientists, doctors, and politicians. But, the Marshallese give different meanings to the English words, and in doing so, demonstrate their resistance to the narrow scope of damages and injury resulting from the testing program that the U.S. government maintains. The result is a unique radiation language that provides a way for the radiation survivors to communicate their experiences to each other and to reflect the history and lived experiences of the people. The next chapter continues to investigate the Marshallese radiation language by looking specifically at the language of women.

7/Uncovering Themes in Linguistic Data

Language provides rich data for anthropologists to consider what people think about human actions. In the case of the Marshall Islands, I will analyze the language used during interviews with radiation survivors to get insight into their thoughts about the testing program and its consequences. I conducted more than 200 interviews that show a consistency in terms of the medical problems afflicting communities, and people's discontentment with the level of U.S. government support and assistance for damages and injuries linked to the testing program. In this chapter, an in-depth analysis of just three of the interviews demonstrates how variables such as sex, atoll of residence, and degree of U.S. medical attention contribute to the different experiences of one subset of the radiation population, the women. Due to the intimate content of the interviews and the linguistic taboos that make it forbidden for many of these women's male relatives to read these accounts, I want to protect the identity of the women. Therefore, the names used in the interviews, including the name of one woman's husband, are pseudonyms.

The unique experiences Marshallese women face as a result of their exposure to radiation is evident in the first interview with Kita and her husband, Kino. Closely bonded, the couple sat very near to one another, finished each other's sentences, continually expressed concerns about the other's medical conditions, and even used a singular verb form to refer to the two of them as a single unit. Kita and Kino's joint construction of their experiences with radiation enhance the interview because they exchange their memories together. Kita's depiction of the birth anomalies she experienced is among the most devastating accounts I encountered during more than a decade of work in the Marshall Islands. By the same token, her language indicates that she received almost no medical care for or information about her illnesses. Because Kita's family is from Likiep Atoll, which the U.S. government defines as "unexposed" to radiation from the testing program, Kita is not eligible for any U.S. medical monitoring or care programs currently provided to the legally "exposed" population. Like many subpopulations in the Rongelap community, the Likiepese represent another undocumented radiation population.

The second interview is with a woman named Jakori who also lived on Likiep Atoll during the testing program, but currently lives in the capitol, Majuro. It is clear from the interview that Jakori has a better understanding of the medical effects of radiation. I believe Jakori's improved understanding of radiation effects results from her command of the English language and her ability to access at least limited health care services provided by the RMI government (unlike Kita, who remains on Likiep where there are no medical facilities). Although the hospital in Majuro lacks the human, financial, and technical resources to deal adequately with radiological illnesses, Jakori, unlike Kita, had access to some medical care during her acute reproductive crisis.

The third interview describes the experiences of Ertilang, a resident of Rongelap Atoll. Ertilang was on Rongelap during the Bravo test and experienced the heavy radioactive fallout and relocation to Kwajalein 54 hours after the event. Ertilang was also one of the Rongelapese enrolled in Project 4.1, the research project to study the response of human beings to radiation from nuclear weapons. Unlike Kita, Ertilang is extremely familiar with U.S. physicians and researchers because of her participation in Project 4.1. Ertilang and the Project 4.1 subjects gravely needed medical attention after their acute radiation exposure; instead, decades later, they learned that the U.S. government enrolled them without their consent in an extensive medical and environmental research program. Consequently, Ertilang's discourse is much different than that of her counterparts from Likiep Atoll who did not receive U.S. government medical care.

Linguistic data from the three interviews demonstrates that Marshallese women have numerous social realities that overlap. Language provides the vehicle for Marshallese to construct and negotiate their historical, medical, and cultural experiences with radiation. These social realities are evident in three different themes that the women touch on: blame, powerlessness, and reproductive abnormalities. Although the women express these themes differently, linguistic evidence once again demonstrates the use of a Marshallese radiation language to convey the women's experiences. The fact that the themes of the radiation language exist and remain inaccessible to all but Marshallese-speaking outsiders is critical to understanding Marshallese resistance to constructions of the effects of radiation exposure presented by the U.S. government.

ASSIGNING RESPONSIBILITY[1]

Like many island nations in the Pacific, speakers in the Marshall Islands often avoid assigning blame because interpersonal communication in the Pacific tends to be passive (Brenneis and Myers 1991:20). For example, I remember several occasions over the years when I directly asked one person what time it was. Instead of responding in the first person when they did not know the time, people often replied in the collective plural with *"jenok,"* or "we don't know," even if there was no one else around. Responding with a "we" rather than an "I" enabled the speakers to divert the directness of my question and share the burden of the response with a fictitious other

[1]Anthropologists generally use the term *agency* to describe what this section calls *blame, cause,* or *assigning responsibility.* To research agency, anthropologists look at other societies to see how people "interpret actions and assign responsibility for events . . . [or] how people think about their own and others' actions" (Ahearn 1999:13).

or me, rather than field my question alone. Eventually I learned to ask "What time do we have?"

In small Pacific communities where people must live and work together on tiny islands, preserving harmony is essential to survival. Consequently, people often conceal direct accusations and prefer to express their feelings to a third-party mediator. Use of the Marshallese language to define their experiences enables the radiation populations to ascribe blame for their problems and to vent their anger while avoiding direct confrontation with U.S. government representatives. Avoiding direct confrontation is important because it preserves the integrity of the bilateral relationship between the Marshall Islands and the United States. Despite the history of abuse and neglect during the Cold War, the Marshall Islands remain extremely loyal to the United States and views the United States as its closest friend. The anger that people feel about the weapons testing program has not led to any community or nationwide anti-Americanism, but is an individual manifestation.

As is evident from the text of the interviews, there is absolutely no question of ambiguity in the minds of the three women about who did what to whom. The radiation language enables the Marshallese to speak directly about their feelings in a culturally appropriate manner. Table 7.1 provides a partial list of the pronouns and verbs used by one interviewee, Ertilang. Ertilang speaks directly to convey her perceptions about who caused the radiation, who is affected by the radiation, who makes the decisions, and who is affected by the decisions.

There is little doubt in Ertilang's mind that the Rongelapese, "we," experience radiation exposure, illness, dislocation, and false reassurances from the U.S. government about their safety and health. According to Ertilang, the United States government, or "they," is the clear agent of the Rongelapese people's suffering. Statements such as "they said they were helping" indicate that the U.S. government representatives portray themselves as helpful to the Rongelapese. If Ertilang really believed the sincerity of U.S. government efforts to "help," she likely would say "they were helping." Also, the introduction of the word "should," in conjunction with statements about taking medication and eating or avoiding certain foods, demonstrates that Ertilang believes she was simply following orders rather than receiving care. This is substantiated in the interview by the fact that Ertilang does not completely understand what treatment she received or the reason for taking medication. If Ertilang felt like she was a participant in her medical care, she probably would use words more along the lines of "the doctor gave me medicine to help with my medical problems."

Ertilang's statements of blame reflect the history of the Rongelap people. In 1957, the U.S. government assured the Rongelapese that the main island of their home atoll was safe for reinhabitation after a three-year absence due to high and persistent radiological contamination from the Bravo test. As discussed in Chapter 5, the Rongelapese experienced death and profound illness after returning to Rongelap because of the radiation they ingested from their environment. These experiences, in all likelihood, contribute to Ertilang's skepticism and cynicism about any U.S. government pronouncements regarding radiological safety or the health status of the Rongelapese.

It is clear that the radiation populations' feelings about accountability for their sufferings, and a clear blaming of the U.S. government for injuries and damages suffered by the Marshallese people, transcends to the community at large. When I was teaching at the College of the Marshall Islands, my class put together a community

TABLE 7.1   EXPRESSIONS OF BLAME CONVEYED BY ERTILANG

we were bombed	they bombed us
we were evacuated	they examined us
we were sick	they checked us
we were resettled	they told us it was okay
we were evacuated again	they told us our illnesses are not related to radiation
we were still sick	they told us everything was okay
	they said we should take medicine
	they said they were helping
	they said we should go to the U.S.
	they said the food was okay to eat
	they said we should not eat certain food

celebration for Nuclear Victim's Remembrance Day, a national holiday observed March 1, on the anniversary of the Bravo shot. As part of the commemoration, we asked Marshallese students to write essays about youth perspectives on the testing program. While the content of the essays is interesting, they do not provide as much information about the lived experiences of the students as interviews do. Nonetheless, the essays provide powerful examples of the blame Marshallese youth ascribe to the United States government. The students who wrote these essays were not alive during the testing events. They did not witness the events, but many of them belong to communities that the testing program displaced; many of them belong to families where people are sick, or died from radiological illnesses. The clear ascription of blame and the effects of direct exposure to radioactive fallout that the students describe demonstrates that the older generation passes information, using the Marshallese radiation language, to the younger generation:

> *Ri-pella . . . relukun in kometortor. . . . Ri-pella rekanooj in bwebwe. . . . elukun lap an ri-American kakkure kij. Unin er kar kamelmel bomb nan ailon keni konke rej ba erik aelon kein ad, im ke rerik ren itok jen ailon kon aer im itok me kakkure im ko-poisen ene kein ad. Rejab etal kamelmeli bomb nan ailon kon er ak retook im kamelmeli nan koj. Raan kein elon armij in Marshall rekanooj in jorren ak tairot im cancer. Unin jorren konke armej in America rar jolok bomb nan ailon kein ad, im poisen menin mour im lojet im ebar einwot menin eddok. Rar lukun jaje manet. Ebar lon ajiri ro rejorren im elon lellop im lollap re-cancer im tairot. Ri-Marshallese relukkun jorren* (Amani 1998).

Americans . . . really harass people a lot. . . . Americans they are really crazy. . . . The Americans really did a lot of damage to us. The reason they tested their bombs on these islands of ours is because they said our islands are small and because they are small they can come from their country and come to do harm and poison these islands of ours. They don't go and test bombs on their own land but they come and explode [bombs] on us. These days many Marshallese people are really sick with thyroid and cancer. The reason they are sick is because Americans dropped bombs on our islands, and poisoned the animals in the ocean and also the plants. They really behaved badly. There are also many children who were affected and many old women and old men who have cancer and thyroid [disease]. Marshallese are really suffering (Amani 1998).

Some of the phrases in this young student's essay particularly emphasize the blame placed on the United States for the problems resulting from the testing program. The student uses expressions such as:

Marshallese:	*itok*	*me*	*kakkure*	*im*	*ko-poisen*	*ene*
	kein	*ad*				
Literal translation:	come to	do harm	and	make poison	islands	
	here	of ours				
Meaning:	come to	do harm	and poison	our islands		

or

Marshallese:	*retok*	*im*	*kamelmeli*	*nan koj*
Literal translation:	they come	and	make explosions	to us
Meaning:	they come	and	explode [bombs]	on us

The radiation populations' thoughts about illness and radiation exposure, and the blame they ascribe to the United States for their health problems, also transcends to Marshallese youth. From the lived experiences of the Marshallese, the radiation populations believe that the weapons testing severely compromised the health of their offspring. As evident in the previous essay and the following essay, students express anxiety about children who die or are affected by radiation:

> *Bomb eo ear komman bwe aolepen menin eddik ko ijo ren jorren. Kon wot paijin eo ekar elon armej rar naninmej im jet ian ajirii ro rar mej. Kon an lap paijin, etal im mej King Juda* (Lang 1998).

> The bomb made it so that all our plants would be damaged. From just the poison alone there were many people who were sick and some children who died. Because there is so much poison, King Juda died (Lang 1998).[2]

In the class I taught at the College of the Marshall Islands, Nuclear Testing in the Pacific, guest speakers often came to the class to share their experiences and thoughts with the students. One of the more provocative speakers was Rubon Juda, the son of the legendary "King Juda." Rubon talked candidly about the suffering the people of Bikini endured during their exile. Before the United States government tested weapons on Bikini, the U.S. government relocated the Bikinians to Rongerik Atoll where food and water supplies were insufficient to sustain the people. The people nearly starved to death. Eventually, the U.S. government moved the Bikinians to Kili Island, a single island rather than an atoll, an area that once again could not sustain the people from its resource base. During Rubon's presentation to the class, I recorded expressions he used to assign blame on the United States for the sufferings of the Bikinians:

[2]The Marshallese do not traditionally use the term *king*, but in this case the student borrows the term often used by the United States. The King Juda the student refers to was the leader of the Bikinians when the U.S. approached the community to request use of their islands for the tests, as discussed in Chapter 5.

Rar kalimor im ba: "Kem naaj lo kom."
The [Americans] made a promise to us and said: "We will take care of you."

Lukun kwole. Rej jab retok im lale koj. Kem kar ioon juon jorren laplap. Kemim lukun jorren.
Really hungry. They didn't look after us and care for us. We encountered extreme suffering. We really suffered.

Amedka eriab. Rej riab. Amedka ekar mone kim. Naan in riab. Rar jab mool nan kij. Jan im entan.
America lies. They lie. America tricked us. The words are lies. They weren't truthful to us. Crying and suffering.

Aolep men renana kemim kar ioone . . . im jorren kake.
Every bad thing that exists we encountered . . . and suffered from.

Reriab . . . bwe ren bok jikier en kojerbali.
They lied . . . so they could take our land and use it.

Kim mijak er. Eben ba jab.
We were afraid of them. It's hard to say no.

Kemim kar kaddok ik. Ejjelok ik kar emman. Elon rar mij jen kwole.
We got fish poisoning. None of the fish were safe. Some people died from hunger.

Many of the Bikinians share Rubon Juda's direct ascription of blame on the United States government for the sufferings of the Bikinians. The late senator from Bikini, Henchi Balos, stated on a national radio broadcast that the problems resulting from radiation are not the RMI government's fault, and, therefore, not the RMI government's responsibility to address. Senator Balos firmly and directly placed responsibility on the U.S. government with statements like: "The Government of the Marshall Islands didn't bomb Bikini," and "The Government of the Marshall Islands didn't lie to the Bikinians in 1968 [and say] that we could safely return home. It was the U.S. government." The late senator's reference to 1968 refers to the U.S. government's premature resettling of the community on their home atoll. Like the Rongelapese, the U.S. government assured the Bikinians it was safe to resettle their home atoll although the atoll remained highly contaminated. After ingesting more cesium than any known human population (Balos 1995), the Bikinians, like the Rongelapese, left their home atoll. The mistrust of U.S. government assertions about radiological safety fuels the strong sense of blame that many individuals in the radiation populations direct at the U.S. government.

POWERLESSNESS

Power and powerlessness are topics of intense scrutiny in the field of anthropology. In this section, I will show ways in which the language of the radiation populations reflects the subordination they feel from the U.S. government, and their relatively low status, vis-à-vis their asserted right to control the parameters of radiological injury and damages.

Radiation populations express deep feelings of powerlessness based on their inability to alter the circumstances resulting from their radiation exposure and exile, or to receive the type of medical care and explanations about their exposure they feel they deserve. Many people feel powerless to achieve good health now that radiation invaded their bodies, and powerless to challenge the narrowness of the U.S. government's programmatic assistance for radiation-related problems intended to address the consequences of the testing program.

The three women interviewees express frustration about their inability to understand the medical changes in their bodies. For example, Kita and Kino explain the confusion they felt when U.S. government representatives tried to explain why thyroid disease began to emerge after the weapons testing program. Kita and Kino remember that they could not understand the explanations of the U.S. government officials that visited Likiep Atoll:

> *Na ijab melele ta wawen aer kar itok im etale im buki naninmij ko ke ejjelok jabrewot men reba nan [kij].* . . .

> I don't understand why they came and took tests of different sicknesses because they didn't say a single thing to us. . . .

> . . . *rej konono tok ak komro jaje ta ko . . . rej ba.*

> . . . they spoke to us but we didn't know what . . . they said.

Kita seems reluctant to come to terms with the pervasiveness of medical problems throughout the community even though the Likiepese talk freely about illnesses in their population. Kita will not speculate beyond her family's immediate radiation exposure:

> . . . *ijela wot ke ekar wor jorren ko kar walok nan ajiri eo kab komro.* . . .

> . . . the only things I know about are those things that happened to our child and the two of us. . . .

Similarly, Ertilang acknowledges that she did not understand the medical procedures to which the U.S. government subjected her and her fellow Rongelapese. The Rongelapese view themselves as the subjects of U.S. medical practitioners rather than the patients of doctors concerned about their well-being. When I asked Ertilang what she thought about the medical care she receives from U.S. government contractors, she replied:

> *Ekwe, ijaje. Rej toktaiki kij. Jenaaj ba ta bwe ejjelok ke—jejaje waween bwe ejjelok—kij jej jaje tokta, kij jej jaje ta eo rekomani nan kij. Re lo ta? Ak kij, jenok. Boj—jej jaje tokta. Jej jaje lale anbwinin armej ejab ainwot er. Ke rej toktaiki kij, jej tokta, ak jenok. Kio emman, kio rej ba emmanlok. Ke relok toktaiki kij rej ba enanin ejjelok paijin ippad, bwe etan men ko rekonnan ba? Jej jaje bwe jelikjab jen men dein.*

> Well, I don't know. They treated us. What can we say, nothing—we don't know about anything because we can't—we don't know a thing about medical care, we don't know what kind of [medical] procedures they do to us. What do they see? But us, we don't know. It's just—we don't know about medicine. We don't know how to examine the human body the way they do. Because they treat us, we visit the doctor, but we don't know. Now it's good, now they say [we're] better. When they treat us they always say there is no radiation with us, what is it they always say? We don't know because it's hard for us to understand these things.

Ertilang recognizes that the Rongelapese needed care after the initial near-fatal exposure to radiation, and they continue to need care for long-term and latent illnesses linked to their radiation exposure. Ertilang also realizes that she is at the mercy of her doctors. The repeated use of the phrase *"jej jaje,"* or "we don't know," under-scores the extent of Ertilang's lack of understanding of the medical procedures the U.S. government performed on her. Ertilang has a scar that extends from her jawbone down to her clavicle. When I asked her about the scar, she said she did not know what procedure the U.S. doctors performed on her thyroid. It turns out that Ertilang had her entire thyroid gland removed without her knowledge or permission. Ertilang recalls the feeling of powerlessness she felt when the U.S. government doctors exam-ined her, especially during her numerous trips to the United States. Without a trans-lator or Marshallese companion during one trip, Ertilang recalls: "I was afraid . . . [but] what can we do when we have no choice?". Ertilang's statement demonstrates that the language of radiation populations in the Marshall Islands embodies the his-tory of U.S. and RMI interactions and the relative powerlessness of the Marshallese to alter the decisions and activities of the United States government.

Ertilang seems resigned to the fact that she has no means to influence even basic decisions about her own health and well-being. Ertilang is ill. She needs highly spe-cific and very expensive medical care for her radiation-related illnesses, and she depends on the U.S. government to provide all of her treatment. She has no choice; the RMI government does not possess the capability or the human and financial resources necessary to treat radiation-related illnesses, such as Ertilang's brain tumor. The RMI is no closer now than it was when the Trusteeship ended to respond-ing adequately to health care needs linked to the testing program. Once Ertilang leaves the Marshall Islands for the care that is not locally available, Ertilang enters a foreign country, with a foreign language and alien medical procedures. Ertilang describes her experiences with the U.S. government doctors and medical facilities in the United States that diagnosed and treated her brain tumors:

> *Ijab enjake ke elon tumor ippa. Ak ke rar etale io im pijaike io wot im etal. Kwo lo ke leo ekar bok eddo in AEC, [tokta Robert] Conard, ear ba nan na ewor juon men ej eddek bara. Ear lukun ba nan na. Iar etal im bar pija ilo Hawaii, im rar bar etale io inem ibar rool [nan Ebeye] bwe e ba, "Rool im ped im lok en jet iio inaaj bar kur iok. . . . Ekwe, emoj lok en ta eo juon im ruo iio ke, ekwe rekur io bwe na en tok im etal. Etal wot im kaju nan New—men, Washington [DC] . . . Boke io lok nan Washington. Im drore. Ij make wot. . . . Ekwe, ij etal im rej jerame io aolep raan. Aolep jibbon.*

> I couldn't feel my tumor. They would just come and examine me and take X-rays and go away. You know the guy who was in charge of the AEC, [Dr. Robert] Conard, he told me I had something growing in my head. He said this directly to me. I went to Hawaii for more X-rays and they also examined me. And then I returned [to Ebeye] because he said: "Return and stay, and after a few years I will call you again. . . . Well, after what, one or two years, one year, right, well they came and told me to go. I went and head straight to New—Washington [D.C.]. . . . Took me to Washington. And stay put. I was by myself. . . . I went and they gave me shock treatment everyday. Every morning.

Ertilang uses sentences such as, *"Ear lukun ba nan na"* ("He said this directly to me") to make it perfectly clear that the U.S. government doctor told her directly that she had something growing in her head. The use of the word *"lukun"* in this situa-tion provides a subtle but clear modification of the verb so that there is no doubt to the listener that Ertilang heard these words and that the doctor said them.

Ertilang was clearly frightened by her experiences in the care of U.S. doctors and researchers. Still now, she has no understanding of her medical condition and no medical file that explains her treatment either in the Marshallese or English languages. Either her medical file remains highly confidential and inaccessible, or it no longer exists. According to multiple sources in the RMI government and people I interviewed, fires destroyed all of the medical files of the acutely exposed Rongelapese and Utrikese. Three separate fires—fires in St. Louis, Majuro, and Ebeye—destroyed all the records detailing the illnesses and treatment of the patients (T. deBrum 1994). On several occasions the RMI government asked the U.S. government for an explanation. The U.S. government never investigated the fires. A Marshallese medical practitioner I interviewed (in English), Dr. Esra Riklon, described the fire that destroyed the files in Majuro (E. Riklon 1994):

> **Esra Riklon:** [t]here was a group of [American] physicians hired by our government to come and take over the hospital's management, mostly the budget. So we moved from the old hospital to the new hospital and they burned all the [medical] charts except maybe less than a few—a hundred charts let's say.

> **Holly Barker:** Purposefully?

> **ER:** Well, we asked them. You know, one of our boys who used to take care of these charts was mad. He said: "Why did you burn these charts? They are important files." And they said: "Because we are going to take on a new system of charts—filing charts." And he said: "You didn't have to burn them, all you do is change the number, or change the folder, whatever. But, you need all the information available on the chart or it's going to be handicapped every time a physician goes to take care of these people."

Use of the English language by U.S. government officials contributes to the subordination of the Marshallese. Although the Trusteeship officially ended, the systematic control of information and medical knowledge by the U.S. government enabled the U.S. government to specifically define the scope of damages and injury in the post-colony. The U.S. government, not the RMI government or the radiation populations, determined which people demonstrate illnesses related to the testing program, and which people are eligible for medical care. In addition to denying medical care to thousands of people, this control of information left patients, such as Ertilang, vulnerable to experimentation. As long as the U.S. government retains the rights to define the medical effects of radiation, it will continue to ignore medical conditions that the Marshallese people complain about, like reproductive abnormalities, and the numerous subsets of the radiation population that need medical attention.

WOMEN'S REPRODUCTIVE ILLNESSES

Without question, one of the greatest concerns of the women exposed to radiation is their reproductive health. Although it is one of their greatest concerns, it is also one that they do not feel free to discuss. Research by medical anthropologists and the medical profession demonstrates that every culture creates its own stigmatization for illnesses that are not socially acceptable. Because of stigmatization, people anticipate rejection from society even before rejection takes place. As a result, even those individuals who successfully mask their illnesses tend to internalize feelings of shame associated with their medical conditions (Kleinman 1988).

Women exposed to radiation in the Marshall Islands suffer from an array of reproductive problems. They feel a sense of shame, and stigmatization as a result of their illnesses. Ertilang, Jakori, and Kita all miscarried, and/or gave birth to grossly deformed children who lived for only a short time before dying. During their interviews, Kita and Jakori specifically discussed the humiliation women experience when they give birth to grossly deformed children. The humiliation that these women feel often means that women will quickly take these children away after they die to bury them and hide their shame from the community, and even their spouses. Jakori's description of the birth and burial process provides linguistic evidence about the speed with which these events take place. This is demonstrated by the closeness of the verbs, as seen in the sentence:

> *Im ien eo wot elotak emij rej kalibwene.*
>
> And the moment   it was born   it died   they   buried it.

Jakori also linguistically demonstrates the rapidity of events following her birth of "grapes" with the sentence:

> *Eliktata ij kolotak, rej kwalok kiraap ko, im rej jolok jikin ninnin eo ao.*
>
> Finally, I gave birth, they showed me the grapes, and they removed my reproductive system.

There is no description of activities between the birth of the grapes and the hysterectomy, but it is clear from the linguistic signals that Jakori's hysterectomy occurred very quickly after her birthing abnormality.

In addition to her own birthing experiences, Jakori describes the deformed babies she heard about but did not see. Birth is usually a very public experience for Marshallese women. Female relatives and care providers come in and out of the birthing area, and frequently the community will gather nearby to see the baby or hear news after the baby is born. The fact that Jakori did not see these deformed children with her own eyes once again shows the humiliation linked to these births and the women's efforts to cover up their experiences. In her interview, Jakori described Kita's birth:

> *Ekwe, ajiri ro ilok kar ron, rej ba ekojak baran. Im ien eo wot elotak emij rej kalibwene. Rejab kwaloke nan armej. Ne ainwot Kita eo, ij ron elotak—im bar juon kora rej ba ainwot baran tepil ajiri eo nejin. Na iar jab loi bwe rej lotak wot rej noeji im kalibwener.*
>
> Well, the children who are born, according to what I hear, their heads are funny. When one [of these deformed children] is born it dies [and] they bury it. They don't show it to people. . . . Like Kita, I heard it was born—and one other woman they say [gave birth to a baby] like a Devil, that child of hers. Me, I didn't see them because they gave birth, they hide them, and they bury them.

In a highly Christian country, there is an interesting link between the deformed child and the devil that shows an association between these births and biblical images of immorality. On a few occasions, Marshallese women told me that if a woman gives birth to a deformed child it is evidence that she is unfaithful to her husband, and therefore, subject to the retributions of her husband and the community. The wife of the health assistant on Likiep Atoll expressed these sentiments when trying to account for the deformed babies she knew about:

> I was terribly, terribly upset. I cannot explain exactly what my feelings were except remembering the horror and compassion I felt for the women. I wondered to myself if those monsters [the women] gave birth to felt any pain or had any of the human qualities

we all share. I suspected black magic and wondered what those women may have done to offend someone to such a degree that the spell cast on them was so profound and terrible (E. deBrum 1994; translated by Newton Lajuan).

Women suffering reproductive abnormalities feel stigmatized by virtually everyone around them, including (as seen from the statement above) other women in their communities. The U.S. government obviously has no interest in recognizing the sufferings of women since its purpose is to minimize the scope of its responsibilities, most notably its financial responsibilities. The Marshallese men who account for the vast majority of politically elected seats in the Marshall Islands often do not know about the degree of suffering experienced by women. The information contained in the interview above also reveals that women cannot find solace for their burdens even from one another if other women think birthing abnormalities are the result of bad behavior on the part of the birthing mothers, not radiation exposure.

The interview with Kita provides more evidence about the suffering Marshallese women endure as a result of their reproductive problems. Kita had difficulty describing and talking about her own experiences and uses repetition to convey intensity and emphasize certain points. For example, Kita highlights the fact that many women experience reproductive problems:

> *Ellon, ellon armej ar jorren, im ellon kora ar kiraap nejeer. . . .*
>
> Many, many people were injured, and many women had "grape" babies. . . .

When Kita talks about the numerous miscarriages following her exposure to radiation, she uses the phrase *"Mij wot, mij wot"* ("[they] just die, just die"). The repetition in words mirrors the repetitive miscarriages Kita sustained. The repetition occurs again when I asked Kita about the causes of her ailments: *"paijin eo, paijin eo"* ("the radiation, the radiation"). There is no doubt that Kita makes a direct link between radiation exposure and reproductive abnormalities. When Kita tries to describe the two-headed child she gave birth to, she stammers: *"Ainwot e, ainwot e . . . ,"* or "it's like, it's like . . ." and she goes on to say *"ainwot armej . . . ainwot armej,"* meaning that the child "resembled a person . . . resembled a person" but was not quite a human being in her eyes. Sensing his wife's difficulty describing the event, and clearly wanting me to witness their testimony about their experiences, Kino takes over for his wife to describe the child Kita gave birth to. Like Kita, Kino's repetition of phrases denotes his personal difficulty discussing the birth and the need to underscore important aspects of the story:

> *Ien eo ewotlok baam eo elikin enaninmej kon ajiri . . . elok tak ajiri eo, ewor ruo baran ajiri eo. . . . Ruo bar. Einwot ruo bar. Juon eped ilun kab baran. Ijo (ejibwe baran bwe en kwalok ia) e walonlok im ainwot jidik wot, ewor jidik men ijo (ejibwe baran) im bar eo eped ijo (ebar jibwe baran). . . . Ewor juon bar eo edik jen bar eo, ainwot ruo—ejab bar men eo ak ainwot baran armej. Ear jab mour ajiri eo. Lotak inem mij. . . . Emenono jidik wot ien ke ej lotak. Emaron wot—ejab awa, jet wot minute.*
>
> After the bomb testing she got pregnant with a child. . . . when the baby was born, it had two heads . . . two heads. It was like two heads. One was on top of the other. . . . Here (touches his head to show where) it was really small (touches head). . . . There was a small thing coming out of the head, like two—it wasn't a head but it was like a head that thing. That child didn't live. Born and died. . . . It breathed for a short time after it was born. Maybe only—it wasn't an hour, only a few minutes.

Women on every atoll where I conducted interviews over the years experienced extreme birth deformities—deformities and experiences that not a single one of my friends or relatives in the United States ever encountered.

In contrast to Jakori and Kita's experiences as part of the "unexposed" populations outside the parameter of the U.S. government's radiological consideration, the Rongelapese women were not surprised by the birth of deformed children nor did they feel the same type of shame as the Likiepese women. The U.S. government told the Rongelapese women to expect birth abnormalities because of their exposure to radiation (Emos 1999). The Likiepese women felt shame and hid their deformed babies because they did not know and were not told that their exposure to radiation would result in birth deformities. In the case of the Rongelap community, the U.S. government acknowledged that the community was exposed to radiation and planned its research to document the human effects of radiation exposure. The U.S. government prepared the community and told them that birthing abnormalities would occur. Consequently, the Rongelap community publicly buried and grieved the loss of the deformed children; the women did not hide them and hurry them off for secret burials the way the Likiepese women did.

During her interview, Ertilang focused on the medical problems experienced by the Rongelap community that the U.S. government does not recognize as radiation related. Ertilang is unwilling to accept the U.S. government's dismissal of medical problems that the Rongelapese connect to their radiation exposure. Ertilang questioned me, as an American, to display how she contests U.S. government pronouncements about radiation-related illnesses. On different occasions in the interview, Ertilang describes medical problems experienced by the Rongelapese that are outside the U.S. government's tight parameters of radiation injury. She follows her descriptions with curt and confrontational questions. For example, Ertilang said in a somewhat sarcastic tone: *"Ak iar bar tumor, kwo jela ke?!"* ("Well I had a [brain] tumor, did you know that?!"). Another time, Ertilang looked me directly in the face, which Marshallese usually find uncomfortable or even rude, and asked:

> *Ainwot ke jet rane ajiri ro relotak, relotak ke jet ainwot armej ak jet jej lale re kamour kiraap, ekwe ta?!*
>
> Some of the children who are born here, when they are born they resemble humans but when we look we see they give birth to "grapes," well what is that?!

Ertilang's questions were rhetorical, but the tone and content of her speech clearly demonstrated her anger and frustration. Her challenging and direct manner also signal that Ertilang was trying to gauge whether or not I believed her experiences to be valid and truthful, or whether I, as an American, would give her a reason, other than radiation, for the cause of her troubles, as she has become accustomed to from Americans. I remember asking a U.S. government doctor at the Brookhaven National Laboratory (the contractor with responsibility for monitoring the health of the Rongelapese and Utrikese) about reproductive abnormalities experienced by the women. This doctor, a woman, told me that the birthing abnormalities are probably because of incest and inbreeding, and that the populations were too small to make any statistically relevant conclusions linking radiation to birthing abnormalities. I cannot begin to imagine how Ertilang would feel if this same doctor told her that her problems—problems she never experienced before the testing program—are the result of incest and inbreeding, not radiation exposure. No wonder Ertilang feels the need to vent her feelings! I find Ertilang's bitterness appropriate given the amount of suffering she endures as a result of her brain tumors, a thyroidectomy, birth anomalies, radiation treatments in foreign hospitals where they subjected her to "shock treatments" without any explanations or the benefit of a translator.

My interview with Ertilang did not end with a sense of hostility or anger. Instead, Ertilang openly reflected on the futility and powerlessness she feels as a Marshallese woman exposed to radiation. She does not understand the physical changes to her body, or what the future holds. With sadness in her voice, Ertilang said:

> *Elukun oktak mour jen jeamaan. Aolep men ijaje kio.*
>
> Life is extremely different than the old days. I don't know anything anymore.

The high incidence of reproductive abnormalities described in the ethnographic data I collected corresponds with, and builds on the important research undertaken by medical anthropologist Glenn Alcalay. Alcalay studied the incidence of miscarriages and reproductive abnormalities in the Marshall Islands after the testing program and found a direct correlation between the frequency of birthing problems and distance in residence from the ground-zero test sites (Figure 7.1). Instead of incest and inbreeding, Alcalay's work demonstrates that the closer a community lived to Bikini and Enewetak atolls, the more radiation the population received, and the greater the incidence of birthing problems experienced by Marshallese women (Alcalay 1995).

Women throughout the Marshall Islands complain about reproductive abnormalities linked to radiation exposure. The ethnographic data I collected between 1994 and 2001 indicates that phenomena such as "jellyfish" and "grape" babies are widespread. Women in the far northwestern corner of the country—close to where the testing occurred—as well as women in locations farthest from the test sites understand what "jellyfish" and "grape" babies are and use these words to explain these reproductive phenomena. The existence of the word *kiraap* (grape) in the language indicates that the Marshallese assigned a nonhuman word to describe new phenomena in the post-testing era. If Marshallese women experienced these types of reproductive illnesses before their radiation exposure, the illnesses would have proper Marshallese names, instead of descriptive English names. For example, *jibun* and *ko* are the terms used for stillbirths by the Marshallese before the testing era and terms which they continue to use today. These birthing problems remain constant, even if women believe they are more frequent in nature because of their exposure to radiation, but the names of the condition have not changed and indicate that these are not new ailments the way "jellyfish" or "grape" babies are.

Jellyfish babies describe a phenomena that is widespread enough to warrant a name, and for women to understand what the word means throughout the country. Jellyfish babies are children that are born with no bones in their bodies. Witnesses say the skin of the babies is transparent so onlookers can see the hearts beating in the babies' chests, and the pulsing of the blood moving through the babies' brains and other organs. During an interview, a Marshallese medical practitioner described the appearance of a jellyfish baby he witnessed:

> [T]he baby was very funny looking. The legs and arms were there, but they were kind of larger than normal, and shorter than normal. You can see the body, but there was no skull . . . and there was no skull except a membrane of the brain, but you can see the brain with your own eyes. You can see the brain is moving—and the baby, the heart was beating also.

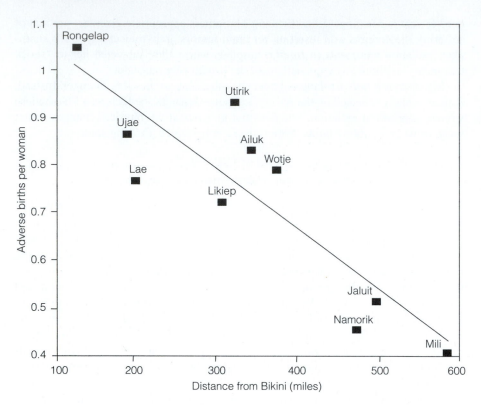

*Figure 7.1 Link between atoll of residence and reproductive abnormalities in the RMI.
Source: Alcalay (1995).*

After 24 hours the baby passed away, and the baby was quite shorter than normal. Kind of thick and big (E. Riklon 1994).

In addition to the terms "jellyfish" and "grape," Marshallese use other nonhuman words from their environment or local realm of experiences to describe the less-than-human "monsters" they give birth to, such as "turtle," "octopus," "devil," or "apple head" babies. Another interviewee on Wotje Atoll described a deformed baby as *"lejikan,"* or marlin fish. The spine of the baby, like the marlin fish, protruded out of the body in big bumps (Komram 1998). A woman from Ailuk Atoll, an atoll adjacent to Utrik yet outside the U.S. government's scope of consideration, said she gave birth to a clam-like child:

Two [of my children died]. One of them was born defective. It didn't look like a human. It looked just like the inside of a giant clam (Anonymous 1994).[3]

A woman from Likiep gave birth to a child that resembled a coconut:

I will now confess that I, too, gave birth to something less than human. What I gave birth to was normal in every aspect except that the top of the skull had not fused and remained open like the cracks of a coconut that has not completely split (Anonymous 1994).

[3]As with the testimonies of Kita, Ertilang, and Jakori, the speakers' are not identified because the reproductive information is too personal.

The U.S. government clearly did not try to describe the types of deformities the women would see because there are no English loan words and no English equivalents for the types of births these women experienced. Therefore, the Marshallese women searched for nonhuman words in their environment to describe the nonhuman children they gave birth to, such as *coconut, insides of a giant clam*, or *marlin fish*.

A UNIQUE MARSHALLESE RADIATION LANGUAGE

After the devastating consequences of radiation exposure and the resulting exile because of persistent contamination, the Marshallese needed to develop ways to communicate their experiences to each other. This need to communicate new experiences began with the populations most affected by radiation and exile, but eventually migrated into the population at large so that children and non-affected populations in the Marshall Islands could talk about the events that took place in their country.

Many Marshallese have lost faith in the U.S. government's ability to inform them about their health and safety. There is an inherent conflict of interest in having the U.S. Department of Energy (DOE), which is directly responsible for the human and environmental exposure of the Marshallese, have a say in determining who is and is not harmed by this exposure. The hierarchical nature of the Trusteeship system allowed the U.S. government to control access to information, to conduct human radiation experiments, and to serve its own security and scientific interests. For the Marshallese, this colonial domination continues to translate into physical and emotional suffering more than a decade after the Trusteeship was terminated.

Even though both the language of political and scientific domination is English, the English language cannot express the social and cultural realities of the Marshallese people and their experiences with radiation. As a result, the Marshallese borrow words from English, combine them with existing Marshallese words, and create new words to allow them to express their full range of experiences with radiation and the effects of nuclear weapons testing. These three distinct features characterize the Marshallese radiation language and are evident in the following passage spoken by an atoll senator,[4] Alvin Jacklick, during a formal *Nitijela* debate regarding the effects of radiation on the second generation. By breaking this passage into parts and considering the *literal* translation of the words, the characteristics of the radiation language become clear:

> *Kon   komelmel   an Amedka . . . enaaj lon armej   ilo Majol*
>
> Because making explosions by America . . . there will be many Marshallese people
>
> *renaaj claimi   naninmej.   Jet kein in*
>
> they will claim [for compensation to the Tribunal] illnesses. Some kinds of
>
> *naninmej re ped ippen ri-Majol   rebar ped ippen jekeke jet,*
>
> illnesses they occur with Marshallese   they also occur with some others.

---

[4]Alvin Jacklick was a senator when I recorded this debate, but he is now Minister of Health and Environment for the RMI government.

armej ro ilo Arizona im Utah, jet armej ro rar winddowner

people from Arizona and Utah, some people they were downwinders

ilo komelmel an Amedka ijen. . . .   Paijin eo rar boktok

in making explosions by America there . . . .   The poison they brought

ilo Bikini in Majol   ej ped wot nan rainin

to Bikini in the Marshall Islands it still remains until today.

In this passage all of the characteristics of the radiation language become clear. First, the language borrows from the language introduced by the U.S. government to discuss the activities and consequences of the testing program, English. The senator uses the word *claim*, for instance, to indicate that Marshallese will file claims with the Nuclear Claims Tribunal to receive compensation for their radiation-related injuries. Prior to the testing program, the Marshallese had no use for the word *claim*, as there were no situations where people received monetary payments for damages. Second, the senator alters English words to adapt them to a uniquely Marshallese language context. The senator's modification of the word *downwinder* to *winddowner* reflects the Marshallese preference for a noun followed by a descriptive term as well as a significant change in the structure of the English word. Third, the senator demonstrates the Marshallese creation of new words from Marshallese that enable speakers to express their full range of experiences with radiation and the effects of nuclear weapons testing. Prior to the testing program, the word *komelmel* did not exist in the language. *Komelmel*, which means "to make explosions," is a new Marshallese word.

As evident in linguistic data from interviews and popular songs, the Marshallese created their own radiation language to convey the havoc that entered their lives in the aftermath of the U.S. nuclear weapons testing program. In addition to communicating the social and cultural realities of the Marshallese, the radiation language is a form of resistance to the scientific-political-militaristic paradigm of the U.S. government that insists that radiation adversely affected only very few Marshallese. Through their unique radiation language and its themes of agency, powerlessness, and medical and reproductive abnormalities, the Marshallese construct the linguistic means to convey the social realities that U.S. definitions of radiation exposure deliberately ignore. For radiation populations that the U.S. government ignores because their experiences fall outside the U.S. government's constructed space and definition of radiation exposure, the major avenue available for them to convey their experiences is their language of resistance.

Marshallese constructions of their social and cultural realities do not distinguish between "exposed" and "unexposed" groups. It is obvious that Marshallese people from both of these imposed U.S. categories suffer from the same types of illnesses. The interviews with Jakori, Kita, and Ertilang demonstrate the parallels between the medical problems women in both categories experience. Although Ertilang is the only legally "exposed" woman of the three, each of the interviewees and the women in their communities experience severe reproductive abnormalities. Linguistic evidence also indicates that the women feel ashamed about their illnesses in the legally "unexposed" atolls, and, therefore, conceal the deaths of their deformed children from each other and from their communities.

Linguistic evidence indicates that the reproductive problems experienced by the Rongelapese women did not occur before the testing program and their exposure to radiation. Instead of using Marshallese words to describe the illnesses, the interviewees use nonhuman words from their local environment to describe their birth anomalies, such as "octopus," "grapes," or "hermit crab" to describe the deformed children. If these reproductive problems existed before the testing program, they would have proper Marshallese names like other illnesses experienced by the Marshallese before the testing program (Barker 1997), such as normally occurring (albeit with a smaller incidence level) *jibun,* or stillbirths.

In the case of the "grape" babies discussed by the women in the ethnographic data, the experiences of the women mirror the descriptions in the medical literature of hydatidiform molar pregnancies. During these pregnancies, cells stop dividing and swell to the size of grapes. The enlarged cells attach themselves to the uterus of the women and are often miscarried several months later, giving the impression of a birth of grapes. It is interesting to note that U.S. government scientists observed the same phenomena in plants exposed to radiation. Dr. Laurence Donaldson from the University of Washington observed the changes in plant life in 1950 and noted that: "cell division ceased and the cells enlarged and took on an abnormally mature appearance" (Donaldson 1950:9). Judging from incidence levels of reproductive problems detailed by Glenn Alcalay, the observations of U.S. government scientists, and the creation of a new word to describe a new phenomenon, there is a direct link between the "grape" births experienced by the Marshallese women and their exposure to radiation.

Despite the links between the medical problems of the three women highlighted in this chapter, the interviews underscore the disparities of medical care available to each of the women. Because Ertilang is from the "exposed" community of Rongelap, Ertilang continues to participate in U.S. funded medical programs. Questions remain in Ertilang's mind, however, about the efficacy of these U.S. programs that cause her to feel powerless and at the mercy of her medical practitioners. Jakori, on the other hand, experienced an ailment that is common enough in the Marshall Islands to warrant the creation of a name despite the relatively rare rate of occurrence in the United States. Despite the fact that Kita suffered through multiple miscarriages and the birth of a two-headed child, and that Jakori nearly died while delivering "grapes," both Jakori and Kita, as well as other women and populations outside the 226 originally "exposed" people of Rongelap and Utrik, remain ineligible for radiation-related health care. Extension of U.S. government health care remains linked to the U.S. government's narrow, legal construction of the boundaries defining which atolls comprise the "exposed" area.

The Marshallese language reflects the unique historical and social identities of the people. Because of the evolving relationship between the U.S. and the RMI governments, and the continued emergence of latent radiation-related illnesses, there is little doubt that the radiation language of the Marshallese will continue to evolve and reflect the changing social and cultural realities of the lived Marshallese experience with radiation. U.S. government responsibility for the health of the radiation survivors also needs to evolve to include the previously ignored radiation populations.

CONCLUSION

Language reflects the history and lived experiences of the Marshallese. The radiation language developed by radiation survivors provides clues about the changes to Marshallese life and culture as a result of the U.S. nuclear weapons testing program. Furthermore, language use transcends from those with experiences linked directly to the weapons testing program to the population at large, including the generation born after the testing program.

The women I interviewed did not believe they had any ability to either get access to information about their health, or to influence decisions about their own medical care. Control of information and patient treatment is one way that the U.S. government retained full authority to account for the consequences of the weapons testing program during the Trusteeship and into the post-colony. Women in the Marshall Islands experience multiple burdens as a result of their exposure to radiation; their own health is compromised, the health and well-being of their offspring is affected, and community stigmatization makes the women feel shame for their conditions. Consequently, it is often easier for women to hide their burdens than to share them. Very few women hold elected political posts in the Marshall Islands. Consequently, Marshallese women's experiences with radiation are rarely a part of bilateral discussions to address problems related to the weapons testing program by the overwhelmingly male U.S. and RMI government officials.

Linguistic evidence also demonstrates that women from all atolls outside of the U.S. government's narrow confines of radiation exposure suffered from a lack of medical care for and community understanding of their radiation-related illnesses. They had no preparation prior to their birthing problems, no doctors to care for them, and no support or understanding from the community for their experiences. Therefore, although the radiation groups all suffer from their undocumented experiences with radiation exposure, the groups with acute exposure and U.S. government attention suffered differently from the atoll populations, like Likiep, who received less initial exposure to radiation but no medical or U.S. government attention.

Linguistic data demonstrate that radiation populations use the Marshallese language, not English, to convey blame, powerlessness, and women's experiences with reproductive abnormalities. Radiation and its effects are a clear part of the consciousness and lived experiences of the Marshallese people. The exposed communities insist on discussing radiation and its effects in a Marshallese context even when they borrow words from the English language. Both the existence of the themes and the refusal to give up a Marshallese-speaking context indicate that the radiation populations created a language of resistance to thwart U.S. government attempts to impose a post-testing reality on the Marshallese people.

8/Changed Circumstances
A Petition to the U.S. Congress

During the original negotiations to terminate the Marshall Islands' trust territory relationship with the United States, the Reagan administration reached an agreement with the Republic of the Marshall Islands (RMI) on a full and final settlement of claims arising from the U.S. nuclear weapons testing program in the Pacific. The Compact of Free Association and the nuclear claims settlement (Section 177 Agreement) state that the purpose of the settlement is to "create and maintain, in perpetuity, a means to address past, present, and future consequences of the nuclear testing program."

The settlement agreement submitted to Congress by President Reagan included a "Changed Circumstances" provision authorizing the national government of the RMI to petition Congress if it believes developments since approval of the settlement render the assistance and compensation provided by the United States manifestly inadequate. In order to receive a settlement package from the U.S. government for damages and injuries from the testing program, the RMI had to terminate pending claims in U.S. and RMI courts, including a major claim for damage and loss of land by the people of Bikini Atoll. The settlement also established the Nuclear Claims Tribunal in the Marshall Islands as an alternative adjudicative forum to ensure the adequacy of remedies and finality of the settlement.

Congress approved the RMI nuclear claims settlement in 1985. The RMI made its settlement based on information provided by the U.S. government about the extent of damages and injury from the testing program. At the time, the RMI had no independent scientists or medical practitioners to provide alternative conclusions about the consequences of the testing program; the RMI government had no choice but to accept the U.S. government's findings about the extent of damage and injuries that became the basis for the Section 177 Agreement of the Compact (Chapter 3).

In the years following the termination of the trust territory relationship when the Compact of Free Association came into effect, it became clear to the citizens and government of the RMI that the assistance provided by the United States for damages and injuries from its nuclear weapons testing program is manifestly inadequate. The current agreement omits entire segments of the RMI population from receiving

assistance for their suffering, loss, and illness as a result of the nuclear weapons testing program. These segments of the population include many discussed in the previous chapters: the Marshallese workers who helped clean up and prepare highly
radioactive islands for resettlement; populations that the U.S. government prematurely resettled on highly contaminated islands; the people of Ailuk, Likiep, and
other atolls that are not as close to Bikini and Enewetak as other atolls, but are close
enough to receive substantial and dangerous levels of fallout from the weapons tests;
and the people from Rongelap used by the U.S. government for human radiation
experiments.

Some critics of this conclusion maintain that the Compact provides medical care
in the form of the 177 Health Care Program (HCP), a program available to anyone
from the four atolls affected by the testing program, and anyone to whom the Nuclear
Claims Tribunal awards a claim for a radiation-related illness. U.S. government
funding for the 177 HCP was terminated on October 31, 2001. The Tribunal provided
$2 million annually to keep the 177 HCP operating during 2002 and 2003, but this
takes money away from claimants, is not the responsibility of the Tribunal, and is not
a funding source for the future. Furthermore, because of the large number of people
from the four atolls affected by the testing program—either directly through exposure to radiation, or indirectly from their inability to access off-limits land and
resources—the 177 HCP operates on a budget of less than $12 per patient, per month.
Radiological illnesses are expensive and complicated; the 177 HCP is unable to provide adequate care for its patients. Furthermore, the 177 HCP does not provide monitoring or care for groups like the workers or the people from Ailuk and Likiep. It is
only after a person develops an acute radiation illness recognized by the Tribunal that
they become eligible for care. No preventative treatment is available. In the case of
women, the Nuclear Claims Tribunal does not recognize the vast majority of reproductive illnesses as radiation related. Therefore, women like Kita and Jakori cannot
petition the Tribunal for a claim or participate in the 177 HCP. The only other medical program provided by the 177 Agreement is the Department of Energy (DOE)
medical program that currently serves approximately 125 people exposed to radiation from the Bravo test.

When the Clinton administration began to declassify information about U.S. government activities in the Marshall Islands during the testing program, the U.S. government provided the RMI government with new information about the
consequences of the testing program. This information was not known to the RMI at
the time of the Compact negotiations. The declassification process, therefore, ful-
filled the requirements necessary for the RMI to petition the U.S. Congress for additional assistance for the damages and injury resulting from the testing program. The
changed circumstances provision of the Compact specifies that the RMI has the right
to petition the U.S. Congress for additional assistance if it can prove that it has
(1) new and additional information about the consequences of the testing program,
(2) that this information was not known during the negotiations to terminate the
trust territory status, and (3) that this information renders the $150 million one-time
settlement provided by the U.S. government manifestly inadequate.

Toward the end of the 15-year terms of the first Compact agreement, the RMI
government determined that it could easily meet the three criteria for filing a petition
for additional assistance with the U.S. Congress. The former president of the
Marshall Islands, Imata Kabua, hired a law firm in Washington, DC, to draft a peti-

tion for the RMI government. The firm wrote a draft petition, but it was not submitted to the U.S. Congress because of a change in leadership in the RMI government. When the current president of the RMI, Kessai Note, came to power, his administration called together representatives from the major groups in the RMI with an interest in the changed circumstances petition. President Note's Minister of Foreign Affairs, Gerald M. Zackios, established the Advisory Committee on Changed Circumstances to consider the submission of a petition to Congress.

ADVISORY COMMITTEE ON CHANGED CIRCUMSTANCES

Under the leadership of Ambassador Banny deBrum, the RMI embassy in Washington, DC, took the lead in bringing together members of the Advisory Committee on Changed Circumstances (ACCC). Members of the ACCC included the ministers of foreign affairs, and health and the environment; representatives from the Utrik, Bikini, Rongelap, and Enewetak local governments; a representative from Ailuk atoll to represent the interests of atolls outside the scope of U.S. government assistance; representatives from the Nuclear Claims Tribunal; and independent scientific and medical advisors hired by the RMI government.

The Note administration asked the ACCC to draft a petition for submission to the U.S. Congress. In September 2000, the RMI government formally submitted a changed circumstances petition drafted by the ACCC to the U.S. Congress, with a copy to President Clinton. After the change in U.S. administrations, the RMI government resubmitted its petition to Congress and to President Bush in November 2001.

CONTENT OF THE PETITION

The RMI's changed circumstances petition to the U.S. Congress has four sections.

1. **Legal issues.** The legal component of the petition establishes the statutory requirements for submitting a claim to the U.S. government and how the RMI meets each of these requirements. The legal brief uses independent scientific research to establish that the atolls of the RMI received far more radiation from multiple tests than was previously recognized. In addition, scientific and medical research demonstrates that much lower doses of radiation are more harmful to human beings than the levels thought to be dangerous at the time of the Compact negotiations.
2. **Personal injury awards.** The Nuclear Claims Tribunal has awarded over $72.6 million for personal injuries to more than 1,600 individuals, all of whom had medical conditions directly linked to the nuclear testing program. Because of the severity of the claims, and the sheer number of individuals harmed, the Tribunal awarded over $26.9 million more than the total available for payment during the Compact period. The Changed Circumstances Petition asks Congress to authorize and appropriate funds so that the Tribunal can make full payments to those still living and to the estates of those already deceased.
3. **Land claims.** By the time the RMI resubmitted the petition to the U.S. Congress in 2001, two communities, Enewetak and Bikini, successfully adjudicated property claims with the Tribunal. The Tribunal made awards to the communities to compensate them for damages. Like the personal injury awards,

the Tribunal is unable to disperse the awards due to a shortfall in the Nuclear Claims Trust Fund. The Changed Circumstances Petition asks Congress to authorize and appropriate funds to settle the two adjudicated claims. The Tribunal is expected to make a decision on pending land claims for the communities of Rongelap and Utrik; other communities are in the process of developing claims. If the Tribunal makes awards to these communities, the RMI government will add them to the changed circumstances.

4. **Medical care.** The Compact envisioned that the U.S. government would provide adequate health care for the impacted populations and the awardees of personal injury claims from the Tribunal. Unfortunately, the current program is manifestly inadequate. The program expected to deliver care through the RMI health infrastructure, a system not prepared or equipped to deliver the necessary level of care (Table 8.1). Also, current levels of funding are grossly inadequate to provide health care. With only $2 million appropriated annually (which equals an average per patient expenditure of $12 per month), the 177 Health Care Program for the communities of Enewetak, Utrik, Rongelap, and Bikini did not provide the services people need during the years it received funding. For comparison purposes, an average monthly expenditure for a patient health care program in the United States is $230 (Table 8.2). The petition requests that the U.S. government establish a sustainable medical care system for the country in order to provide adequate care for the people most severely affected by the U.S. nuclear weapons testing program.

Based on the information provided in the four categories listed above, the RMI government makes six specific requests to the U.S. Congress in the Changed Circumstances Petition:

1. $26.9 million to pay for personal injury awards made by the Tribunal
2. $386 million to pay for the property damage award made by the Tribunal to the people of Enewetak. The compensation included awards for loss of use of their land, for restoration (nuclear clean-up, soil rehabilitation, and revegetation), and for hardship (for suffering the Enewetak people endured while being exiled to Ujelang Atoll for a 33-year period). Subtracting compensation provided to the people of Enewetak in the past, the Tribunal determined that the net amount of $386 million is required to provide the Enewetak people with just compensation.
3. $278 million to pay for the property damage awards made by the Tribunal to the people of Bikini ($563 before subtracting compensation previously received by the community). The Tribunal made its award for the loss of use of property; costs to restore the land; and consequential damages for hardship suffered by the Bikinians resulting from their removal.
4. $50 million to cover the initial capital costs to build and supply a medical infrastructure that could provide adequate primary and secondary care to the affected populations.
5. $45 million annually for the next 50 years to provide a health care program for the affected communities and awardees of personal injury claims.
6. Extension of the U.S. Department of Energy medical monitoring program for exposed populations to any groups that can demonstrate high levels of radiation exposure.

TABLE 8.1   COMPARATIVE HOSPITAL EXPENDITURES

	Number of Acute Care Beds	Population Served	Annual Operations Budget	Cost per Bed per Day
USAKA* Hospital	13	2,500	$5,300,000	$1,117
Ebeye Hospital (old)	25	15,000	$280,000	$31
Ebeye Hospital (new)	35	15,000	$280,000	$22
Majuro Hospital	103	40,000	$2,700,000	$72

Source: Palafox 2002a

*U.S. Army Hospital on Kwajalein

TABLE 8.2   COMPARATIVE MEDICAL COSTS

1997 Per Capita Annual Health Expenditure Data

Republic of Palau	$320
Commonwealth of the Northern Marianas	$614
Guam	$510
American Samoa	$369
177 Health Care Program (RMI)	$163
National health care system, RMI	$128

Source: Institute of Medicine in Palafox 2002a

The total amount the RMI government requests in its Changed Circumstances Petition is $2,990,900,000, or roughly $3 billion. While this figure may seem staggering and unrealistic, this is the equivalent of two years' funding by the U.S. Congress for the clean-up of the Hanford plutonium manufacturing facility in Washington State, despite the fact that the DOE has not contained the radiological contamination problem at Hanford (Chapter 9). Yes, damages and injuries resulting from nuclear weapons testing are expensive, but do the people of the Marshall Islands deserve anything less than the people adjacent to Hanford, or any other U.S. citizens?

REVIEW OF THE PETITION

Although the Compact requires that the RMI government submit the petition to Congress, Congress looked to the administration for input. In a letter from former Chairman of the Senate Energy Committee, Frank Murkowski, to the White House, the U.S. Congress directed the Bush administration to review the petition and report to Congress about whether the U.S. government has further obligations to the RMI under the nuclear claims settlement. Representatives from several U.S. government agencies, including the departments of Energy, State, Interior, Justice, and Health and Human Services began a review of the RMI's Changed Circumstances Petition. The administration anticipated that it would complete its review of the petition by October 2002, but the U.S. embassy in Majuro recently informed the RMI government that it will delay its response for at least a year.

Recently, the RMI government decided to hire an independent contractor to review the Nuclear Claims Tribunal's process for awarding claims for personal injury and property damage. The RMI government contracted a prominent Republican attorney, one with credibility and respect in the Bush administration, former governor and attorney general Richard "Dick" Thornburgh. Thornburgh finished his review in January 2003 and determined that the Tribunal followed procedures similar to those of a legal institution in the United States and that its awards are credible. Thornburgh also noted that U.S. government funding for the Tribunal is manifestly inadequate.

CONCLUSION

From recently declassified information and independent scientific and medical research, the RMI government knows that radiation from the U.S. government's weapons tests caused substantially greater injury to people and to land than was previously known or made public. The Nuclear Claims Tribunal, created by Congress to settle claims as an alternative to judicial means, does not have adequate funding to make the awards it is supposed to. Additionally, the health care system envisioned as part of the compensation for the affected communities is inadequate to handle the growing health care needs of the communities impacted by the nuclear testing program.

It is clear that neither Congress nor the administration is prepared to deal with the RMI's Changed Circumstances Petition in a timely manner, but the petition and the needs of the RMI will not go away. People in the RMI continue to die without receiving compensation for their radiation-related illnesses. Some families cannot afford to pay for the funeral services of the claimants who died without funding. Entire communities remain in exile where their hardships continue because no funding is available to clean up and restore their home islands.

The RMI requires a response and fair consideration of the issues outlined in the petition. Even if the U.S. government believes that it has no continuing obligation to the RMI, it still must explain its reasoning to the RMI and to the public. The large fiscal request of the petition is not a reason for the U.S. government to ignore or dismiss the RMI's requests, despite economic downturns in the United States—the U.S. government already agreed to take responsibility for the consequences of its testing program and needs to meet that obligation.

The RMI still considers itself a close friend of the United States and is a nation that sacrificed its land and its people for U.S. defense interests. The U.S. government owes it to the Marshallese people to help those who were injured in the process. The U.S. government must assess its obligations to the Marshallese people fairly, equitably, and in a timely manner. As of July 2003, the U.S. government has yet to respond to the petition first submitted by the RMI almost 3 years ago.

9/Other Case Studies

Sadly, the Marshallese story is certainly not the only tale of acute radiation exposure, exploitation, exile, and cover up. For comparison purposes, this chapter provides brief descriptions of international and domestic crises involving radiation, including Hiroshima/Nagasaki, French Polynesia, Chernobyl, Nevada, Hanford, and U.S. government-sponsored human radiation experiments. In all of these cases, radiation exposure dramatically altered the lives of the affected populations—populations that had no ability to protect themselves from exposure.

HIROSHIMA/NAGASAKI

After Japan attacked Pearl Harbor on December 7, 1941, President Roosevelt accelerated efforts to create the world's first atomic bomb. The Manhattan Project was the name given to the highly secret scientific effort to build the atomic bomb, headquartered in the middle of the desert in Los Alamos, New Mexico. On July 16, 1945, the United States conducted the world's first nuclear weapons test, the Trinity test. Just nine days later, the U.S. government issued an order to drop an atomic bomb on Japan. On August 6, 1945, the United States obliterated the city of Hiroshima with an atomic bomb (Figure 9.1). A second atomic bomb destroyed Nagasaki three days later.

Japanese survivors, known locally as *hibakusha,* which literally means "explosion-affected people" in Japanese, report that target areas erupted in huge fires and explosions. The force of the explosions hurled thousands of people through the air—their clothes burned off and their skin peeled away. Black rain full of radioactive soot and dust fell to the ground and contaminated large areas around the cities. People who did not die immediately from the blast suffered from extreme burns, broken bones and lacerations from the blast, and damage to skin and internal organs caused by radiation exposure. In addition to the immediate and acute effects of the blasts, radiation exposure caused a wide array of problems for the exposed population, including leukemia, cancer, reproductive problems, blood and digestive tract disorders, and genetic effects. There are no conclusive statistics for the numbers of lives lost, but estimates generally conclude that 140,000 people died in Hiroshima during

Figure 9.1 Hiroshima's devastation

the first year, and 200,000 died by the end of five years. Estimates for Nagasaki are similar, but slightly lower.

Initially, the U.S. government did nothing to help the Japanese survivors of the atomic weapons. Similarly, Japan prevented any public discourse about the bombs and their effects. The Japanese government did not establish medical or other programs until 1952. The U.S. government waged a large-scale campaign to justify the bombing, a debate that continues to this day as many historians believe the bombing was unnecessary because an invasion of Japan as well as a Japanese surrender from the war were imminent at the time.

To collect data about the effects of radiation on the Japanese population, the U.S. government sponsored the Atomic Bomb Casualty Commission (ABCC). The ABCC was under the auspices of the National Academy of Sciences, and funded by the AEC. In later years, the Japanese National Institute of Health became affiliated with the ABCC, but this did not diminish the impression that the organization was for American research interests (Lifton 1991:345). Like the early years of the DOE medical program in the Marshall Islands, the ABCC's primary purpose was to conduct research, although the organization presented itself as a medical care facility for the *hibakusha.*

In 1995, I traveled to Hiroshima as part of a class sponsored by the Nuclear Studies Institute at American University. A Hiroshima *hibakusha,* Akihiro Takahashi, shared his experiences with our class:

On August 6, 1945, I was a second-year middle school student of 14 years old. I was one of some 150 students who were exposed to the atomic explosion in the schoolyard, 1.4 kilometers from the hypocenter. The entire place around me turned pitch dark with a tremendous roar. After a while smoke vanished and the schoolyard lightened up. I was blown about 10 meters toward the back from the impact; all of my classmates were also blown away and lay scattered all around. The school buildings were leveled to the ground. Not only neighboring houses but also distant buildings disappeared, leaving only very few buildings standing. A thought instantly ran through my mind; "Hiroshima has gone!"

Recovering myself, I looked at my body. My uniform was all burned and tattered. The back of my head, my back, arms, and legs were badly burned. Especially the skin covering the back of my hands was hanging loose like rags and the flesh was exposed to the air. Several parts of my body were pierced with glass fragments. I was seized with indescribable terror. I hurried my way to the street in the direction of the river. After a while I heard a voice calling my name from behind. Turning around, I saw a classmate, Tatsuya Yamamoto, who lived in my hometown and usually went to school with me. Tatsuya was crying for help. He kept crying; "Mother! Mother! Help! Help me!" I said to him, "Stop crying! Crying won't help you a bit. Let's get out of here as soon as possible." While we made our way to the river, I scolded or encouraged Tatsuya to cheer him up.

I saw A-bomb sufferers dizzily dragging their legs and walking in line. Arms were dangling forward, and clothes frayed. Some were virtually naked. They did not look human; the procession was ghostly. In line was a man who was covered with pieces of glass from the waist up. The skin of another man's upper body had peeled off and red flesh under it was exposed. With an eyeball dangling out of its socket, a woman was covered with blood. Beside a mother whose own skin was completely gone, a similarly peeled baby was crying loudly. A number of corpses were also lying on the ground. There was a dead woman whose innards had burst out to the ground. It was horrifying; it was hell on earth. We ran as hard as we could to the river.

Yet we could not get there easily with all streets and paths to the river bank blocked by debris of collapsed houses blown up by the blast. We desperately crawled over the debris and finally managed to get to the riverbank. We saw there a small wooden bridge that mysteriously survived the blast. We tried to cross the bridge but a fire broke out from collapsed houses. The fire quickly turned the scene into a sea of fire. Long flames shot up into the air making thunderous noises, just like erupting volcanoes. We were fortunate to be out of the fire. But then I had lost sight of my friend, Tatsuya Yamamoto.

Getting to the other side and being relieved, however, I felt my whole body burning hot. I still remember dipping myself in the river several times to ease the heat. The cool river water felt like treasure on my hot body. "That was close!" I said to myself. It was not until then that I broke into tears and just couldn't stop crying. After coming out of the river, I went to a temporary rescue center built in a bamboo forest on the hill. I received emergency aid and rested for a while. Then rain started falling. It was "black rain;" something I had never seen in my whole life. I watched the black rainfall wondering whether such a thing as black rain existed in this world. I set for home after waiting for the rain to let up.

As I was picking my way, I heard my name called again. It was a classmate, Tokujiro Hatta, who also lived in my hometown and went to school with me everyday. He was crouching and groaning for help; "Help me! Help me! Please take me home with you!" Somehow the skin of Tokujiro's soles had been so burned away that the flesh was exposed. There was no way he could walk with the burns. Although I myself was seriously burned,

I couldn't leave him there and go home alone. I was determined to take him home by all means. "How can I possibly take Tokujiro home who cannot walk?" I considered the possibilities for a while. Fortunately the burns and wounds of his body except of his soles were not so serious, so I had him crawl on his hands and knees for some time, and then I helped him walk on his heels, supporting him. In this way we began our trek home.

We sat and rested by the road when we were too tired to go any farther. When I happened to look back, I saw my great uncle and great aunt walking toward us. I called out to them as loudly as I could. It was only coincidence that we met; they were on their way home from a Buddhist service in the countryside; they rescued us and took us to our respective homes.

After my return, I fell unconscious and remained so for three weeks. Later, I was able to receive treatment for my burns twice a day in the morning and the evening by an ear and nose specialist who visited my home. Ordinarily this type of specialist would not treat burns, but in the state of virtually complete lack of physicians and nurses in the city, I believe I was fortunate to be treated by someone who was a medical practitioner. Wandering between life and death during the period of treatment, I was bedridden for a year and a half but narrowly escaped death after all. I later found out that Tatsuya Yamamoto died a month and a half after reaching home and Tokujiro Hatta a week after the fatal day. They both succumbed to acute radiation sickness.

I have survived to this day. Still, my right elbow and four fingers except my thumb stay bent, and I have keloid burns on my arms, legs, and back. My ears were deformed because cartilages in them festered with bleeding and pus. A black nail continues to grow on my right index finger. . . . I was also afflicted with chronic hepatitis, believed to be an aftereffect of atomic radiation, and have been hospitalized 10 times since 1971 when I was certified as an A-bomb victim. Recently my hepatitis has worsened and I get an IV every day. I suffer from many ailments other than hepatitis and feel apprehensive about my life every day. At times my frail health has almost made me lose all hope. I often asked myself, "Why should I keep on living with all these sufferings?" However, I have lived to this very day thinking positively that as I was allowed to survive the disaster, I must live as long as I can.

Of about [more than] 60 classmates of mine, about 50 were ruthlessly killed. To date I have confirmed 13 including myself alive. I'm one of the very few students who survived the bombing. We should never let our friends' deaths be wasted. It is our mission and responsibility as survivors to hand down to future generations the voiceless voices of the victimized. I have lived imprinting this conviction in my heart and encouraging myself to comply. My friends were killed by the atomic bomb in extreme pain before their adulthood. They were too young to die and their life was too short to be terminated (Takahashi 1995).

As with the Marshallese, Japanese *hibakusha* face a lifetime of ill health and social stigmatization as a result of their exposure to radiation. In many cases they feel uncertain about marriage because they do not want to risk giving birth to children with major health problems or deformities. For the severely burned *hibakusha,* their scars often elicit unwanted stares and nervous behavior from the public (Lifton 1991).

FRENCH POLYNESIA

There are many similarities between the nuclear testing conducted by the United States government in the Marshall Islands and the tests conducted by the French government in its Pacific territory, French Polynesia. Similarly to the Marshall Islands, the people of French Polynesia were powerless to stop the military activities of the colonizing nation. (See Figure 9.2.)

The French government turned to French Polynesia for its nuclear weapons testing in the 1960s after France's former colony and nuclear weapons testing location, Algeria, gained its independence. Between 1966 and 1995, France conducted 44 atmospheric tests and more than 140 underground tests on Moruruoa and Fangataufa atolls.

Immediately after France decided to use French Polynesia for its nuclear weapons testing, France infused its small territory with money as a means to "encourage local acquiescence" (Henningham 1992:127). In the 1960s, military spending accounted for 32 percent of the gross domestic product of French Polynesia, and 28 percent of the GDP in the 1970s. The money that France poured into the area abruptly shifted the entire economy from one based on agriculture and traditional living practices to a wage economy.

The Maohi people (the indigenous population that accounts for roughly 82 percent of the nation's 200,000 people) vehemently protested France's use of their nation for nuclear weapons testing. The international environmental organization, Greenpeace, assisted the Maohi people with their protest. Greenpeace sent its flagship, the *Rainbow Warrior*, to French Polynesia in 1985 just after relocating the people of Rongelap in the Marshall Islands from their contaminated home islands. French secret service agents bombed and sank the *Rainbow Warrior*, killing one crew member, when the ship arrived in French Polynesia to protest a nuclear weapons test by France. During rioting in 1995 at the airport in Faa'a, Tahiti, protestors set the main building of the airport on fire and clashed violently with police forces. The international community also protested France's decision to test nuclear weapons in the 1990s. The French government arrested a U.S. Congressman, Eni Faleomavaega, the representative from American Samoa, on board the *Rainbow Warrior II*.

International scientists, including French marine biologist Jacques Cousteau, expressed concern about the effects of the underground tests on the fragile, coral ecosystem in French Polynesia. Moruroa, the site of 130 of the 140 underground tests is often said to resemble Swiss cheese because it is full of holes and in danger of disintegrating. Scientists remain concerned about the leaking of radioactive materials from the testing holes in the porous coral to the surrounding waters and affecting marine life. Moruroa is reportedly sinking at an artificially fast level because of the military activities. Like the Marshall Islands, local people complain about a high incidence of ciguatera, or fish poisoning, in the areas exposed to radiation from nuclear weapons tests.

Dr. Andy Biedermann, a Swiss doctor working for Greenpeace, conducted interviews in 1987 with former test-site workers and inhabitants of nearby islands. The interviews describe the effects of the tests on their lives and their environment. Many of the people interviewed believe that the tests seriously affected the health of themselves, their children, and their friends. Like the Marshallese, the Maohi people talk about mysterious illnesses, unexplained deaths, stillbirths, and a large increase in the number of disabled children born after the tests began. One of Dr. Biedermann's interviews was with Ruta, a Maohi man who worked on Moruroa Atoll for more than 12 years:

> My first job was waste management. After each explosion . . . we had to go around the
> atoll and clean the dead fish and other rubbish off the beaches. It was usually two to three

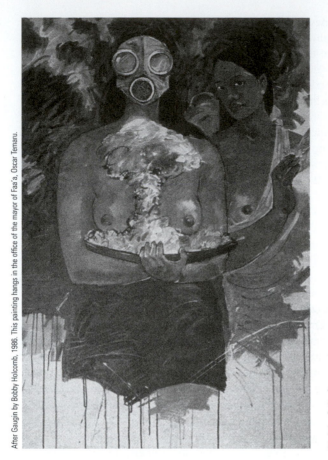

After Gaugin by Bobby Holcomb, 1986. This painting hangs in the office of the mayor of Faa'a, Oscar Temaru.

Figure 9.2 Painting on the cover of a book called Testimonies: Witnesses of French Nuclear Testing in the South Pacific

days after the explosion. Depending on which way the wind was blowing, the fish would be swept ashore in different places—several tons of dead fish at a time. Once, not very long after a test, three dead whales were swept ashore, on the ocean side.

[One time r]adioactive material [was] . . . spread over the atoll by a cyclone. There was a general alarm to let everyone know that a cyclone was coming and to warn us to stay inside. People came out of their houses when it was over and we saw that boats had been lifted on to the rocks and that all sorts of barrels were floating around. The waves had washed them out of the repository where they had been buried. It was hard work to retrieve them and store them away again, this time in the blockhouse. We were not told that they contained radioactive materials.

It's still forbidden to fish at Moruroa, but you can't stop Polynesians from eating fish. Of course, we all knew that it was dangerous to eat fish but the food we got from the military was bad. The fish was old and we always got potatoes. So most of us ate local fish when we were on Moruroa and Fangataufa. And most of us got sick. I remember a group of 10 people on Fangataufa who ate fish. They all got seriously ill and had to be evacuated to Tahiti for treatment.

People died from eating contaminated fish. One of my friends ate a crab and became ill. His skin started to itch and he scratched himself so much that he started to bleed but he couldn't stop scratching. Then he got problems with his eyesight and soon afterwards he died.

I know of four people who have died from eating poisoned fish, and many others who have had symptoms of fish poisoning. When people die on Moruroa they are put in metal coffins and the seams are welded so that nobody can open them any more.

I've had five children. The youngest was born with a kidney missing and no anus. He had to have an artificial intestinal opening made in the wall of his stomach. Hopefully, in a few months time, this artificial opening can be closed and a normal one reconstructed.

I know, of course, that there are a lot of bad things happening on Moruroa but I need the money. There is a lot of unemployment in Tahiti and I have a large family to look after. Before each test everybody was warned not to tell our friends and family about it. If the French find out that I've been talking, I'll be dismissed. But I don't care. I think it is important to tell people what is happening (Greenpeace 1990:13–18).

CHERNOBYL

In the same year that the U.S. government relinquished its administration of the Marshall Islands, 1986, a terrible accident took place in Chernobyl. On April 26, 1986, technicians at the Chernobyl nuclear power station in the Ukraine deactivated several major safety systems during a controlled test of the fourth reactor. The routine test triggered a massive explosion that blew the top off the reactor. Unfortunately, the deactivated systems could provide no protection and a fire in the core burned for several days, destroying the reactor core and blowing clouds of radioactivity into the surrounding area.

The Chernobyl accident killed more than 30 people immediately and approximately 2,500 people eventually died from radiation exposure. Once the reactor's core began to burn, it emitted high levels of radiation into a 20-mile surrounding area. The radioactive cloud covered an area the size of Italy. Government response to the incident, which was under the operation of the central Soviet Union at the time, was to keep the accident quiet and not tell the public or the international community for several days. As a result, the people in the highly contaminated areas went about their normal activities and did not take protective measures to reduce their exposure to radiation. Local residents were not aware of a problem until Soviet tanks arrived and ordered immediate evacuation of the area. People had only a few moments to put together one bag of possessions to take with them. The Soviets padlocked their houses, and their villages and cities became part of an official exclusion zone. The Soviet government evacuated approximately 135,000 people to makeshift tent cities and continued to resettle approximately 200,000 people in the years after the accident. Still today, thousands of people cannot return to their homes.

To date, the Chernobyl incident is the world's largest nuclear accident. Seventy percent of the radiation blew to the north over 30 percent of Belarus, an area inhabited by more than 2 million people. In the post-Soviet Union era, the nations of the Ukraine and Belarus lack the financial, scientific, and other resources to clean up areas that will remain contaminated for several generations to come, and to provide adequate medical care to the exposed populations.

As a result of the lingering radiation in the environment, people still drink and wash in contaminated water. When the Soviet Union ceased to exist, controls on the distribution of foods disintegrated. People who live in areas not affected by the Chernobyl accident have no assurance that they are not eating contaminated foods shipped into local markets.

The population in the contaminated area reports a high incidence of radiation-related illnesses, particularly in children, such as leukemia and cancer of the thyroid. Researchers also note a decrease in the IQ of exposed children. Other conditions include thyroid disorders, brain tumors, and malignant tumors of the mammary glands, lungs, bladder, and kidneys. People also report the birth of many babies with substantial deformities, and a general decline in the birth rate throughout the contaminated area. Studies are underway to determine the scope of genetic damage to both human and animal populations.

Hundreds of thousands of workers came to Chernobyl from all over the Soviet Union to assist with decontamination efforts. These workers scrubbed the areas around the reactors and helped build a protective casing for the burned reactor. The Soviet Union launched a massive effort to wash contaminated houses, remove topsoil, and to hose down pavement, roads, and railway lines in the city of Kiev and outlying areas. These clean-up efforts were not adequate, however, since radiation falls to the ground randomly and creates unpredictable hot spots that clean-up teams could not locate.

Like the Marshall Islands and other areas exposed to radiation, the accounts of the survivors help us understand the consequences of the disaster for the people it affects. Here is a story by Emma:

> It's not so easy for a mother and granny to share sad experiences, especially if they concern children. The emotional damage to our people is a terrible thing.
>
> Two weeks after the accident I was returning home by train from visiting my son in Moscow, who was serving time in the army. There were four of us in the compartment. I have very vague memories of two men who were in the same compartment with me, but the face of the third stands out quite vividly in my memory. He was a soldier, a boy of 19. He was overwhelmed with sorrow; there was no joy in his eyes. He couldn't forget the last couple of days of his life. He was one of those participating in burying the perished from Chernobyl. Here is his story:
>
> Five dead firemen were brought to the cemetery in Moscow. There were five groups of soldiers, so-called teams, who were to perform the funerals of the dead. . . . All of us had to wear special suits and masks for the burials. The worst part was telling the relatives of the perished that they could not come close to the bodies of their dead. Mothers were crying because they were forbidden to hug their precious sons and husbands and to say the last "good-bye." The bodies and the coffins were highly radioactive and dangerous.
>
> As soon as one of the victims had been buried in a locked and covered coffin into an unusually deep pit, the first group of young soldiers, including me, was made to rush into a special bus that took us to some kind of a sauna where we quickly took off the suits and had a shower. Our reward is ten days' leave home, but I don't feel any joy about it any more.
>
> Three years ago I had to spend a lot of time in the hospital myself with cancer and saw with my own eyes and lived through the sufferings of some of them. I knew a girl, Lida by name, 14 years old, who suffered so much because she had to wear a kerchief all the time, even when the weather was hot. She lived in Chernobyl itself and became completely bald. It is a new disease from Chernobyl and they say it has no cure. She didn't want to see her classmates; she refused to see even neighbors. She felt ashamed, but why should she? There were many very small children in Borovlyany hospital at that time from the contaminated zone. The majority of them had physical defects; they couldn't walk,

radiation affected their bones. Their poor Mummies had to carry them in their hands, even to the building where patients got radiation treatment.

When a patient gets this treatment, he or she has to lie motionless. Can a little child of three or four or five do that for four minutes? No, of course not. And because of this every day the poor little children were made to sleep with drugs. I can't imagine how their mothers' hearts could bear that. When you are waiting for your turn, you can watch those who are getting the radiation treatment on a television screen. Even men couldn't stand that; their eyes were full of tears.

Another thing that struck me there was the children's indifference to everything and everybody. When they were given toys or sweets, they wouldn't even look at them, wouldn't turn their heads. Some remained indifferent in their beds even if their mothers tried to entertain them by telling funny stories. They would lie staring into the ceiling or window. It was hard to say whether they were alive or not. Our hearts were bleeding. I can tell you frankly that we women cursed Chernobyl and those who were guilty for the lack of medicine. I'm sure that many of those little ones who died would have survived if they had been given the actual treatment they needed.

I feel full responsibility for what I say. Once, two years ago, I was in Druzhny with a group of foreigners as a translator. Druzhny is a settlement that was erected for the evacuated families. Living conditions there were extremely bad. We visited a family of nine who lived in a flatlet of 24-square meters in total. Moreover, a girl of eleven months had cancer, her granny was in bed with cancer, and her father was very ill. Our doctors couldn't cure the child, but one of the Canadians who had a daughter at home of the same age took the girl to Canada and she was cured!

When the bus with the group of foreigners was ready to leave, many Belarussian mothers surrounded it. All of them had their sick babies in their hands. Crying, they addressed the Canadian, pleading: "Take mine, please take mine. Cure mine. My baby is dying. Let me even not see him ever again, but let him be healthy and live in another country . . ." Can you imagine? Mothers so desperate to save their children that they would give them away to a stranger! It is terrible (Roche 1996. Reprinted by permission of Chernobyl Children's Projects.).

In addition to the majority populations affected by the Chernobyl accident, anthropologist Sharon Stephens illuminated the social and economic consequences of the event for the Sami reindeer herders in Sweden (Stephens 1992). The Sami people depend on plant, animal, and water resources from their environment for survival, and particularly reindeer. The reindeer that are a staple of the Sami diet feed on the grasses contaminated by radiation from the Chernobyl accident. Stephens noted the conflict that occurs between the women who are afraid to consume the reindeer meat and the advice of outsiders, such as international scientists who claim that the meat is safe to eat. Because of the way labor is divided among the Sami, women have an increased risk of radiological contamination from the environment. As in the Marshall Islands, scientific explanations about radiation exposure produced by outsiders confuse local communities who prefer to express their experiences with radiation in terms or visible changes in their daily lives. Radiological contamination of the environment affects subsistence communities in unique and different ways from the public at large because they depend on contaminated food sources from their local environments for survival and for their livelihood.

NEVADA

For 12 years, beginning on January 27, 1951, the U.S. government conducted 126 atmospheric atomic weapons tests at the 1,350 square-mile Nevada Test Site. Radiation from these tests contaminated all of the continental United States and reached into Canada and Mexico. Each of the 126 tests contained radiation levels equivalent to those released by the Chernobyl explosion in 1986 (Gallagher 1993).

The Atomic Energy Commission chose the Nevada Test Site for the same reason it tested nuclear weapons in the Marshall Islands; the AEC operated under the assumption that it could conduct secret tests and reduce threats to the American public by testing weapons in what the AEC perceived as a remote, harsh, uninhabited landscape. Like the Marshall Islands, the weapons testing sites exposed people downwind from the testing area, people who subsisted from the local resources for generations to high levels of radiation. In the case of the Nevada Test Site, the tests exposed Native Americans, cattle ranchers and farmers, test site workers (often migrant laborers who could not find employment in other states), and U.S. servicemen (those from the ranks, not the elite, often straight out of high school) to radiation. Like the Marshallese, the AEC considered all of the above mentioned populations expendable; any injuries sustained by these people was of less importance than the military and strategic values of the tests.

Immediately following many of the detonations, the AEC would march U.S. servicemen into the testing area to simulate battle scenarios and to assess the men's ability to cope with the physical and psychological effects of the tests. The servicemen who survived their radiation exposure refer to themselves as the Atomic Veterans. At the age of 17, the AEC marched Robert Carter and his company into the test site of the biggest atmospheric test conducted in Nevada on July 5, 1957:

> I remember the ground was so hot that I couldn't stand on it, and I was just burning alive. I felt like I was being cooked.
>
> I had a huge sunburn, and I remember being in a lot of pain going back to the base on the bus. The doctor told me that he thought I had radiation illness because I was nauseated, dizzy, disoriented. They don't do anything for radiation illness, they just watch you die. (Carter in Gallagher 1993: 57–58).

After the weapons testing began, downwinders in Nevada, Utah, and Arizona complained about cancer and other illnesses affecting people and animals. The AEC and the U.S. government dismissed concerns and any link to the nuclear weapons testing. Women who complained about radiation burns and the loss of hair were told they suffered from neurosis (Gallagher 1993). Sheep farmers who reported high incidences of death, stillbirths, and miscarriages among their flocks, as well as the birth of some animals with their hearts outside their chests or other bizarre conditions never witnessed by the local population, were told that the problems were due to "mismanagement, malnutrition, and perhaps poisonous plants on the range" (AEC in Gallagher 1993:xxiv-xxv). The U.S. government consistently told the downwinders, as it did the Marshallese people, that radiation presented no danger to them, as discussed by Delayne Evans, a sheep herder:

> Have you ever seen a five-legged lamb? I did. Have you ever seen a one-eyed lamb? I did.

We would have a prevailing wind from the southwest all the time, and it brought it right over where we run our sheep, just over the fence from the atomic range. The Atomic Energy Commission drove up in a station wagon and said, "You better get the hell out of here, it's hotter than a firecracker out there," then drove off. They wouldn't stay there five minutes. I said, "Where the hell am I going to move 2,000 head of sheep?" They'll only go two miles an hour, that's as fast as a sheep will walk, and where could you go? The thing of it was, they stayed there for another 30 days and ate the shrubbery with all that stuff on it. That's how the ewes got it in their thyroids and that's what killed the lambs. Those sheep of mine had scabs from it on their ears and noses and their feet. They were burnt, and every spot on those sheep that didn't have wool over it had radiation burns on them.

I bet there wasn't one sheep that was out there in '53 that didn't die within two years because I was buying sheep all the time to replace them. I had to mortgage my home to buy more sheep to start out again.

Have you ever seen a young animal that was born completely rotten? I did. They'd be bare. I had little lambs born that absolutely didn't have one speck of wool on their bodies. They were transparent and you could see their little hearts a-beatin' until they died. I never seen anything like that in my whole life until then and I've been in the sheep business from the time I was a little boy on the farm. . . .

They [the AEC] thought we were a bunch of old stupid sheep herders but there's nothing stupid about us. . . . Then they tried to tell us that our sheep were dying from malnutrition! Hell almighty, we were feeding them every day, hauling water to them to keep them in good shape, and they were fat! . . . (Evans in Gallagher 1993:247–249)

It is interesting to note that Delayne Evans' account of the sheep born without wool, and with transparent skin mirrors the description of the "jellyfish" babies born in the Marshall Islands.

It was not only the downwinders and the Atomic Veterans injured by the release of radiation from the Nevada Test Site. In 1962, the U.S. government dumped 15,000 pounds of radioactive soil from the Nevada Test Site near Point Hope, Alaska, without the legally required containers. As they did in the Marshall Islands, U.S. government officials dumped radioactive soil near the community to study the movement of radionuclides through the ecological and human food chains.

In the 1980s, the Nevada Test Site became a manufacturing location for nuclear weapons. The radioactive waste from the weapons production created additional environmental problems for the area. Although many nations in the world continue to create radioactive waste from military and commercial enterprises, there still is no safe and long-term solution for the storage of this waste. Nuclear waste is the product left over after nuclear fuel is spent. In the United States, nuclear waste comes primarily from nuclear power plants and from military facilities used to create the radioactive materials used in nuclear weapons. Both power plants and the production of radioactive materials for weapons produce radioactive waste. The U.S. government estimates that 85,000 tons of nuclear waste will exist in this country alone by the end of 2030. The U.S. government is currently looking for a permanent repository site to store the waste. Yucca Mountain in Nevada is the only site currently under consideration.

The U.S. government has begun to dig out a large area of Yucca Mountain in Nevada and plans to begin filling it with nuclear waste as early as 2010. Yucca

Mountain is on federally owned land—land that the Shoshone tribe also claims—on the northwestern edge of the Nevada Test Site. It is located in an area at risk for an earthquake, and near a major water source for the Las Vegas area. The storage of nuclear waste at Yucca Mountain creates risk to the entire nation, not just the people who live closest to the area. Any radioactive waste buried at Yucca Mountain must travel to the site by public roadways, railways, or airways.

Again, as with the Marshall Islands, the U.S. government views the area designated for radiological contamination as a useless, uninhabited landscape fit for the military and economic objectives of the country. To the Marshallese, and to the tribes around Yucca Mountain, such as the Shoshone and the Paiute, these areas are bountiful providers of the plants, animals, and cultural traditions.

HANFORD

As part of the Manhattan Project, the U.S. government designated specific areas throughout the country for the manufacturing of the radioactive materials needed for its nuclear weapons. To produce weapons-grade materials, the U.S. government needed enormous amounts of cold water to run and cool the reactors needed for plutonium processing. It turned to the nation's largest cold water river, the Columbia River. The U.S. government established Hanford, a 560-square mile plutonium processing facility in eastern Washington State, 51 miles of which run alongside the Columbia River. From 1944 through the late 1980s, Hanford produced plutonium for the U.S. government's nuclear arsenal, including plutonium for Fat Boy, the atomic bomb dropped on Nagasaki, Japan, and the world's first atomic weapons test, Trinity, in New Mexico.

Through the bombardment of uranium fuel with neutrons, and the separation of plutonium from irradiated uranium, Hanford produced massive amounts of bomb-grade plutonium, as well as radioactive by-products. U.S. government researchers released some of these by-products into the environment through Hanford's smoke stacks.

The making of plutonium at Hanford was a messy operation. Plant managers pumped water from the Columbia River into Hanford's reactors. After cooling the reactors, Hanford operators pumped the contaminated water back into the river making the Columbia River perhaps the most radioactive river on earth at the time. Hanford researchers monitored the high levels of radiation in the fish and ducks downstream from the facility but failed to notify the public or to restrict fishing and subsistence activities along the river. Many Native Americans in the area received high levels of radiation exposure from the fish they consumed as fish from the Columbia River was a staple in their diet. Hanford operators dissolved spent fuel rods from the reactors in nitric acid to separate out the plutonium. Plant operators dumped contaminated liquids on the porous and sandy soil adjacent to the facility where it seeped into and contaminated the groundwater below Hanford.

Hanford is now home to approximately two-thirds of the nation's high-level radioactive waste, including cancer causing by-products, such as cesium and strontium, substances dumped into 177 underground tanks. About 54 million gallons of high-level radioactive and chemical waste remains in the tanks, approximately 12 miles from the Columbia River. As many as 70 of the 177 tanks have leaked over the years, spilling a million gallons of waste into the soil. Some of the leaking waste reached the groundwater, which eventually flows into the Columbia River. Researchers estimate that the waste could reach the Columbia River within seven years time. Contamination of the river will affect the health, environment, and economy of the entire region yet the U.S. Department of Energy has no immediate plan to intercept the waste before it reaches the river.

In addition to the 177 underground tanks, Hanford also contains two indoor pools holding 2,300 tons of corroded, highly radioactive spent nuclear fuel under water, called K Basins. K Basins store 2,300 tons of spent nuclear fuel rods—80 percent of DOE's national inventory of spent fuel rods—just 400 yards from the Columbia River (Yarrow 2002). Like the underground tanks, the K Basins have leaked millions of gallons of radioactive water into the groundwater that flows into the Columbia River (*ibid*). An earthquake the size of the one experienced by nearby Seattle in 2001 could crack the pools open and spill the radioactive water into the river. The type of fuel in these pools will burn if exposed to the air and would quickly create a radioactive cloud. The potential dangers of the K Basins make them one of Hanford's most pressing environmental problems. Although the 177 underground tanks and the K Basins are two of the largest waste sites of concern at Hanford, there may be as many as 1,400 to 1,700 total waste sites at the facility (*ibid*).

Beyond the high-level radioactive waste produced and stored at Hanford, the Atomic Energy Commission and the contractors who operated the Hanford facility also released radiation from its smoke stacks into the atmosphere. Airborne radiation traveled across Washington State, moved into northern Oregon, crossed Idaho, and entered Montana and parts of Canada. Some of these emissions were accidental. The AEC planned other emissions to study the pathway of radiation to the environment, to the grass that the nearby dairy cows fed on, into the milk consumed by downwind communities. The Green Run in 1949, was an intentional release of radioactive iodine. Trisha Pritikin's story gives us a glimpse of what many Hanford downwinder families and individuals contend with as a result of the Green Run experiment and their exposure to radiation:

> I was born in Richland, Washington, on the Columbia River, in late 1950. I spent a very happy childhood playing in the cold waters and on the islands in the river, being an average kid in Richland's newly planted parks, and attending Sacajawea Elementary School, right across from my "F" house on Stevens Drive.
>
> Richland is the community immediately adjacent to the Hanford nuclear weapons facility, in the desert of eastern Washington State. Beginning in the mid-1940s, Hanford produced the plutonium that was used as the trigger for the Trinity nuclear test in 1945, and for the atomic bomb detonated over Nagasaki later in the same year. Production of plutonium generated massive amounts of radioactive iodine and a range of other potentially harmful radioactive substances, secretly released, often at night, onto the surrounding communities. Some of the radioactive substances, particularly radioactive iodine, traveled across Washington State, into parts of Oregon, Idaho, and Montana, and into Canada. Over 950,000 curies of radioiodine was released from Hanford.
>
> Richland, the community closest to Hanford, is located near two accompanying small towns, Kennewick and Pasco. Together, these three towns were called the "Tri-Cities." Hanford, part of the Manhattan Project, and the Tri-Cities, were isolated in the vast expanse of the eastern Washington desert. As revealed by documents declassified in later years, this isolation was intentional on the part of Manhattan Project planners in order to limit the area which would be contaminated should a nuclear "event" occur at

Hanford. Death and sickness which might result from radioactive contamination, should such a disaster occur, would thus be limited to those of us within the three communities. I grew up in a nuclear sacrifice zone, blanketed by radioactivity, drinking milk infused with radioactive iodine cows had taken up in their pasture grass, enjoying a worry-free childhood.

All the houses in Richland looked alike. We lived in a "F" house, which was essentially a small, two story "box." Floor plans of the government homes in this Atomic Energy Commission town read like the alphabet: A, B, C, D, and F. I think that was the choice. My friends lived in Bs and As. Richland, along with Kennewick and Pasco, developed into what seemed on the surface to be an idyllic three-town community. We had a newly established symphony and theater, several schools, restaurants, and other amenities for Hanford nuclear engineers, chemists, and other workers and their families. Businesses were established, called the Atomic Laundry, Atomic Bowling, and Atomic Foods.

My family spent most summer weekends on the Columbia River. I loved to swim in the areas of the river where the water always seemed to be warmer than the rest of the river. From what we've learned in later years, it appears that the warmer parts of the river were where the warmer effluent, or liquid waste products, from the nine reactors that were operating at Hanford, went into the river. So I was probably swimming in the effluent. Not a choice my parents or I would have made had we been given the choice.

We often traveled in our family boat to the beach and the islands in the middle of the Columbia where I would play like any little kid would, in the fine sands. I made mud pies and all of the things that little kids like to do, like eating some of the mud pie I had made, enjoying the texture. It was beautiful out there with the wind and the birds. Much to my dismay, I have since learned that the islands were covered with Cobalt-60 from Hanford wastes entering the river upstream. One of the target areas of Cobalt-60 in the body is the intestinal tract. It's really hard to so often discover something new about my childhood exposures and wonder how many cancers I am at risk for now.

I was exposed as well to a range of radioactive substances my parents unknowingly tracked home from work. They would come home from work with stuff on their clothes, stuff you couldn't see. Stuff on their lunch boxes, stuff on the tires of their car. There were hundreds of radionuclides released from Hanford. Who knows which of those were stuck to my parents' clothing, as particles, which got tracked home to the rug of my F house. They tracked the contaminants home and I crawled through this stuff when I was a baby. Babies do that sort of thing. Crawl, put my hand on the rug, put my hand in my mouth. Heaven only knows how much stuff I got that way. This is just horrible when you think about the fact that little innocent babies were put in harm's way.

Not even the huge tumbleweeds crashing through town, or the gritty sand of desert windstorms dampened my enjoyment of a happy childhood in what had all the appearances of a normal American town. I felt safe and protected. Had my parents known of the silent clouds of radiation blanketing the community during my infancy and childhood, the most vulnerable time of life, they would have moved our family immediately.

But they didn't know. Only those at the top of the Hanford management chain and at high government levels knew. They knew of the health hazards of the radioactive substances they were releasing. They told the families of management to give their families, and particularly their children, iodized salt to prevent the uptake of radioiodine by their developing thyroids. Radioiodine was known at the time to cause thyroid cancer and other debilitating thyroid diseases. They didn't tell people like my Dad, a new, entry level engineer, about these protective measures. My thyroid took up so much radioiodine that it no longer works at all, and I am dependent upon daily synthetic thyroid medication the rest of my life. Without thyroid replacement, I would pass into a life threatening hypothyroid coma.

Hanford's offsite release of radioactive substances was not made public by the Department of Energy until the late 1980s. When my family finally learned, in 1988, from an article by Karen Dorn Steele, in the *Spokesman Review* in Spokane, Washington, that radioactive iodine had been released, over and over, into our community during the years we lived in Richland, my father and mother were in disbelief. And, with that knowledge, as I began my almost 15 years of work to make the government and Hanford's contractors do the right thing for all of us harmed, my mother and father were not supportive of my work. For, if Hanford had indeed harmed us and so many like us, this meant that my father's livelihood, his professional life, had harmed his own family. He was a Navy man, a patriot, who had taken great pride in his efforts at Hanford. And now, he had to come to grips with the news that his government had lied to him, and these lies may have caused harm to his family.

My own thyroid disease was just the start. My father developed hypothyroidism and a nodule on his thyroid. My mother developed hypothyroidism and hyperparathyroidism, a disease of the parathyroid glands, which surround the thyroid. Both glands are very sensitive to radioiodine.

This was unheard of in my extended family, where there was no history of thyroid disease, anywhere. No thyroid disease and no parathyroid disease except in those of us who lived in Richland, in the Hanford downwind sacrifice zone.

My joy is gone. My gentle father died, suddenly and cruelly, far before his time. The nodule on his thyroid suddenly raged malignant, generating tumors throughout his throat, lungs, and brain. To save his life, a tracheotomy was performed in the emergency room of a local hospital when his throat and esophagus quickly closed as tumors blocked the passageways. "I want to live," he scrawled in a message to me on his engineer's pad, his ability to speak ended by the tracheotomy. He subjected himself to chemotherapy, he was irradiated over and over in an attempt to stop the tumors in his brain. As he died, his spirit died too. The day after his death, a letter arrived for him from the Department of Energy. Upon opening it, I learned that he had written to the DOE to ask whether he had been the subject of human radiation experiments. The Department of Energy told him about the Green Run, an intentional massive release of radioactive iodine in 1949. That plus all of his work exposures, all of his offsite exposures.

My mother suffered massively as my father died in pain. He had always taken care of her. Now it was up to me, as she began to suffer seizures and shortness of breath. She was hospitalized over and over. Her mild visual problems suddenly worsened into legal blindness. As my father died, my mother suffered.

My father died February 4, 1996, just months after diagnosis with aggressive, metastatic thyroid cancer. The tracheotomy tube was never removed. My mother never regained her sight. She spent the next three years in darkness, not even able to see the photo of my father that she kept by her bedside. And then, just as suddenly as my father fell ill, my mother, on a Saturday evening, developed stomach pains and by the following Monday, was diagnosed with massive tumor invasion of the liver, resultant from malignant melanoma. She died weeks later. As I tried to tell her I didn't want her to leave me, her breathing stopped and she was gone.

My brother had died shortly after birth, part of a peak of neonatal deaths which occurred within the Hanford downwind area during years of offsite radiation release.

I wish all of this was a dream. I consider myself a very rational person, trapped within life facts which read like science fiction. Logically and reasonably, our government should have apologized to families like mine, and should have helped those of us who suffer so with health care for the diseases and death which are "more likely than not" caused by our exposures. That would at least be a start.

Instead, no apology has been forthcoming. No apology, no help. Nuclear workers, or their survivors, can now file claims under a federal workers compensation program, if they can show that their exposures more likely than not caused their disease. These are challenging hurdles to overcome. My mother, also a worker at Hanford, was not monitored for her exposure. So, it would be impossible to show her exposure caused her disease. And, those of us exposed during our most vulnerable time of life, infancy and childhood (and in utero as well for some of us), have been ignored, left to cope with all of this on our own, invisible and forgotten.

I was brought up by my patriotic parents to believe we live in one of the best societies on earth. I was taught to think logically, and that truth would prevail. My family and families like mine have given their health and their lives in the downwind regions of Hanford, in the service of this country. We are in need of help and it is now our government's turn to take appropriate steps to help us, to show us that we are not forgotten, that our sacrifices are not ignored and disrespected. And, to apologize for blanketing us with radiation, while lying to our parents, who were patriotic Americans who trusted the government's reassurances of safety as they dedicated their lives in the service of this country (Pritikin 2002. Reprinted with permission.).

As with the other areas discussed in this chapter, downwind families, in this case primarily farming families and individuals exposed to radiation when they were children, suffer from illnesses in other areas exposed to high levels of radiation, including intentional radiation exposures for experimental purposes. Many of those exposed live outside the immediate Hanford region as radiation from the facility exposed a vast area. Hanford's downwinders suffer from a variety of illnesses, like those seen in other areas exposed to radiation, including cancers, thyroid disease, stillbirths, and birth defects. If radioactive waste continues to contaminate the Columbia River, health risks in the area will certainly magnify.

Now that the reactors at Hanford are no longer operational, a window of opportunity exists to clean up the area and prevent a colossal contamination of the river that could irreparably harm a watershed of pivotal importance to a large portion of the Pacific Northwest. Hanford is owned by the federal government and managed by DOE. DOE employs 14,000 workers and spends $1.5 billion a year for clean-up. To date, the U.S. government has spent more than $9 billion, although there is almost no evidence of progress toward clean-up. Total cost estimated for clean-up of this site is $230 billion over 75 years.

SUBJECTS OF HUMAN RADIATION EXPERIMENTATION

Although nuclear weapons testing, the production of weapons-grade materials, and accidents from nuclear power plants are the most common scenarios for human radiation exposure throughout the world, these are not the only means. At the height of the Cold War, and into the 1980s, the U.S. government financed and authorized human radiation experiments with American citizens, including citizens of the Trust Territory of the Pacific Islands.

After the U.S. government dropped atomic weapons on Hiroshima and Nagasaki and Japan surrendered in World War II, the American public was elated. This euphoria was only temporary, however, as Americans quickly realized they could not defend themselves from an attack. The need to reassure the people and psyche of the United States ultimately led to additional nuclear weapons tests to understand more about the capabilities of the weapons. Fear and the need to protect the nation became the ideology that shaped four decades of U.S. Cold War history. The role of the Atomic Energy Commission during the Cold War was to assist with the nation's preparedness for a nuclear war by sanctioning research to understand how radiation affects the human body. Universities, hospitals, military facilities, and doctors across the United States willingly conducted experiments that could help the United States prevail in a nuclear war.

The Office of Biology and Medicine of the Atomic Energy Commission conducted much of the research, categorized as "top secret." Overwhelmingly, the subjects of the experiments were the most powerless and vulnerable populations at the time: children, prisoners, African Americans, institutionalized mental patients, pregnant women, the impoverished, and critically ill patients. In most cases, researchers did not ask for consent from the participants. Even if the patients had known about the research, the marginality of some of the populations made it difficult for them to say no to government-supported doctors. In cases where researchers asked for consent, participants were not told about any risks associated with the experiments. In all likelihood, researchers knew the general public would find their experiments unacceptable and assumed it would be easier to target disenfranchised populations for their work.

Examples of the more than 20,000 government-sponsored human radiation experiments include the following: purposefully exposing the armed forces, uranium miners, and Marshallese citizens; injecting newborns with radioactive iodine to determine if the rate of uptake is the same in infants as it is in adults; having pregnant women drink radioactive iron to see if gestation affects absorption; irradiating the the testicules of Washington State prison inmates; giving radioactive milk to employees at General Electric in Hanford, Washington; and tainting children's oatmeal with radioactive iron in the Fernald School outside of Boston, a dumping ground for orphaned, mentally ill, and troubled children. Many of the participants in these experiments were sick and seeking medical care in hopes of recovery. They thought the doctors were treating their illnesses, but in fact, they received doses of radiation that often killed them or made them severely sick. Helen Hutchison, for example, thought she was receiving medication for severe nausea experienced during her pregnancy when her doctor handed her a mixture to drink in 1946:

> "What is it?" she asked.
>
> "It's a little cocktail. It'll make you feel better," she recalled the doctor saying.
>
> "Well, I don't know if I ought to be drinking a cocktail," she responded. . . .
>
> "Drink it all," he told her. "Drink it on down." The concoction was fizzy and sweet, like a cherry Coke. It wasn't bad tasting.
>
> Three months later Helen was rolled into the delivery room. . . . The bizarre health problems that were to plague mother and daughter began several months later. Helen's face swelled up and water blisters appeared on her right side. . . . Then her hair fell out and she began to tire easily . . . [Her daughter] Barbara also felt exhausted through most of her

childhood and now suffers from an immune system disorder and skin cancer . . . (Welsome 1999:220).

There were 828 women, in addition to Helen, who received radioactive cocktails they assumed were nutritious drinks offered to them at a prenatal clinic. What doctors gave them, however, was a mixture containing radioactive iron that immediately crossed the placenta and circulated through the blood of their developing babies (Welsome 1999:221).

The irradiation cases of patients at the M. D. Anderson Cancer Center at the University of Texas, Baylor University, and the University of Cincinnati epitomizes the view that doctors had toward their research subjects. In these cases, Dr. Eugene Saenger irradiated accident victims from the "slums" of Cincinnati. According to Dr. Clarence Lushbaugh, who assisted Dr. Saenger:

> In such typical slums, these persons don't have any money and they're black and they're poorly washed. These persons were available in the University of Cincinnati Center to Dr. Saenger as persons who needed to be total body irradiated, and they were given total body irradiation by Dr. Saenger. I was on his committee, by the way, and I did review what he was doing, and I thought it was well done (Lushbaugh in Welsome 1999:358).

The uncovering of information about these human radiation experiments enraged and concerned the public, and pressure was put on the White House to respond. In January 1993, President Clinton established a White House Advisory Committee on Human Radiation Experiments to investigate the extent of the experimentation and to make recommendations to ensure these abuses would never take place again. The 14-member Advisory Committee issued its final report in October 1995. Although the final report grossly downplays the intentions and consequences of the research, it did provide a broader context for understanding the relation of particular experiments to the government ideology during the time period.

CONCLUSION

Radiation has destroyed the lives and environments of millions of people on this planet, and disproportionately affects the most marginal and vulnerable populations. America's pursuit for strategic power or cheaper forms of energy often outweighs considerations for the vulnerable populations most likely to suffer the burdens.

Anthropology plays, and could play, an even stronger role in analyzing situations of human and environmental degradation. Our tools for analysis do not only apply to the case studies dealing with radiation exposure in this book but extend to a wide array of circumstances. For anthropologists, the approach for considering the consequences of the Exxon Valdez oil spill in Alaska, or the industrial chemical accident in Bhopal, India, are the same as the radiation-related examples in this book.

As anthropologists, we can go to crisis areas and research the consequences for local populations. Anthropology plays a critical role in witnessing and documenting human environmental rights abuses. We can also work with these populations to help them seek the remedies they desire. In addition to studying the relatively powerless populations in these circumstances, as most anthropologists do, anthropology is also useful for understanding the power structures and decision makers of the elite (Gusterson 1993).

Whether researching language, culture, or human environmental interactions, anthropologists identify the issues and problems we care about most deeply as individuals and think about ways we can help. There is an endless supply of human dilemmas with which anthropologists can become involved, and communities can benefit from our time, our research, and our assistance.

10/Methodology and Community Empowerment

What is applied anthropology, and why is it of value to the Marshall Islands? If you boil down the essence of what applied anthropology is, practitioners describe it as research that helps people by helping them solve their own problems. More specifically, applied anthropologists work with communities to better understand problems they face, and to help community leaders take the steps necessary to address problems in culturally and locally appropriate ways. The fundamental concept underlying applied anthropology is *praxis*, or an activity based on anthropological theory conducted with certain moral and ethical standards (Warry 1992). Applied anthropologists work with communities to help them: define their problems, consider alternatives, plan and implement interventions, assess the outcomes of their actions (Wulff and Fiske 1987), and employ ethical standards to ensure that our activities do not create more problems for communities where we work.

In this section I will discuss the research methods I employ as an applied anthropologist working in the Marshall Islands. This is not an accounting of all research tools available to applied anthropologists, but a list of the methods that work best for me in a particular setting.

DEVELOPING BONDS OF TRUST

My first introduction to the Marshall Islands was as a Peace Corps volunteer. By living and working with the Marshallese, and more importantly, becoming an adopted member of a Marshallese family (with all its inherent responsibilities to care for one another), I learned the language, culture, and what the lived experience entails for Marshallese on remote outer islands. Consequently, Marshallese often introduce me to others by my association with my Peace Corps family on Mili Atoll. The fact that I am part of a Marshallese family signals to people that I have commitments to the Marshall Islands. These introductions tell people that I care about the Marshallese people, and that they can trust I will use information acquired to serve their best interests. My Peace Corps experience started my personal relationships with people and paved the way for me to do future fieldwork. Having a strong "bond of trust" (Parker and King 1987:172) is an important component of getting people to trust you with information about their lives, particularly sensitive information such as the medical problems resulting from radiation exposure.

LEARNING THE LANGUAGE

Learning the local language is essential to fieldwork. Working through translators changes the tenor of dialogues. The researcher could miss clues that a translator does not think to point out. My Marshallese language certainly is not perfect, but I function well. Continued learning of the language is an important ongoing research goal (Basso 1995) for me.

ARCHIVAL RESEARCH

Before going into the field, it is important to review existing data and government records about a research topic (Trager 1995). As discussed earlier, I reviewed thousands of recently declassified documents about the consequences of the testing program before going into the field. Understanding more about U.S. government activities in the islands during the testing program provided me with clues about topics to investigate during interviews. For example, some of the declassified documents describe how medical researchers pulled both healthy and decayed teeth from Marshallese citizens to investigate the degree of radiation concentration in their bone/teeth. This was new information to me and an issue no one discussed with me in the Marshall Islands. After reading this information, I talked to several informants. I learned that researchers from Brookhaven National Laboratory made it appear to people that they were fortunate to receive dental exams. After the exams, people complained to each other that the researchers pulled healthy teeth from their mouths. It was only because I read this information in the archival records that I knew to explore the topic with the interviewees.

ACCESS TO INFORMATION

Before communities can address their problems, they need to understand as much as they can about them. This means that they need access to information.

To make the information in the declassified documents available to people in the Marshall Islands, I wrote a grant to DOE to create a database for the documents and to copy the materials to a digital form for easy transportation to the Marshall Islands. The embassy also urged DOE to establish a Website (*tis.eh.doe.gov/health/marshall/marshall.htm*) containing all of the DOE documents so researchers and interested Marshallese citizens could gain access to the information.

BUILDING ON THE WORK OF OTHERS

In addition to archival records, it is important to familiarize yourself with related research. Reviewing the work of anthropologists Jack Tobin, Leonard Mason, Robert Kiste and Glenn Alcalay as well as linguist Byron Bender gave me a foundation for beginning my work. Tobin, Mason, and Kiste provided me with important information about the multiple and far-reaching problems that occur when you take people away from areas where they have land rights. The entire social structure in the

Marshall Islands is based on land rights; when you take people off of their land and put them on someone else's land the community loses its social structure (Johnson and Barker 1999, Johnson and Barker 2001). Alcalay provided me with the most relevant research about the effects of the testing program by examining a portion of the population I am particularly interested in, the women. Alcalay's work inspired me and helped me understand the utility of anthropology. Finally, Bender's cataloging of Marshallese place names and their meanings, as well as the Marshallese dictionary that he and several Marshallese colleagues wrote, helped me take a deeper look at the meaning of the Marshallese words used to describe people's experiences with radiation.

LIFE STORY AND ORAL HISTORY COLLECTION

From my research experience in 1994, I came to understand the value and the breadth of information a researcher can acquire from open interviews. I conducted both life story interviews and oral histories with as many people as possible. "Oral histories" (or "life histories") are verbal accounts or reflections of a person's life. "Life stories" represent the shorter experiences within the life of a person. Because of my particular interest in linguistics, interviews also capture moments of language use, and preserve these tape-recorded moments as text and linguistic data to consider in conjunction with the Marshallese lived experience.

I conducted all of the interviews at the site of linguistic construction as a means to "investigate speech behavior in [its] natural settin[g]" (Winford 1994:52). This relaxed approach makes the interviews similar to managed conversations (Hart 1996). Whenever possible, it is important to use the language of the respondents to conduct interviews (Bernard 1995) so interview subjects will feel comfortable and so they have the capacity to express themselves as fully as possible. With the exception of two interviews, I conducted all of the oral histories and life stories in Marshallese. A Marshallese research partner accompanied me for the vast majority of the interviews. In order to create an atmosphere conducive to a free exchange of information, it helps to use open-ended, informal questions, and to allow the informants to guide the discussion in a relaxed and flexible manner (Beebe 1995, Bernard 1995, Netting et al. 1995, Portelli 1997). Whenever possible, I conducted interviews in the homes of the people to create the most culturally appropriate and natural means of exchanging information. By being in the homes of the informants, I also picked up important clues about the lives of the people that helped me interpret the texts of the interviews. Researchers need to understand what happens outside of the texts if they want to fully understand what takes place in the texts (Basso 1995). I placed emphasis on developing a bond of trust and a rapport with each of the informants.

When conducting interviews, ethnographers must consider how the narrator and the audience co-construct the texts of the interviews (Basso 1995). This notion of co-construction acknowledges that many factors, most notably the physical, biological, cultural, linguistic, and political traits of the ethnographer, shape the texts in a variety of ways. For example, my presence as an American affected the content of the interviews since people sometimes speak to outsiders differently than they do to members of their own community. Because the informants spoke to me, knowing I am a citizen of the country responsible for the nuclear testing, the interviewees sometimes saw me as a conduit to transmit their information and feelings to the U.S. public and policy makers in Washington, DC, where I lived and worked at the time. I think the respondents partially shaped their messages to reflect what they wanted policy makers to know about their experiences.

I was also aware of how my sex and the sex of the interviewees affected the texts of the interviews. On a few occasions, my Marshallese male counterparts had to leave the interview area so I could discuss medical and reproductive illnesses alone with the informants. In these cases, my sex positively influenced the interviews. In other cases the failure of male relatives of the subject to remove themselves from the interview areas meant that I could not explore reproductive matters with their female relatives because of customary taboos restricting these discussions in front of certain relatives. Without knowing the family history of everyone present during an interview—and I should point out here that conducting an interview in private is difficult; usually several people wandered in and out of the interview area or sat to listen to the stories—I avoided any discussion about reproductive issues unless I was alone with the women or I received a cue from the speakers.

LOCAL COUNTERPARTS AND KEY INFORMANTS

Whenever I conduct interviews in the Marshall Islands I always work with at least one Marshallese colleague. Local counterparts can serve as key informants (people who are particularly knowledgeable about the experiences of their communities) to help get access to people and information. Equally as important, working with local colleagues demonstrates to the informants that the information gathered during interviews is not for the researcher to take away and analyze, but for the researcher and the community to analyze together. In every situation where I gathered data, my colleagues and I both benefited from discussing information obtained during the interviews and from a partner approach to research.

PUBLIC EDUCATION AND TRAINING OF STUDENTS

Since I had an abundance of linguistic and ethnographic data from my fieldwork in 1994, I decided to focus my 1997–1998 research on gathering data from interviews conducted by Marshallese. I find these interviews important from a linguistic perspective because they produced texts in which both the interviewer and the informants are native Marshallese speakers. Comparing data that I collected to data gathered by Marshallese interviewers allowed me to test the validity of my own data, and more important, to provide training to Marshallese researchers. Involving local people in my research also provides me with a check to make sure that my investigations are of value to the communities.

Many Marshallese remain sensitive to the exploitative research conducted in the Marshall Islands by outsiders, particularly researchers linked to the testing program. In a few cases, Marshallese openly expressed disdain for the actions of some researchers who came into their communities and failed to consider the best interests of the Marshallese. The history of research and abuse in the Marshall Islands underscores the need to create a generation of Marshallese researchers who can conduct their own investigations. Human capacity building is an essential ingredient of community empowerment and development.

In 1998, the Ministry of Foreign Affairs allowed me to volunteer some of my time at the College of the Marshall Islands. I worked with the former president of the college, Alfred Capelle, to establish a Nuclear Institute to study the consequences of the testing program from a Marshallese perspective. I taught the Institute's first course, the History of Nuclear Weapons Testing in the Pacific Region. The first director of the Nuclear Institute, Mary Silk, was a student in my class before she became the director.

By working with students and faculty at the College of the Marshall Islands, I helped train local counterparts in techniques of data collection, analysis, transcription, and translation. At the same time, people learned more about their nation's history with nuclear weapons. As part of the course requirement, students researched the challenges facing different radiation communities in the Marshall Islands. The students chose to work in groups and to research three specific populations: Marshallese workers sent to the test-site areas, the people of Mejit Atoll, yet another community downwind from the test sites, and the generation of Marshallese born after the testing period. In addition to archival research, students collected life stories from the respective populations. Students collected, transcribed, translated, and analyzed their interviews. Both the students and I benefited from the project. They learned research techniques and valuable information about their communities, and I gained additional insights into the research I conduct for the RMI government. Students gave final copies of their reports to key informants and to the policy makers/leaders from the various communities, such as the senators and mayors.

After their data collection projects, my students were anxious to share their knowledge about the testing program with the community at large. We invited the public to hear guest speakers discuss various aspects of the nuclear legacy, and we filmed guest speakers to create a video archive. We sponsored a national essay writing contest and a public ceremony commemorating Nuclear Victim's Remembrance Day on the anniversary of the Bravo test. To disseminate the ideas espoused by the writers, the winners of the national essay contest for each grade level read their winning submissions over the public radio.

For their final exam, students conducted a live, nationally broadcast radio program to discuss nuclear issues and their findings from their class research projects. This program reached thousands of people in the urban centers and remote outer islands. Each student covered a particular testing-related topic in detail. At the end of their presentations, the students fielded questions from the public for more than an hour. People called in by telephone or by a radio transmitter from the outer islands. The public gave the students tremendous support and encouragement for their project. After hearing the discussion on the radio station, people drove down to the station to congratulate the students after their show, others called the radio station to express their congratulations, and still others wrote to the local newspaper to say how impressed they were that young Marshallese knew so much about the issues that dramatically affect the nation. One woman from Utrik who was alive during the testing said she learned a great deal from the students, including basic information such as the number of tests conducted and their yields. The fact that even those who lived through the testing program do not understand the nature of U.S. government activities at the time illustrates the need to disseminate information from the declassified documents and ethnographic data to the public.

Positive feedback, together with the outpouring of community support, bolstered the students' desire to learn more about testing-related issues and signaled to them that their communities value the study of nuclear issues. Inspired by the success of the radio show and the need to create an ongoing opportunity for students to explore nuclear issues, the students established a Nuclear Club at the college. The goal of the club is public education. Students use skits, songs, films, and lectures to educate people about the U.S. nuclear weapons testing program in the Marshall Islands and its effects. Several members of the Nuclear Club joined a summer study program operated by American University in Hiroshima and Nagasaki, Japan. After returning from Japan, the participants shared what they learned with other members of the Nuclear Club. The Nuclear Club decided to make regular presentations to the public middle and high schools in the Marshall Islands, and to the outer islands when funding provides, to share what they learned with as wide an audience as possible. The presence of peer educators motivates younger Marshallese to learn about their history.

Based on the successful contributions of the students at the College of the Marshall Islands in RMI government–sponsored research, the RMI embassy in Washington, DC, established its own training program. In 1995, the embassy invited interns to live and work in the embassy in exchange for internship credit at their colleges. The embassy gives preference to Marshallese students, although students from Japan and the United States have also participated in the program. Interns at the embassy do not answer telephones and assist with administrative tasks. Instead, they become active members of the team and assist with efforts to educate the U.S. government about problems and needs in the RMI. Two of the interns created a permanent photo exhibit about the weapons testing program that is still on display at the embassy. Other interns wrote speeches and letters to Congress, developed informational brochures, gathered film footage about the testing program from U.S. government archives, and assisted with the preparation for hearings on Capitol Hill. Both the embassy and the students benefit from these experiences, and the more students understand the events that took place in the Marshall Islands, the more they want to get involved in efforts to assist people whose lives were dramatically altered by the testing program.

TRANSCRIPTION AND TRANSLATION

A number of individuals, including myself, influenced the texts of the interviews during the transcription and translation processes. After my preliminary fieldwork, I turned over copies of my interview tapes to the RMI government. The government funded the project and, therefore, owned the information. The RMI government hired two Marshallese men to undertake the enormous task of transcribing and translating the majority of the interviews. I also transcribed and translated several of the particularly important interviews myself. As I reviewed the interviews, I found several important omissions in the transcriptions and translations of the government-hired workers. Reviewing the transcription and translation work of others gave me the opportunity to make important corrections to my data.

Elizabeth Cruz, a woman who was on Likiep Atoll during the weapons testing program assisted me with some of my translations in Washington, DC. She was particularly helpful because she was a child during the testing program and remembers many of the experiences described by the narrators in the interviews. Because she left the Marshall Islands as a young woman, her day-to-day use of the Marshallese language reflects a more traditional manner of speaking consistent with the language use on a remote, outer island where she grew up in the 1950s. In the early 1950s, the English language and the vocabulary of globalization were just beginning to influence the Marshallese language. Because she was away from the Marshall Islands during a period of modernization of the language, Elizabeth has a rich Marshallese vocabulary that characterizes the speech of many older Marshallese who grew up on the outer islands, such as the elderly radiation survivors. Elizabeth has not traveled back to the Marshall Islands for decades and her language use does not reflect the modern changes, and increased use of English words found in contemporary Marshallese. I found her assistance in transcribing and translating invaluable, especially with the interviews I conducted with elderly radiation survivors on the outer islands.

In addition to the woman from Likiep, a number of Marshallese interns at the embassy also assisted with the transcription and some of the translation. All of the students said they enjoyed listening to the interviews because they learned about the effects of the weapons testing, and that they were interested in learning more about their country's history during the Cold War.

OBSERVATION

Unlike participant observation, which maintains distance between the observer and the subject (Bernard 1995), I augmented my interviews with close observation. Close observation allows anthropologists to get as near as possible to their research subjects while still maintaining the ability to step back and reflect. This method worked well for me since it makes no clear division between researcher and subjects, and instead assumes that a researcher needs to participate in the life world of his or her subject to better understand what it entails. Observations are particularly important to ethnographic research with radiation communities, as it is often difficult for people to express physical disabilities using only words. Oral testimonies captured on a tape recorder do not amply convey the physical challenges described or experienced by the people. As seen in the interview with Kita and her husband in Chapter 6, notations of hand gestures people use to help explain deformities or changes to their bodies as a result of radiation exposure are important to document.

Although photographs and videotapes can obviously help convey some of the physical difficulties experienced by radiation survivors, I find them troubling. First of all, they take away the anonymity of the informant if they wish to keep their experiences confidential. Secondly, they change the dynamic of an interview. In my experience, people suddenly feel like a specimen when the camera comes out. In an interview, an ethnographer can make her respect for her informants quite clear. When cameras emerge on the scene, the photographic subject becomes an object rather than someone with whom you share a respectful dialogue. In some instances during my fieldwork, informants asked me to take their photographs because they wanted to produce evidence that would help other people understand the hardships they endure. This was the case when I interviewed Jalel John, the grandmother of a girl on Ailuk with no knees, a missing arm, and missing fingers (Figure 10.1). In her grandmother's view, this girl embodies the effects of radiation on human beings.

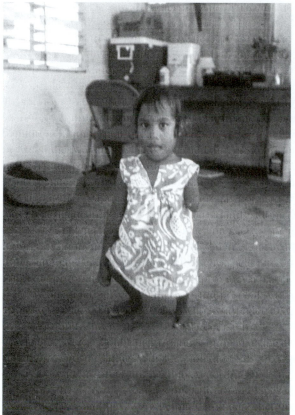

Figure 10.1 An unidentified girl from Ailuk Atoll

EXPECT TO BE CHALLENGED

Over the years, several of the radiation survivors openly challenged me and my presence in their communities. In my interview with Ertilang discussed in Chapter 8, I told Ertilang I was conducting research for her government, and her leaders, and I had a Marshallese counterpart with me who verified my role with the RMI. Still, Ertilang challenged me and made sure the interview was not easy for me. Although I found this interrogation uncomfortable, I also welcomed it. I know Ertilang's experiences with radiation exposure and exile are not easy for her and painful to discuss. Ertilang certainly should not share her experiences if she is not completely comfortable.

When entering a community, I always convene a community-wide meeting to discuss the reasons for my research, get input from the community, and to allow community members to question me. By peppering me with questions, community members have an opportunity to ask me whatever is necessary to determine whether they are satisfied that my presence is useful and understood by all. Anthropologists, particularly those working with exploited and injured populations, should expect to have their presence and intentions challenged by the communities; this challenging provides the community with however many responses it takes for them to feel comfortable with our presence. The community's comfort level is an important component of our research.

FIELDNOTES

During my fieldwork, I recorded on-site observations and thoughts each day in my fieldnote journals. I took these fieldnote journals with me everywhere I went. I made quick notations during interviews of thoughts raised by the informants that I wanted to explore further. I try to save my follow-up questions for the end of interviews so I do not disrupt the thoughts and flow of the speech set by the informants. I also used my fieldnote journals to make notes to myself about topics to pursue in the archival documents, or additional people who might be good sources of information. When it comes time for analyzing the data from the interviews, I always find it helpful to review my fieldnote entries and to recall the physical context of the interviews as well as any thoughts I had at the time. When I return home from the field and review my notes, I often find themes—themes that I was unaware of while in the field—that help me with my analysis of the data.

REPEAT VISITS TO THE FIELD

The first time I collected ethnographic data in 1994, I thought I had a wealth of information that would keep me busy for a lifetime. When I examined the content of the interviews more closely, I could identify places in the dialogues where I failed to follow up on important clues, or where I did not delve deeply enough into an issue. Repeat visits to the field are important because they allow researchers to reach deeper levels of complexity in their research, and to maintain close working relationships with the communities. After 1994, I returned to the field for half a year in 1997, and again in 1998, 1999, 2000, and 2001. The RMI embassy in Washington, DC, fully supported and paid for all the expenses of my earlier trips because I was collecting data for the RMI government to use as a means of convincing the U.S. government to meet its obligations to the communities affected by the weapons testing. The Public Advocate at the Tribunal funded my more recent interviews to help construct Rongelap's land claim.

THE POLICY REALM

My main role as an anthropologist working for the RMI government is to help leaders convey the needs of the communities affected by the weapons testing to the U.S. Congress and administration. In this capacity, I often act as a cultural broker "translat[ing] one culture/society into terms comprehensible to another" (Nalven 1986:34), or as a liaison trying to bridge understanding between the U.S. and RMI governments.

Without question, the most powerful way to convey the needs of the radiation communities to the U.S. government is to allow RMI government and community leaders to speak for themselves during bilateral meetings. Prior to these meetings, I brief Marshallese leaders about the issues I research, and I help them develop a technique for effectively conveying their problems and needs to U.S. government representatives. During the meetings, I am able to sit quietly behind the Marshallese leaders and let them speak for themselves. Only when necessary do I whisper information into their ears. I view my work as successful when my input is not needed at these meetings.

In one instance, RMI government leaders used data about the nuclear weapons testing to convince DOE to put the contract for the medical program out to bid so other providers would have the opportunity to consider how they would construct the medical program. The RMI wanted to remove Brookhaven National Laboratory, the institution responsible for the human radiation experiments in the Marshall Islands.[1] RMI national and local governments insisted on participating in the drafting of the proposal for a new medical provider to ensure that the program considered aspects of health care delivery of importance to the recipient communities. RMI national and local government officials also used data from the research in testimonies to the United Nations, to the White House, to the U.S. Congress, in ceremonies in Japan remembering the victims of Hiroshima and Nagasaki, in meetings with Pacific Island heads of state, in the *Nitijela* and in other venues.

By giving the information I gather to the leaders, helping them to digest it, and helping them use the information to advance their policy and political goals with the U.S. government, knowledge is given back to the communities. Human capacity building is an essential and important component of applied anthropology because it makes communities stronger and better able to fend for themselves in the future. Communities where anthropologists work should benefit from our interactions with them long after our working relationships come to an end.

METHODS OF THE NCT PROJECT

To provide a specific example of how I employ research methods while in the field, I will discuss the methods that Dr. Barbara Rose Johnston and I developed for the Rongelap land claim project with the Nuclear Claims Tribunal. The methodology we developed for our project drew on my 12 years of experience and connections with people in the affected communities, and Barbara's experience in human environmental impact assessment and reparations research. It also drew on Barbara's and my shared commitment to community participation in every phase of research.[2]

Prior to the arrival of the anthropological team to the Marshall Islands, we worked with the Public Advocate for the Nuclear Claims Tribunal, William Graham, to put together a Marshallese advisory committee to assist our team with every phase of our research.[3] I discussed the composition of a Marshallese advisory committee with Bill. Like me, Bill was a Peace Corps volunteer in the Marshall Islands. He served in the 1960s, married a Marshallese woman, and has been an integral part of the community for four decades. Bill convinced an *iroij* from Rongelap to join the advisory committee. This *iroij*, *Iroij* Mike Kabua, is respected throughout the

---

[1] Any comments in this book about the problems relating to the DOE medical program relate to Brookhaven National Laboratory, and not the new contractor, PHRI, that recently assumed responsibility for the program.

[2] Cultural anthropologist Stuart Kirsch also assisted with initial discussions of the Marshallese value of land and provided information on other compensation cases in the Pacific region involving loss of a way of life.

[3] During the first phase of our research in March 1999, Dr. Kirsch joined our team.

country for his cultural revitalization efforts and his knowledge of traditional Marshallese lifestyle. In addition to *Iroij* Kabua, a Rongelapese woman, Lijohn Eknilang, and a Rongelapese man (who was also an *alap*), George Anjain, joined the advisory committee. Lijohn and George provided us with a wealth of information about subsistence practices on Rongelap and key events that affected the peoples' resource relations and the socioeconomic consequences of the damages and loss the community suffered. The committee was rounded out by two well-respected Marshallese with extensive knowledge about traditional agricultural and fishing practices, *Iroij* Wilfred Kendall, and handicraft production, Mary Lanwi.

In March 1999, our anthropological team met with the advisory committee to discuss our research plans, to get feedback from them, and to refine our plans before presenting them to the community. Before beginning our research, we worked with the Rongelap local government to convene a community-wide meeting to introduce ourselves, explain the purpose of our research, and to make sure people understood that we were gathering data to support the community's land claim to the Nuclear Claims Tribunal. Community members asked many questions and agreed to assist us with our work.

From March to April 1999, I conducted interviews with members of the community who lived on Majuro and Ebeye; I also conducted interviews during a visit to Rongelap (for the community to see the results of a restoration project that was under way). I had two Marshallese research partners who accompanied me for the interviews, Tieta Thomas and Kristina Stege. Tieta is an assistant to the Public Advocate who lives on Ebeye and knows many of the Rongelapese who reside there, and on Mejatto Island. Kristina majored in sociology in college and did her senior report about the plight of the Bikinians. She is a natural and gifted ethnographer and made substantial contributions to the project. By the end of our data collection, Tina conducted some of the interviews entirely by herself. Tina eventually went on to conduct her own research on the displacement of communities moved off of their home islands by the U.S. government for defense missile tests, and will likely continue her own research in the future.

In May and June of 1999, I analyzed data from my interviews and reviewed information contained in other interviews I conducted with some members of the Rongelap community in 1994. Barbara continued the documentary review, and examined similar cases of environmental damage and the socioeconomic implications from other communities. Barbara and I then produced a draft report of our research for the Public Advocate.

In July 1999, Barbara and I returned to Majuro to present the preliminary findings in our report, to elicit comments and feedback from Rongelap contributors, to conduct follow-up interviews, and to track down remaining documentary sources. We distributed our draft report for comment to the advisory group, informants, and key contacts in the Marshall Islands as well as several environmental social science colleagues throughout the United States.

In 2001, the Public Advocate asked Barbara and me to revise our report to focus specifically on the hardships and consequential damages experienced by the Rongelapese as a result of their exile and their involvement in U.S. government human experiments. I conducted follow-up interviews in April 2001 in Majuro and in July 2001 in Hawaii. Many members of the Rongelap community, particularly those who want access to a better quality of health care in the United States, live in Hawaii. Barbara explored U.S. government documents to find support for the painful

Figure 10.2 Members of the Rongelap community singing about their losses and their land at the end of their hearing before the NCT

memories expressed by the informants. In July 2001, the RMI and the DOE convened an annual meeting in Hawaii to discuss issues and problems related to DOE's environmental and medical programs in the Marshall Islands. The senator for Rongelap, Abacca Anjain-Maddison, arranged for group meetings with many of the Rongelapese women residing in Hawaii. Senator Anjain-Maddison actively participated in the group discussions and facilitated the women's discussion of the difficulties they face in managing their radiation-related illnesses and getting access to medical care as required by the 177 Agreement of the Compact of Free Association.

By September 2001, Barbara and I submitted our second report to the Public Advocate. This report became the basis for the Rongelap community's claim to the Nuclear Claims Tribunal for hardships and consequential damages. In October 2001, Barbara and I flew to Majuro to participate in the hearing before the Tribunal. For several days prior to the hearing, I worked one on one with Rongelapese witnesses to review their experiences and to prepare them to appear as witnesses before the Tribunal judges. At the hearing, witnesses from the Rongelap community shared their experiences with the judges. I asked the witnesses questions in English because two of the three judges do not speak Marshallese and so a Marshallese interpreter could make certain that the witnesses fully understood the questions. The witnesses responded in Marshallese and the interpreters translated for the English-speaking judges (Figure 10.2).

At the end of the hearing, the Rongelap community felt elated because people finally felt as if they had had their day in court, and a chance to tell their stories from their own perspectives. They felt confident that the judges would understand the pain and suffering the community endures. The community also added its distinctive flavor to the hearings. The Rongelapese insisted on opening the hearings with a prayer and a song as is customary in the Marshall Islands. They also wanted to read the names of all their community members who suffered from the effects of radiation exposure but were not present at the deliberations because they had passed away. A councilwoman read the names of the deceased one by one. Although the reading of the names was not an official part of the hearing, it reminded all who were present of the human losses each family struggles with. The Rongelapese shaped the tone of the hearing, and participated fully in its three-day proceedings.

CONCLUSION

For anthropologists interested in empowering communities to better manage and respond to their problems, applied anthropology provides an array of tools to meet this challenge. Applied anthropologists have an obligation to serve the interests and needs of the communities where they work. We can do this by collaborating with

local counterparts and communities during every phase of our research, and by giving the results of our work back to the communities. These methods ensure that our
research is for the benefit of the recipients.

As an applied anthropologist working for the RMI government, I work with
Marshallese leaders and atoll attorneys to produce tangible outcomes for communities and the nation—whether in the form of a piece of legislation passing the U.S.
Congress, a change in the executive branch's policy toward the RMI, or a chance for
the RMI to present its views to the United States or the international community.
More important than the tangible outcomes, however, are the community empowerment efforts. I consider my role with the RMI government a success only if its leaders become more self-reliant and better able to manage their radiation-related issues
and problems in the future. By training local counterparts, disseminating information, and teaching leaders how to present themselves and their issues effectively to
the U.S. government, Marshallese leaders become increasingly skilled at advancing
their bilateral interests.

11/A Broader Understanding of the Consequences of the Testing Program

The history of the Marshall Islands represents the extreme in colonial domination where the powerful decided that the powerless should sacrifice their health and their lands to science, medicine, and global political and strategic interests. Although the U.S. government literally made a Hollywood production out of its effort to ask the Bikinians for permission to use their land for testing, it is clear that the Marshallese people had no ability to refuse the United States. The U.S. government chose the location to test its nuclear weapons, not the Marshallese. The U.S. government told the Marshallese their relocation would be temporary and that they could return home after the testing program. Fifty years later, the entire communities of Rongelap and Bikini, as well as half of the Enewetak population, remain in exile. The U.S. government also promised to look after the health and well-being of the citizens in the trust territory. Still today, those directly exposed to dangerous levels of fallout from the Bravo incident lack complete medical care and thousands of Marshallese people exposed to radiation have not been recognized or received care. The United States government—by its own admission in the Compact of Free Association—has a legal and moral obligation to take full responsibility for the damage and injuries caused by the testing program.

The price of clean-up, adequate medical care, and compensation in the Marshall Islands is expensive, unquestionably, but it is a fraction of the $1.5 billion annual cost the U.S. government spends on contemplating clean-up of the Hanford facility. If the U.S. government can locate funding to conduct its military activities, surely it can find the resources to remedy the resulting damages and injuries. The U.S. nuclear weapons testing program in the continental United States and the Marshall Islands cost American taxpayers approximately $5.8 trillion. Of that figure, only 0.04 percent reached the victims of the weapons testing programs (Schwartz 1998).

The scientists who invented the nuclear bombs knew they had created weapons of genocide. These weapons inflicted incalculable damage during a war with Japan, and, later, on the Maohi of French Polynesia, downwinders in Nevada and Hanford, and numerous other communities, including the RMI. In the case of the Marshall Islands, throughout the Trusteeship and into the post-colony era, the strategic and research interests of the United States outweighed concerns for the safety, health, and well-being of the Marshallese people and their islands. U.S. government representatives used their power to arrange for the tests to occur, to control or suppress information about the testing program, to determine which people and islands legally constitute an "exposed" group, and to decide which communities would receive compensation or U.S. government programmatic support for their radiation-related injuries or damages. Doctors and scientists vigorously pursued their research agendas with little or no thought about Marshallese knowledge and experiences with radiation.

From a Marshallese perspective, the inadequate response of the U.S. government to the problems created by the testing program demonstrates to the Marshallese that the U.S. government considers them an expendable population, one whose sufferings and pain are part of the price of Cold War politics. The U.S. government has a history of exploiting and trampling the values of others, such as its own Native American populations, in order to pursue its own domestic self-interests. The Marshallese people still struggle to cope with the devastation of their fragile coral islands they depend on for survival and to come to terms with the pervasive deaths and health problems resulting from radiation exposure.

Studying historical events helps us, as anthropologists, understand the factors that shape modern life in the areas where we conduct research. The U.S. nuclear weapons testing program, conducted five decades ago, affects virtually every aspect of Marshallese life today. As discussed earlier in the book, it is impossible to separate the Marshallese radiation language from the history and relationship of the Marshallese people to their immediate surroundings, a world filled with invisible contamination and observable problems. The testing program affected men, women, youth, the elderly, the legally exposed population, the test-site workers, and the people from atolls such as Ailuk, Likiep, Wotje, and Mejit, but affected them differently. We see death and illness, and psychological problems in the population. We see an economy that can not utilize large portions of its resources base and land. We see a political system that does not include representatives from the land, and for the people rendered inhabitable by the weapons testing, such as Rongerik. We see a social structure weakened and changed by the introduction of radiation into the most valued possession of all, Marshallese land.

In spite of the pain and problems resulting from the testing program, we can also see the incredible resilience and resistance of the Marshallese. The Marshallese protested the testing program and its consequences to the United Nations, and the U.S. government. Much to their credit, the Marshallese refuse to accept U.S. government explanations about the minimal effects of radiation exposure. The Marshallese continually and actively challenge U.S. government policies that limit their inclusion in much needed medical and environmental monitoring programs.

FLAWS IN THE U.S. GOVERNMENT'S ACCOUNTING OF HISTORY

By comparing the U.S. government's history of the U.S. nuclear weapons testing program with the documentary and ethnographic records, the cracks in the history imposed by the United States begin to emerge and point the way to a new narrative of history. The U.S. government used its power to control all information relating to the testing program to carefully construct a very limited range of damages and injuries resulting from the testing program. Through the independent work of scientists, lawyers, journalists, anthropologists, and others, RMI government leaders can refute the U.S. government's accounting of events with a new narrative of history, a history that includes Marshallese experiences with radiation during and after the testing period. The new narrative of history debunks long-held, legally binding assertions by the U.S. government. There are many examples of faulty U.S. government assertions about the consequences of the testing program. Here are just three examples.

U.S. Assertion #1: The exposure of Marshallese populations to radiation from the Bravo test was the result of an accidental wind shift   Given the extensive meteorological data from previous tests and knowledge about the unpredictable nature of the trade winds in the Marshall Islands, it was not an "accident" that wind blew radioactive fallout over inhabited islands. While there is no documentary proof that the U.S. government purposefully exposed people to radioactive fallout, the U.S. government conducted human radiation experiments with vulnerable U.S. populations without their consent or knowledge and failed to take any precautions to minimize injuries. Furthermore, the U.S. government evacuated residents from atolls downwind from smaller tests as a precaution, but failed to evacuate people for what was planned to be the biggest and dirtiest test of all time. At a minimum, the U.S. government grossly failed in its duty to protect the residents of the Trusteeship from harm. After all, if the events on March 1, 1954, were an accident, why didn't the U.S. government conduct an investigation?

U.S. Assertion #2: The U.S. government provided adequate medical care to the injured populations after their exposure to Bravo   Although the U.S. government did give medical attention to the people from Rongelap and Utrik after their exposure to Bravo's fallout, the U.S. government used these populations to further its own medical and scientific interests. For example, the U.S. government documented and photographed (Figure 4.1) the radiation burns received by the people of Rongelap, but did not offer them pain medication even when the burns reached and exposed the bones in people's feet (Eknilang 2000). The U.S. government did not ask the people of Rongelap and Utrik for permission to include them in studies even though their participation resulted in increased exposure to radiation and harm. In the case of the Rongelapese, the White House Advisory Committee on Human Radiation Experiments acknowledged that U.S. government researchers injected Marshallese subjects with radiation, or had them drink an irradiated substance.

For both the Rongelapese and the Utrikese, the U.S. government's decision to return them to contaminated homelands to study the transfer of radiation from the environment to human beings exposed these populations to additional radiation. The U.S. government also prematurely resettled the Bikinians on their homelands. In all these cases, the U.S. government systematically measured cumulative levels of radioactivity in the environment and in the urine of the people. The bioaccumulative contamination in the marine as well as terrestrial ecosystem that islanders relied on for food increased the harm they experienced from the testing program. The U.S. government monitored the increased radiation burdens, primarily through urinalysis samples, but failed to report this increased burden until years later. Furthermore, failures to restrict local consumption of foods with high levels of radioactivity led to increased radiation exposure for the residents of the contaminated islands and to people throughout the nation who received gifts of food as customary in the Marshall Islands.

Medical care and medical studies are not the same thing, particularly when the caregivers are not interested in treating the problems identified by the people, such as blisters in their mouths from eating contaminated foods, or reproductive abnormalities.

U.S. Assertion #3: The only people exposed to harmful levels of radiation from Bravo were the people who resided on Rongelap or Utrik on March 1, 1954   Within the communities of Rongelap and Utrik, it was not only the Bravo test and not only exposure to external fallout that exposed the people to radiation. In addition to the external exposure people received from Bravo's fallout on March 1, 1954, everyone who resettled their contaminated homelands received internal exposure to radiation.

The testing program exposed everyone residing in the Marshall Islands to radiation. The U.S. government ignores the needs of many populations exposed to levels of radiation sufficient to warrant U.S. government medical assistance. Examples of these populations include the Marshallese test-site workers; the people of Ailuk, Likiep, Mejit, and Wotje; the generation of Marshallese born on contaminated islands, or prematurely resettled on contaminated islands; the offspring of people with genetic and chromosomal abnormalities resulting from their exposure to radiation; and the subjects of human radiation experiments.

A NEW NARRATIVE OF HISTORY

Historical and ethnographic data demonstrate that the U.S. government ignored or covered up an array of knowledge critical to the history of the Marshall Islands' intersections with the Cold War. This erased and covered-up knowledge includes both U.S. government knowledge recorded in written documents and ethnographic data detailing the lived experiences with radiation of the Marshallese people. The location of this erased knowledge highlights the flaws in the U.S. government's representation of the history of the U.S. weapons testing program.

The U.S. government's construction of history fails to include critical aspects of a complete history. As discussed above, the U.S. government does not include multiple exposed populations in its definition of people harmed by exposure to radiation. Additionally, the U.S. government's version of history does not acknowledge human environmental rights abuses such as allowing populations to resettle and remain on contaminated islands despite the fact that researchers were aware of increased radiation burdens received by the resettled communities. Furthermore, the U.S. government does not acknowledge the problems caused by exile and land loss, and the ways it affects women, men, youth, the elderly, and the entire social structure of the communities. Women experience loss of power associated with land rights, and suffer reproductive abnormalities. Men lost the ability to provide for their families. The youth have no understanding of or connection to their future land holdings. The elderly lost customary respect accompanying knowledge about the environment as well as the dignity to die and be laid to rest on their own land. The *iroij* and social structure lost the ability to accumulate power and disperse resources to people because land and resources now lay dormant.

It is clear that the official U.S. government accounting of events espoused in the Compact of Free Association and the 177 Agreement is incomplete and erroneous. The RMI government has replaced the colonial version of history that oppresses the needs and experiences of the people with a new history that includes the voice and experiences of the all the radiation populations in the Marshall Islands, including those that the U.S. government erased from consideration. To provide a complete history of the events in the Marshall Islands would take years of research orchestrated by all the radiation communities in the RMI, but it is clear that a new narrative of the history of the testing program is emerging—a history that includes a much broader accounting of the damages and injuries caused by the testing program to all of the affected populations in the RMI.

The collision of the histories of the U.S. government and the Marshall Islands resulted in a large strategic gain for the United States and extensive damage, injury and death for the Marshallese people and their land. The powerful nation gained unquantifiable military advantage and secured its superpower status in the Cold War. The relatively powerless nation was left with severe, long-term health and environmental catastrophes; displacement of entire communities; and psychological, social, cultural, political, and economic problems. The U.S. government asserted its military objectives on the Marshall Islands and the Marshallese paid for it with their lives and livelihoods.

By acknowledging a more complete history of the testing program, the U.S. and RMI governments can recognize the full scale of injustices, injuries, and damages experienced by the Marshallese. The RMI and U.S. governments must work together to jointly address these problems. In the near future, the RMI government's Changed Circumstances Petition to the U.S. Congress provides an opportunity for additional monetary compensation, and to change the existing U.S. government policies that severely limit medical and environmental programs in the RMI. Addressing the issues presented in the RMI government's Changed Circumstances Petition to Congress provides an immediate vehicle to embrace the new narrative of the history of the testing program, a history that now includes the complex, wide breadth of problems facing a variety of radiation populations in the Marshall Islands.

Now that there are two competing constructions of history, the Marshall Islands has little choice but to present its case to Congress so it can weigh the facts and determine which scenario is correct. Unfortunately, elected officials who constantly face reelection tend to pursue the interests of their constituents. Facing America's responsibilities in the Marshall Islands is not a priority for any constituent group in the United States. As a tiny country with few resources, little or no power in international politics, and no voice in the U.S. Congress, chances that Congress will spend the time required to investigate the U.S. government's lingering responsibilities to the Marshall Islands are slim. With the exception of a few champions from the Pacific region, most notably Congressional representatives from Hawaii, Guam, and American Samoa, few members of Congress take the time to learn about issues in the Marshall Islands even when the bilateral relationship between the Marshall Islands and the United States falls under the jurisdiction of their committees.

LOOKING TOWARD THE FUTURE

The Marshallese have become actively engaged in challenging the U.S. government's version of history, in redefining history to include their own experiences, and in pressuring the U.S. government to change its policies and take full responsibility for the consequences of the testing program. The Marshallese are not victims; they are survivors. A victim is paralyzed by his or her situation and unable to care for himself or herself. A survivor, on the other hand, is one who endures.

With independent research and strong leadership, the Marshallese feel empowered to demand justice for their nation and its people. Calls for justice come from many survivors who feel angry and resentful toward the United States for its exploitation of the Marshallese people. For real and meaningful healing to take place in the Marshall Islands, the U.S. government must acknowledge the full extent of the injuries and damages resulting from the testing program and take full responsibility for the problems it caused.

Applied anthropologists can continue to play a role in assisting the radiation survivors in the Marshall Islands. By documenting the experiences of the radiation populations and creating ethnographic data, it is possible to capture and amplify a portion of the voices of the undocumented radiation populations. While not attempting to speak on behalf of the radiation populations, the ethnographic data demonstrates that there is more to the narrative than the history perpetuated by the U.S. government. In this case, ethnographic data serves as an anthropological tool for demonstrating the existence of radiation populations in the Marshall Islands with needs outside the narrow parameters of injury and damages currently addressed by the U.S. government.

Anthropologists are uniquely qualified both to understand and articulate problems facing communities and to take actionable steps to assist communities, particularly in the policy realm. We consider how global interests affect the specific communities where we work. Given the unique history of the RMI, and the abusive research that took place in the past, anthropologists and all researchers need to employ rigorous ethical and methodological practices. If our research is going to help the people, it must be owned by them. It is essential to include the people we work for in every phase of our work, from designing a research approach, to gathering and analyzing data. As applied anthropologists we can work with communities to help them use our research effectively in their efforts to address local problems.

Bibliography

Advisory Committee on Human Radiation Experiments. 1995. Final Report. Pittsburgh: U.S. Government Printing Office.

Ahearn, Laura M. 1999. Language Matters in Anthropology: A Lexicon for the Millennium. Alessandro Duranti, ed. *Journal of Linguistic Anthropology.* Vol. 9, Nos. 1–2. Pp. 12–15.

Alcalay, Glenn. 1992. The United States Anthropologist in Micronesia: Toward a Counter-Hegemonic Study of Sapiens. In *Confronting the Margaret Mead Legacy: Scholarship, Empire, and the South Pacific.* Lenora Foerstel and Angela Gilliam, eds. Pp. 173–204. Philadelphia: Temple University Press.

———. 1995. Testimony to the White House Advisory Committee on Human Radiation Experiments regarding dissertation research on the incidence of reproductive abnormalities experienced by Marshallese women. Washington, DC.

Almej, Kanike. 1999. Presentation to the Nuclear Studies Institute by a historian from the Alele Museum about why the Marshallese allowed the weapons testing to take place in the country. Majuro: College of the Marshall Islands.

Alperovitz, Gar, et al. 1996. *Decision to Use the Atomic Bomb.* New York: Knopf Publishing Group.

Amani, Shake. March 1, 1998. Essay from Marshall Islands Middle School in recognition of Nuclear Victims' Remembrance Day.

Anjain, Jeton. 1989. Testimony to the Committee on Interior and Insular Affairs regarding the safety of Rongelap Atoll. Washington, DC: U.S. House of Representatives.

Applied Fisheries Laboratory. December 30, 1955. Radiological Survey of Rongelap Atoll. Seattle, WA: University of Washington Press.

Atomic Energy Commission. 1952. Memo to Brig. Gen. K. E. Fields, Director of Military Applications from George P. Kraker.

———. 1953. Memorandum from the Commander of Task Force 7.1 detailing the general concept of Operation Castle. August 17, 1953. New Mexico: Los Alamos National Laboratory.

———. 1954. Operation Castle: Report of the Manager, Santa Fe Operations. Pacific Proving Grounds (DOE #30).

———. 1956. Minutes of the Advisory Committee on Biology and Medicine. January 13–14, 1956. AEC: New York.

Bair, William J., John W. Healy, Bruce W. Wachholz. 1982. The Meaning of Radiation for Those Atolls in the Northern Part of the Marshall Islands That Were Surveyed in 1978. Washington, DC: U.S. Department of Energy.

Balos, Henchi. 1995. Testimony to the White House Advisory Committee on Human Radiation Experiments regarding the people of Bikini. Washington, DC.

Barker, Holly. 1997. Fighting Back: Justice, the Marshall Islands and Neglected Radiation Communities. In *Life and Death Matters: Human Rights and the Environment at the End of the Millennium.* Barbara Rose Johnston, ed. Pp. 290–306. London: Alta Mira.

———. 1998. Fieldnotes from 1997 to 1998 Ph.D. dissertation research conducted in the Republic of the Marshall Islands.

Barker, Holly, interviews:
Alfred, Tempo. September 8, 1994. Ailuk Atoll.
Alik, Alion. August 14, 1994. Likiep Atoll.
Allen, William. August 22, 1994. Majuro.
Anjain, John. March 16, 1999. Ebeye.
Anonymous. August 14, 1994. Likiep Atoll.
Boaz, Boney. March 17, 1999. Ebeye.
Boaz, Ellyn. August 26, 1994. Mejatto, Kwajalein.

Bobo, Aruko. August 27, 1994. Ebeye.

deBrum, Agnes. August 14, 1994.
Likiep Atoll.

deBrum, Esra. August 19, 1994.
Majuro. Translation by Newton
Lajuan.

deBrum, Kramer. August 19, 1994.
Majuro.

Eknilang, Isao. October 31, 2000.
Majuro.

Eknilang, Isao. June 13, 2001.
Honolulu.

Eknilang, Lijohn. March 28, 2001.
Majuro.

Emos, Dorothy. March 18, 1999.
Ebeye.

Ertilang (pseudonym). August 26,
1994. Mejatto, Kwajalein.

Gideon, Kaleman. September 2, 1994.
Majuro.

Jakori (pseudonym). September 1,
1994. Majuro.

Jenwor, Jerkan. March 17, 1999.
Ebeye.

Jibas, Catherine. August 23, 1994.
Majuro.

Jili, Lontak. September 3, 1994. Ailuk
Atoll.

Jilon, Dikjen. September 2, 1994. Ailuk
Atoll.

Job, Mijua. March 10, 1999. Rongelap
Atoll.

John, Jalel. September 5, 1994. Ailuk
Atoll.

Joniber, Seiko. September 1, 1994.
Majuro.

Joseph, Nerje. March 8, 1999. Majuro.

Kebenli, Mwenadrik. March 16, 1999.
Ebeye.

Kebenli, Norio. October 29, 2001.
Majuro.

Kita and Kino (pseudonyms). August
14, 1994. Likiep Atoll.

Kolnij, Timako. March 18, 1999.
Ebeye.

Komram, Likotar. February 12, 1998.
Majuro.

Matayoshi, Almira. October 29, 2001.
Majuro.

Matayoshi, Almira. June 13, 2001.
Honolulu.

Riklon, Esra. August 18, 1994. Majuro.

Saul, Joe. August 22, 1994. Majuro.

Sneid, Rine. September 5, 1994. Ailuk
Atoll.

Takia, Kanji. September 5, 1994. Ailuk
Atoll.

Barker, Holly, Barbara Rose Johnston, and
Stuart Kirsch group interviews:

Anjain, George. March 3, 1999.
Majuro.

Eknilang, Lijohn. March 2, 1999.
Majuro.

Eknilang, Lijohn. March 3, 1999.
Majuro.

Eknilang, Lijohn. March 4, 1999.
Majuro.

Kabua, Mike. March 2, 1999. Majuro.

Kabua, Mike. March 4, 1999. Majuro.

Kebenli, Norio. October 31, 2000.
Majuro.

Kedi, Ken. March 1, 1999. Majuro.

Kendall, Wilfred. March 2, 1999.
Majuro.

Kendall, Wilfred. March 3, 1999.
Majuro.

Kendall, Wilfred. March 5, 1999.
Majuro.

Matayoshi, James. March 1, 1999.
Majuro.

Riklon, Johnsay. February 28, 1999.
Majuro.

Basso, Ellen B. 1995. *The Last Cannibals:
A South American Oral History.*
Austin: University of Texas Press.

Beebe, James. 1995. Basic Concepts and
Techniques of Rapid Appraisal. *Human
Organization* 54:42–51.

Bender, Byron. 1963. A Linguistic Analysis
of Place Names of the Marshall
Islands. Unpublished Ph.D.
dissertation, Indiana University.
Available at the Alele Museum in
Majuro or the Pacific Collection at the
University of Hawaii.

———. 1978. *Spoken Marshallese.* Second
printing. Honolulu: University of
Hawaii Press.

Bernard, H. Russell. 1995. *Research
Methods in Anthropology: Qualitative
and Quantitative Approaches,* Second
Edition. London: Alta Mira.

Bertell, Rosalie. 1989. Testimony to the
Committee on Interior and Insular
Affairs regarding the safety of
Rongelap Atoll. Washington, DC: U.S.
House of Representatives.

Brenneis, Donald Lawrence and Fred R.
Myers, eds. 1984. Language and
Politics in the Pacific. *Dangerous
Words: Language and Politics in the
Pacific.* Pp. 1–19. New York: New
York University Press.

Bugher, John C. 1959. Memorandum to
Dr. Charles Dunham, Director of the

Division of Biology and Medicine, Atomic Energy Commission, regarding the genetic effects of cumulative doses of radiation.

Clarkson, D.W. 1953. Memorandum by the Commander of Joint Task Force 7 attached to a pre-Bravo weather forecast by Elbert W. Pate and Clarence E. Palmer.

Conard, Robert, et al. 1958. March 1957 *Medical Survey of Rongelap and Utrik People Three Years after Exposure to Radioactive Fallout*. Upton, NY: Brookhaven National Laboratory.

———. 1965. March 1964 *Medical Survey of Rongelap and Utrik People Ten Years after Exposure to Radioactive Fallout*. Upton, NY: Brookhaven National Laboratory.

Cronkite, Eugene. April 21, 1954. Memorandum to the Atomic Energy Commission, Division of Biology and Medicine, regarding future exposure to radiation by the Rongelapese.

deBrum, Oscar. 1999. Testimony to the House Resources Committee regarding the Nuclear Claims Tribunal. Washington, DC: U.S. House of Representatives.

deBrum, Tony. 1994. Testimony to the White House Advisory Committee on Human Radiation Experiments.

Deines, Ann C., et al. 1991. Marshall Islands Chronology, 1944–1990. Rockville, MD: History Associates, Incorporated (DOE #430).

Donaldson, Lauren R. 1950. Radiobiological Survey of Bikini, Enewetok, and Likiep Atolls, July–August, 1949. Seattle: Applied Fisheries Program, University of Washington Press.

Duranti, Alessandro. 1991. Lauga and Talanoa: Two Speech Genres in a Samoan Political Event. In *Dangerous Words: Language and Politics in the Pacific*. Donald Lawrence Brenneis and Fred R. Meyers, eds. Pp. 217–242. New York: New York University Press.

Eisenbud, Merril. 1956. Comments reflected in the minutes of a meeting of the Advisory Committee on Biology and Medicine of the Atomic Energy Commission. New York.

Franke, Bernard. 1989. Testimony to the Committee on Interior and Insular Affairs regarding the safety of Rongelap Atoll. Washington, DC: U.S. House of Representatives.

Gallagher, Carole. 1993. *American Ground Zero: The Secret Nuclear War*. New York: Random House.

Gilliam, Angela, and Lenora Foerstel, eds. 1992. Margaret Mead's Contradictory Legacy. In *Confronting the Margaret Mead Legacy: Scholarship, Empire, and the South Pacific*. Pp. 101–156. Philadelphia: Temple University Press.

Government of the Republic of the Marshall Islands. 1978. Constitution of the Marshall Islands. Majuro.

———. 1999 Census Data. Marjuro: Office of Planning and Statistics.

———. Petition to the Congress of the United States of America Regarding Changed Circumstances Arising from U.S. Nuclear Testing in the Marshall Islands. Submitted to the President of the United States Senate and the Speaker of the House of the United States House of Representatives. September 11, 2002.

Greenpeace. 1986. Report on the Marshall Islands by Henk Haazen and Bunny McDiarmid. Auckland: Greenpeace New Zealand.

———. 1990. *Testimonies: Witnesses of French Nuclear Testing in the South Pacific*. Auckland: Greenpeace International.

Gusterson, Hugh. 1993. Exploding Anthropology's Canon in the World of the Bomb: Ethnographic Writing on Militarism. *Journal of Contemporary Ethnography*, Vol. 22, No. 1. Pp. 59–79.

Hanlon, David. 1994. Patterns of Colonial Rule in Micronesia. In *Tides of History: The Pacific Islands in the Twentieth Century*. K. R. Howe, Robert C. Kiste, and Brij V. Lal, eds. Pp. 93–118. Honolulu: University of Hawaii Press.

Hart, Janet. 1996. *New Voices in the Nation: Women and the Greek Resistance, 1941–1964*. Ithaca: Cornell University Press.

Henningham, Stephen. 1992. French Polynesia, 1945–1982: From trading colony to nuclear territory. In *France and the South Pacific: A Contemporary History*. Pp. 117–147. Honolulu: University of Hawaii Press.

Hezel, Francis X. 1995. *Strangers in Their Own Land: A Century of Colonial Rule*

in the Caroline and Marshall Islands.
Pacific Islands Monograph Series, 13.
Honolulu: University of Hawaii Press.

Hills, Howard. 1999. Testimony to the
House Resources Committee
discussing the political nature of the
$150 million compensation figure for
the 177 Agreement. Washington, DC:
U.S. House of Representatives.

House, R.A. 1954. Memorandum for the
Record: Command Briefing, 0000, 1
March 1954. Pacific Command: United
States Air Force.

Jacklick, Alvin. 1998. Discussion before
the RMI *Nitijela* regarding second
generation effects of nuclear weapons
testing. Majuro, RMI.

Johnston, Barbara Rose. 1994. *Pays the*
Price?: The Sociocultural Context of
Environmental Crisis. Washington,
D.C.: Island Press.

Johnston, Barbara Rose and Holly M.
Barker. 1999. Assessing the Human
Environmental Impact of Damage from
Radioactive Contamination, Denied
Use, and Exile for the People of
Rongelap, Rongerik, and Ailinginae
Atolls: Anthropological Assistance to
the Rongelap Land Valuation/Property
Damage Claim. Majuro: Office of the
Public Advocate, Nuclear Claims
Tribunal.

———. 2001. Hardships and
Consequential Damages from
Radioactive Contamination, Denied
Use, Exile, and Human Subject
Experimentation Experienced by the
People of Rongelap, Rongerik, and
Ailinginae Atolls. Majuro: Office of the
Public Advocate, Nuclear Claims
Tribunal.

Joint Task Force 7. 1955. Operation Castle:
Radiological Safety. Final Report, Vol.
I. Washington, DC: Headquarters, Joint
Task Force 7, Technical Branch, J-3
Division.

Juda, Rubon. 1998. Presentation to students
at the College of the Marshall Islands
regarding the conditions that enabled
the U.S. government to test nuclear
weapons in the Marshall Islands.
Majuro.

Kirch, Patrick. 1984. *The Evolution of*
Polynesian Chiefdoms. London:
Cambridge University Press.

Kiste, Robert C. 1974. *The Bikinians: A*
Study in Forced Migration. The Kiste
and Ogan Social Change Series in

Anthropology. Menlo Park, CA:
Cummings.

———. 1994. *Pre-colonial Times. Tides of*
History: The Pacific Islands in the
Twentieth Century. H. R. Howe, Robert
C. Kiste, and Brij V. Lal, eds. Pp. 3–28.
Honolulu: University of Hawaii Press.

Kleinman, Arthur, M.D. 1988. *The Illness*
Narratives: Suffering, Healing, and the
Human Condition. New York: Basic.

Krieger, Herbert W. 1943. *Island Peoples of*
the West Pacific Micronesia and
Melanesia. Smithsonian Institution War
Background Studies, No 16.
Washington, DC: Smithsonian
Institution.

Lang, Harina. 1998. Essay from Marshall
Islands Middle School in recognition of
Nuclear Victims' Remembrance Day on
March 1, 1998.

Lifton, Robert Jay. 1991. *Death in Life:*
Survivors of Hiroshima. Chapel Hill,
NC: The University of North Carolina
Press.

Lodge, William. 1958. Memorandum to the
Secretary General of the United
Nations regarding the delay of
submission of a Marshallese petition to
the Security Council.

Lulejian, N. M. 1954. Memorandum to Dr.
John C. Bugher, AEC Division of
Biology and Medicine, on December
21 regarding radiation fallout in the
Marshall Islands (DOE #83).

Mason, Leonard. 1948. Rongerik Report:
Summary Findings and
Recommendations. Guam: Office of the
High Commissioner of the Trust
Territory of the Pacific Islands.

———. 1968. The Ethnology of
Micronesia. In *Peoples and Cultures of*
the Pacific. Andrew P. Vayda, ed.
Pp. 275–298. Washington, DC: The
Natural History Press.

———. 1989. A Marshallese Nation
Emerges from the Political
Fragmentation of American
Micronesia. *Pacific Studies* 13:1–46.

Mufwene, Salikoko. 1994. On
Decreolization: The Case of the Gullah.
In *Language and the Social*
Construction of Identity in Creole
Situations. Marcyliena Morgan, ed.
Pp. 63–99. Los Angeles: Center for
Afro-American Studies.

Nalven, Joseph. 1987. Measuring the
Unmeasurable: A Microregional Study
of an Undocumented Population. In

Anthropological Praxis: Translating Knowledge into Action. Pp. 26–38. Boulder, CO: Westview.

Ned, Bienthy, and Dorothy Simeon. 1998. Interview with John Milne, President of the Marshall Islands Radiation Victims' Association. Majuro.

Netting, Robert McC., Glenn D. Stone, and M. Priscilla Stone. 1995. The Social Organization of Agrarian Labor. In *The Comparative Analysis of Human Societies: Toward Common Standards for Data Collection and Reporting.* Emilio Moran, ed. Pp. 55–74. Boulder, CO: Lynne Rienner.

Ngugi, Wa Thiong'o. 1986. *Decolonising the Mind: The Politics of Language in African Literature.* Portsmouth, NH: Heinemann.

Niedenthal, Jack. 2001. *For the Good of Mankind: A History of the People of Bikini and their Islands.* First printing. Majuro: Micronitor Printing.

Nuclear Claims Tribunal. 2003. Information regarding compensable illnesses http//www.tribunal-mh.org/claim.html.

O'Rourke, Dennis. 1985. *Half Life: A Parable for the Nuclear Age.* Australia: O'Rourke and Associates.

Palafox, Neal, M.D., MPH. 2002a. Impact on Health Services in the RMI. A position paper for the RMI Minister of Health and Environment in preparation for Compact renegotiation.

———. 2002b. E-mail correspondence with author regarding social problems on Ebeye Island, April 24, 2002.

Parker, Patricia L. and Thomas F. King. 1987. Intercultural Mediation at Truk International Airport. In *Anthropological Praxis: Translating Knowledge into Action.* Pp. 160–173. Boulder, CO: Westview.

Plumbo, Peg. 1999. Pregnancy Loss: Molar Pregnancy. http://www.parentsplace.com/expert/midwife/qua/0,10338,239082_100016,00.html.

Portelli, Alessandro. 1997. *The Battle of Valle Guila: Oral History and the Art of Dialogue.* Madison: The University of Wisconsin Press.

Pritikin, Trisha. November 1, 2002. E-mail correspondence with author.

Roche, Adi. 1996. *Children of Chernobyl.* Dublin Castle, Ireland: Harper Collins. Excerpt from http://www.adiccp.org/projects/education.html.

Romaine, Suzanne. 1994. Language Standardization and Linguistic Fragmentation in Tok Pisin. In *Language and the Social Construction of Identity in Creole Situations.* Marcyliena Morgan, ed. Pp. 19–42. Los Angeles: Center for Afro-American Studies, University of California.

Schwartz, Stephen I., ed. 1998. *Atomic Audit: The Costs and Consequences of U.S. Nuclear Weapons since 1940.* Washington, DC: Brookings Institute.

Stege, Kristina. March 19, 1999. Interview with Malal Anjain. Queen of Peace High School. Gugeegue, Kwajalein.

Stephens, Sharon. 1992. Physical and Cultural Reproduction in a Post-Chernobyl Norwegian Sami Community. In *Conceiving the New World Order: The Global Politics of Reproduction.* Faye D. Ginsburg and Rayna Rapp, eds. Pp. 270–287. Berkeley: University of California Press.

Takahashi, Akihiro. August 8, 1995. Statement to American University students. Hiroshima, Japan.

Tartios, Edma, Raymond Johnson, and Mary Silk. April 17, 1998. Interview with Samos Relang.

Task Group 7.1. November 10, 1953. Outline of Scientific Programs—Operation Castle. Distributed by the Commander of Task Group 7.1. Los Alamos, NM.

Tobin, Jack A. 1953. *The Bikini People, Past and Present.* Guam: District Administrator, U.S. Trust Territory of the Pacific Islands.

———. 1958. *Land Tenure in the Marshall Islands. Series on Land Tenure Patterns in the Territory of the Pacific Islands.* Guam: Office of the High Commissioner of the Trust Territory of the Pacific Islands.

———. 1967. *A Preliminary Anthropological Report—Bikini Atoll Survey.* Guam: Office of the High Commissioner of the Trust Territory of the Pacific Islands.

———. 2002. *Stories from the Marshall Islands.* Honolulu: University of Hawaii Press.

Trager, Lilian. 1995. Minimum Data Sets in the Study of Exchange and Distribution. In *The Comparative Analysis of Human Societies: Toward Common Standards for Data Collection and Reporting*. Pp. 75–96. Boulder, CO: Lynne Rienner.

UN Trusteeship Council. 1954. May 6 Petition from the Marshallese people concerning the Pacific Islands.

———. 1958. Petition from the Marshallese People Concerning the Pacific Islands: Complaint regarding explosion of lethal weapons within our home islands.

U.S. Air Force. 1954. Eyewitness accounts of the weathermen stationed on Rongerik Atoll. Report to Joint Task Force 7.

U.S. Army website: http://www.smdc.army.mil/RTS.html.

U.S. Congress. 1982. U.S. Public Law 99-239, The Compact of Free Association. Washington, DC.

U.S. Department of Interior. 1987. Integrated Renewable Resource Management for U.S. Insular Areas. Office of Technology Assessment. Washington, DC: U.S. Government Printing Office.

Warry, Wayne. 1992. *The Eleventh Thesis: Applied Anthropology Inquiry*. New Brunswick, NJ: Rutgers University Press.

Weisgall, Jonathan. 1994. *Operation Crossroads: The Atomic Tests at Bikini Atoll*. Annapolis: Naval Institute Press.

Welsome, Eileen. 1999. *The Plutonium Files: America's Secret Medical Experiments in the Cold War*. New York: Dial.

Winford, Donald. 1994. Sociolinguistic Approaches to Language Use in the Anglophone Caribbean. In *Language and the Social Construction of Identity in Creole Situations*. Marcyliena Morgan, ed. Pp. 43–62. Los Angeles: Center for Afro-American Studies.

Wulff, Robert M. and Shirley J. Fiske, eds. 1987. *Introduction. Anthropological Praxis: Translating Knowledge into Action*. Pp. 1–11. Boulder, CO: Westview.

Wypijewski, Joann. December 2001. This Is Only a Test. Vol. 303, No. 1819. Pp. 41–51. *Harper's Magazine*.

Yarrow, Ruth. October 31, 2002. E-mail correspondence from the Seattle office of Physicians for Social Responsibility with author regarding radiation contamination at Hanford.

Zackios, Gerald M. 2001. Testimony by the Minister of Foreign Affairs of the Republic of the Marshall Islands to the Committee on Resources regarding bilateral relations between the United States and the RMI. Washington, DC: U.S. House of Representatives.

Appendix

CATEGORIES FOR PERSONAL INJURY AWARDS, NUCLEAR CLAIMS TRIBUNAL

List of compensable illnesses from the Tribunal and award amounts for each illness:

1. Leukemia (other than chronic lymphocytic leukemia) — $125,000
2. Cancer of the thyroid
   a. if recurrent or requires multiple surgical and/or ablation — $75,000
   b. if non-recurrent or does not require multiple treatment — $50,000
3. Cancer of the breast
   a. if recurrent or requires mastectomy — $100,000
   b. if non-recurrent or requires lumpectomy — $75,000
4. Cancer of the pharynx — $100,000
5. Cancer of the esophagus — $125,000
6. Cancer of the stomach — $125,000
7. Cancer of the small intestine — $125,000
8. Cancer of the pancreas — $125,000
9. Multiple myeloma — $125,000
10. Lymphomas (except Hodgkin's disease) — $100,000
11. Cancer of the bile ducts — $125,000
12. Cancer of the gall bladder — $125,000
13. Cancer of the liver (except if cirrhosis or hepatitis B is indicated) — $125,000
14. Cancer of the colon — $75,000
15. Cancer of the urinary tract, including the urinary bladder, renal pelves, and urethra — $75,000
16. Tumors of the salivary gland
    a. if malignant — $50,000
    b. if benign and requiring surgery — $37,500
    c. if benign and not requiring surgery — $12,500
17. Non-malignant thyroid nodular disease (unless limited to occult nodules)
    a. if requiring total thyroidectomy — $50,000
    b. if requiring partial thyroidectomy — $37,500
    c. if not requiring thyroidectomy — $12,500
18. Cancer of the ovary — $125,000
19. Unexplained hypothyroidism (unless thyroiditis indicated) — $37,500
20. Severe growth retardation due to thyroid damage — $100,000
21. Unexplained bone marrow failure — $125,000
22. Meningioma — $100,000
23. Radiation sickness diagnosed between June 30, 1946 and August 18, 1958, inclusive — $12,500

24. Beta burns diagnosed between June 30, 1946 and August 18, 1958, inclusive $12,500

25. Severe mental retardation (provided born between May and September 1954, inclusive, and mother was present on Rongelap or Utrik Atolls at any time in March 1954) $100,000

26. Unexplained hyperparathyroidism $12,500

27. Tumors of the parathyroid gland
    a. if malignant $50,000
    b. if benign and requiring surgery $37,500
    c. if benign and not requiring surgery $12,500

28. Bronchial cancer (including cancer of the lung and pulmonary system) $37,500

29. Tumors of the brain, including schwannomas, but not including other benign neural tumors $125,000

30. Cancer of the central nervous system $125,000

31. Cancer of the kidney $75,000

32. Cancer of the rectum $75,000

33. Cancer of the cecum $75,000

34. Non-melanoma skin cancer in individuals who were diagnosed as having suffered beta burns under number 24 above $37,500

35. Cancer of the bone $125,000

Source: Nuclear Claims Tribunal http://www.tribunal-mh.org/claim.htm.

Glossary

ACHRE White House Advisory Committee on Human Radiation Experiments

AEC U.S. Atomic Energy Commission (preceded DOE)

alap managers of the land

atoll a cluster of islands formed around the lip of a volcano

baam bombed

bwebwenato a Marshallese story

bwij (jowi) clan

ciguatera fish poisoning

Compact of Free Association P.L. 99-239 defining the bilateral relationship and agreements between the Marshall Islands and the United States.

copra dried coconut meat

DOE U.S. Department of Energy

hibakusha Japanese term for atomic bomb survivors

iroij chief

kajin etto historic Marshallese language

kiraap grape, or grape babies

kotan weto boundaries between land parcels

life stories shorter experiences within the life of a person

matrilineal resources passed through women

MIRVA Marshall Islands Radiation Victims Association

meram enlightenment

NCT Nuclear Claims Tribunal

Nitijela parliamentary, government body of the Marshall Islands

oral histories, or life histories verbal accounts or reflections of a person's life

outer islands islands outside of the two urban areas

powder the Marshallese term used to describe radioactive fallout

Ralik western, or "sunset" chain of islands

Ratak eastern, or "sunrise" chain of islands

ri-jerbal workers of the land

ri-paelle foreigners

roro chants

TTPI Trust Territory of the Pacific Islands

weto a parcel of land, usually with both lagoon and ocean access

Credits

This page constitutes an extension of the copyright page. We have made every effort to trace the ownership of all copyrighted material and to secure permission from copyright holders. In the event of any question arising as to the use of any material, we will be pleased to make the necessary corrections in future printings. Thanks are due to the following authors, publishers, and agents for permission to use the material indicated.

Chapter 1. Page 11: From Notes on the Occurrence, Utilization, and Importance of Polynesian Arrowroot in the Marshall Island, Background Study No. 39, by Dirk Spennenman. Majuro: Independent Nationwide Radiological Survey, © 1992. Reprinted with permission.

Chapter 5. Page 74: First National Anthem translated by Lijohn Eknilang and reprinted by permission.

Chapter 6. Page 91: Samos Relang interview reprinted with permission. Page 93: John Milne interview reprinted with permission. Page 96: LoRauut, collected and translated by Abacca Anjain-Maddison, and reprinted with permission.

Chapter 9. Page 130: Emma's story reprinted by permission from Chernobyl Children's Project. Page 136: Statement and E-mail correspondence with Holly Barker regarding experiences with the Hanford Site reprinted with permission.

Index

www.wadsworth.com

wadsworth.com is the World Wide Web site for Wadsworth and is your direct source to dozens of online resources.

At *wadsworth.com* you can find out about supplements, demonstration software, and student resources. You can also send email to many of our authors and preview new publications and exciting new technologies.

wadsworth.com
Changing the way the world learns®